The Ultimate Why Question

Studies in Philosophy and the
History of Philosophy

General Editor: Jude P. Dougherty

Volume 54

The Ultimate Why Question

Why Is There Anything at All Rather than Nothing Whatsoever?

Edited by John F. Wippel

The Catholic University of America Press
Washington, D.C.

The paper used in this publication meets the minimum
requirements of American National Standards for Information
Science—Permanence of Paper for Printed Library Materials,
ANSI Z39.48-1984.

∞

Library of Congress Cataloging-in-Publication Data

The ultimate why question : why is there anything at all rather
than nothing whatsoever? / edited by John F. Wippel.

p. cm. — (Studies in philosophy and the history of philosophy;
v. 54)

Includes bibliographical references and index.

ISBN 978-0-8132-1863-2 (cloth : alk. paper)

1. Ontology   2. Nothing (Philosophy)   I. Wippel, John F.

BD331.U48 2011

111—dc22

                    2010053924

Contents

Acknowledgments

Permission from the respective copyright holders to reprint here the following previously published material is gratefully acknowledged: Nicholas Rescher, "Optimalism and the Rationality of the Real: On the Prospects of Axiological Explanation," *Review of Metaphysics* 59 (2006): 503–16, originally delivered as the Presidential Address for the Metaphysical Society of America at its annual meeting in 2005; John F. Wippel, "Thomas Aquinas on the Ultimate Why Question: Why Is There Anything at All Rather than Nothing Whatsoever?" *Review of Metaphysics* 60 (2007): 731–53, originally delivered as the Presidential Address for the Metaphysical Society of America at its annual meeting in 2006; Robert Cummings Neville, "Some Contemporary Theories of Divine Creation," in Robert Cummings Neville, *Realism in Religion: A Pragmatist's Perspective* (Albany: State University of New York Press, 2009), c. 12, pp. 191–201, originally delivered at the annual meeting of the Metaphysical Society of America in 2006.

I am deeply grateful to all of the authors who have contributed to this book, for it is their efforts that have made it what it is. I would also like to thank my past research assistant, Brandon Zimmermann, who provided valuable assistance in various ways in the preparation of this volume. I must also thank the past director of the Catholic University of America Press, Dr. David McGonagle, for his generous cooperation and collaboration in preparing the volume for publication; Theresa Walker, managing editor of the press, for her able assistance in seeing it through to its publication; Professor and Dean emeritus Jude P. Dougherty, for having accepted it for inclusion in the series Studies in Philosophy and the History of Philosophy; Susan Barnes, for her expert copyediting of the manuscript; Denise E. Carlson for preparing the indices; and finally Professor Thérèse-Anne Druart and my current research assistant, George Walter, for their assistance in proofreading the final text.

The Ultimate Why Question

John F. Wippel

Introduction

The title of this book is in itself controversial and so, too, is the book's theme: "The ultimate why question: why is there anything at all rather than nothing whatsoever?"[1] For some philosophers, that something now exists and therefore that something has always existed is simply a brute fact and needs no explanation. Hence this question should not even be raised. For many other philosophers, however, the question is legitimate, interesting, and worth pursuing. As will be evident from the chapters that follow, even among these philosophers the question is understood in different ways. According to some, it should be limited to an effort to account philosophically insofar as one can for how things are now, how they have come to reach their present status and, if possible, how they may have originated. For others, while this effort is legitimate and praiseworthy, it is not quite enough. Philosophers should also try to explain why it is that anything actually exists rather than nothing whatsoever if they are really addressing the ultimate why question.

Chapters 1–8 of this volume present a number of different responses to this question developed by major thinkers in the history of philosophy, beginning with representatives of ancient philosophy, both Greek and Chinese, followed by Avicenna from the medieval Arabic philosophical period, Thomas Aquinas from the medieval Christian West, Descartes at the beginnings of modern philosophy, Leibniz especially as interpreted by Heidegger, followed by Schelling and Hegel. Three individual contem-

1. Most of the chapters in this book originated from papers presented at the annual meeting of the Metaphysical Society of America, held in March 2006 on the campus of the Catholic University of America.

porary philosophical approaches to this issue are presented in Chapters 9 (Robert Neville), 10 (Brian Martine), and 11 (Nicholas Rescher).

In Chapter 1, Lloyd Gerson turns to Platonism considered broadly enough to include Plato himself, what is commonly known as Neoplatonism (especially Plotinus), and when helpful, Aristotle viewed as a dissident Platonist. Indeed Gerson suggests that the Platonic tradition can "fairly claim to be the *fons et origo*" of philosophical reflection on our question. He begins with Parmenides' well-known rejection of becoming based upon his rejection of the existence and the intelligibility of nothingness (nonbeing). He notes that one might understand the question "why is there something rather than nothing?" in a more restricted sense as asking "why did this property appear here and now?" Then one might with Aristotle propose an answer based on an appeal to relative nonbeing (which is "something" rather than absolute nothingness) in order to account for the reality of change or becoming.

Nonetheless, as Gerson explains, Plato himself had not been satisfied with such an explanation, since he had realized that an explanation of change would not of itself account for the being of anything that possesses being, especially of changeless things. By drawing upon texts from Plato's *Parmenides* and *Republic,* Gerson concludes that for him whatever has being must partake of *ousia* and to that extent must differ in some way from *ousia*. But the Idea of the Good, which provides being *(einai)* and *ousia* to that which is intelligible, is itself beyond *ousia*. Gerson points out the difference between Plato's First Principle, which is said to be beyond *ousia,* and Aristotle's First Principle, the Primary *Ousia* of *Metaphysics* XII.

Gerson shows how these different conceptions of a First Principle gave rise within the Platonic tradition to the issue often referred to as the Problem of the One and the Many: How can the many arise from the One or the composite from that which is not composite? He traces the origins of a fuller answer within the later Platonic tradition to Plato's *Symposium,* where he presents Socrates' report of Diotima's definition of love as desire for the possession of the good forever, and its work as "birth in [the presence of] beauty in the body and the soul." Plotinus applies Plato's conception of love *(erōs)* in describing his own First Principle—the One or the Good—as a "lover of itself." And, Gerson maintains, Plotinus applies Plato's concept of *erōs* to the One "as an abductive inference or *quia* proof from the claim that goodness is essentially self-diffusive." This claim in turn follows from the "self-evident multiplicity of intelligible forms in the universe."

Gerson notes that for Plotinus the Good must love itself and that in the achievement of its desire it produces necessarily. The self-love of the Good or One for itself is expressed by Plotinus as a kind of "gloss" on the fact that it is self-caused *(aition heautou),* whereas anything other than the One is not self-caused but caused by something outside itself. Moreover, Plotinus describes the self-causality of the One as "[making] itself from nothingness *(oudenos)*." Since all things other than Intellect depend upon the One through intermediaries, and even Intellect depends on the One's external activity, the One creates only itself if one restricts the term "creation" to direct existential dependence. Hence, comments Gerson, for Plotinus the self-diffusion of the Good is "the only possible answer to the question 'why is there something rather than nothing?'" And if we ask why the One or Good necessarily produces [Intellect], this is because it necessarily loves itself, which follows from the fact that it is "self-caused."

In Chapter 2, May Sim examines the question of being, nonbeing, and creation *ex nihilo* within Chinese philosophy by critically examining Robert Neville's views on the same, and especially on creation *ex nihilo*. (For more on Neville's position see Chapter 9 below.) While agreeing with those scholars, including Neville, who maintain that the question of being and nonbeing is present in Chinese philosophy, she expresses serious reservations about his claims concerning the presence of creation *ex nihilo* therein. She begins by setting forth Neville's creation hypothesis according to which "determinate beings come from nothing" and "something determinate 'is determinate with respect to some other determinate things.'" Because a determinate thing has features which relate to and contrast with other things, it is complex. Its complex nature is a harmony of its various features, and such harmonious determinate things must be contingent upon a ground or they would otherwise not exist at all. For Neville this means that they are subject to "ontological contingency" rather than merely to the "cosmological contingency" of the interrelations and harmonies of determinate things. Ontological causation is the causation of the world by what cannot itself be determinate, and Neville refers to this indeterminate ground as the "nothing." We can neither think nor speak about this nothing apart from its relation to the beings that come from it, and it is only in relation to them that it is "creative" and the "source" of the world. Because it is indeterminate, it itself needs no ground and its relation to the world is asymmetric. Whereas things in the world depend on ontological creativity for their existence, its existence does not depend upon them. (See Chapter 9 below for Neville's presentation of his own position.)

As Sim points out, Neville compares his views on "creative nothing" and asymmetry with the Chinese views on creation present in the Daoism of Laozi, the Confucianism of Confucius and Mencius, and the Neo-Confucianism of Zhoudunyi and Zhuxi and finds similar positions there. Indeed he writes that his "category of ontological creativity and the categories of the primary cosmology" are illustrated there perhaps even more clearly than in the Western traditions.

Sim grants that for the Confucians, Daoists, and Neo-Confucians the source seems to transcend the limitations of the world and to be asymmetrically related to determinate beings, and that Neville's ontological ground is his reason why there is something rather than nothing. Nonetheless, she then turns to detailed analysis of the Chinese sources in her effort to show that there are also considerable differences between their views of the source and Neville's characterization of his ontological ground.

She concludes that her comparisons of Neville and the Chinese thinkers regarding their views about the origins of beings and the way these beings change do show that the Chinese were also concerned with the question of being, nonbeing, and creation *ex nihilo,* but in ways that differ greatly from Neville's understanding of these concepts.

Jon McGinnis begins Chapter 3 ("The Ultimate Why Question: Avicenna on Why God Is Absolutely Necessary") with the observation that medieval Arabic-speaking philosophers were usually not inclined to ask "Why is there anything at all rather than absolutely nothing?" They were more concerned with the related question: "Why is there a world rather than no world at all?" or more precisely, "Why does the world have the particular features that it has?" He comments that the standard answer to the latter question in classical and medieval times was normally, "God," whether introduced to account for the orderly existence of our world (see Plato's Demiurge), or the motion in this world (see Aristotle's Unmoved Mover), or the unified existence of the world (see the Neoplatonic One). McGinnis notes that all of these approaches begin with a physical fact (order, motion, unification) and appeal to "God" as the cause of that fact.

Ibn Sīnā (980–1037), known in Latin as Avicenna, rejected purely "physical" arguments for God's existence and argued that a "metaphysical" argument was needed. As McGinnis understands his position, Avicenna feared that if an argument for God's existence rested on a mere physical fact, then if that "fact" had not occurred, a necessary premise for the argument would be lacking and so the argument itself would not establish the absolute necessity of God. In order to overcome this weakness, Avicenna wanted to develop an argument showing that if anything whatsoever exists, no matter how it exists, God necessarily exists. This argument would begin with an analysis of existence itself, or of being *qua* being, and the irreducible modal structure of existence. McGinnis, therefore, proposes to present and analyze Avicenna's metaphysical argument for God's existence and then to examine another Avicennian philosophical position—his proof for the eternity of the world. This proof maintains that if it is even possible for anything other than God to exist, the world must be eternal. And if this proof is joined with Avicenna's metaphysical proof for the existence of God, McGinnis maintains that this results in an even stronger proof for God's existence by showing that if anything whatsoever is simply possible, God necessarily exists. This in turn enables Avicenna to provide an answer to the ultimate why question: "Why is there anything at all rather than absolutely nothing?" The answer is: "Because something is possible."

Chapter 4 deals with Thomas Aquinas's views on the ultimate why question, and there I acknowledge that he does not raise the question why is there anything at all rather than nothing in these exact terms, although he has much to say about it. But this question was explicitly raised by one of his contemporaries from the Faculty of Arts at the University of Paris—Siger of Brabant. While commenting on Aristotle's *Metaphysics* IV, chapters 1–2, Siger attempts to reconcile Aristotle's claim that it belongs to the science of being as being to investigate the first principles and causes of being as being with Siger's own remark earlier on to the effect that there can be no cause or principle of being as being. If there were such a cause or principle, it would then be a cause and principle of itself, something which Siger rejects. To resolve this seeming

conflict, Siger replies that in referring to the principles and causes of being as being, Aristotle did not want to speak about being in the absolute
or unqualified sense; he rather intended to say that one should search for
the principles and causes of every *caused* being. As Siger explains, not
every being has a cause of its existence. And "if it is asked why there is
something rather than nothing," this question may be understood in two
ways. If it is restricted to things that are themselves caused, we may respond that this is because there is some First Mover and First Cause for
every caused being. But if we apply the question to all beings, an answer
in terms of causal explanation cannot be given. This would be to ask why
God himself exists rather than not, and no causal explanation can account for that.

Thomas Aquinas himself discusses the subject of metaphysics at
considerable length. For him its subject is being as being. God is not included under being as being (or *ens commune* [being in general]), but is
studied indirectly by the metaphysician only as the principle and cause
of what falls under its subject. Thus, if Thomas were asked why there is
something rather than nothing, he would distinguish different meanings
for the term "something." If it is restricted to what falls under the subject
of metaphysics—being as being—Thomas would argue that all such being is ultimately dependent upon God as the Uncaused Cause of all other
existents. But if the term "something" in our question is extended so as
to apply even to God, Thomas would agree with Siger's reply. No causal explanation can be given for God's existence since as the Uncaused
Cause he has no cause. Nonetheless, Thomas has more to say about this
issue. Once he has demonstrated to his own satisfaction the existence of
God, he finds it necessary to investigate why God has created anything
at all rather than simply not create. He also examines why God created
this universe rather than any other one that is possible. In Chapter 4, I
concentrate on his answer to the first and more fundamental of these
two questions, and in addressing this consider three sub-questions relating to the same: (1) According to Aquinas why did God create anything
at all? (2) Does he offer a causal explanation for God's decision to create,
or perhaps some other account? (3) How would Thomas respond if we
raise the ultimate why question about God himself: Why does God exist
rather than not exist?

Crucial for Thomas's response to the first question is his conviction that God is all good (which Thomas derives from the divine perfection) and that it is owing to a free decision on the part of his will that he creates rather than not. Moreover, Thomas supports this by citing a Neoplatonic axiom to the effect that the good is diffusive of itself *(bonum est diffusivum sui)*, known to him especially through the mediation of Pseudo-Dionysius. Some have argued, however, that Thomas's appeal to the goodness of God and to this axiom should have led him to conclude that God necessarily creates things other than himself rather than freely.

Aquinas, however, interprets the axiom that the good is diffusive of itself not in terms of efficient causality but in terms of final causality. God's will is directed to other things insofar as they are ordered to his own goodness as their end. A will, however, is not necessarily ordered to things that are themselves directed to an end if that end can be perfectly realized without those things. Since the divine goodness is fully realized without the existence of anything else and, being infinite, receives no increase in perfection from the existence of other things, Aquinas argues that it was not necessary for the divine will to produce such things.

In responding to the second question (Does anything *cause* God to will to create other beings?), Thomas introduces an interesting distinction between a reason *(ratio)* and a cause. A reason can be given for God's willing other things, but not a cause. God wills his own goodness as an end, and other things as ordered to that end. His goodness, therefore, is the reason for but not the cause of his willing other things.

In proposing a possible response on Thomas's part to my third question (Why does God exist?), I go somewhat beyond Thomas's explicit texts. While Thomas would deny that there is any efficient cause of God's existence, he holds that God must exist because his essence is identical with his act of existing. Hence he necessarily exists. This, I suggest, is in fact for him to offer a reason *(ratio)* for God's existence, but not a cause.

Tad Schmaltz addresses Descartes' response to the ultimate why question in Chapter 5 ("*Causa sui* and Created Truth in Descartes"). Descartes is to be numbered among those who took this question seriously and, moreover, was not satisfied with accounting for the contingent universe by simply tracing it back to an ultimate cause. Because he was convinced that there must be a "cause or reason" for the existence of everything, he concluded that this must also apply to the ultimate cause (God). While God has no external cause of his existence, his nature must provide a cause or reason which explains why he exists. He must derive his existence from himself or be a *causa sui*.

When faced with the objection that this would require something to be the efficient cause of itself, Descartes struggled to find a consistent response. Thus, as Schmaltz points out, in one text he reasons that because God conserves himself [in existence], it is not improper to refer to him as *causa sui*. And so we may hold that "in some manner [*quodammodo*] he stands in the same relation with respect to himself as an efficient cause stands with respect to its effect, and thus is positively from himself." In responding to Arnauld's criticism of this explanation, Descartes insists that he had never said that God is an efficient cause of his existence, but only that "in some manner" he stands in the same relation to his existence as does an efficient cause to its effect. And now he appeals to Aristotle's notion of formal cause to suggest that God's essence serves as a formal cause of his existence and that it bears a close analogy with an efficient cause and hence may be described as if it were an efficient cause (*quasi causa efficiens*).

In commenting on this text, Schmaltz remarks that here one "has the sense that Descartes was not entirely on top of his game." Nonetheless, Schmaltz proposes that it is "perhaps clear enough" that Descartes did not literally hold that God is the efficient cause of his own existence, but rather that the cause or reason for his existence—the divine power—is the rational ground for the truth that his existence needs no efficient cause. Thus, Schmaltz explains, in the case of God's existence, Descartes ultimately holds that there is a *reason* for God's existence, but one that is not an (efficient) cause of his existence and thus, a reason although not a cause may be offered to answer the ultimate why question: "Why is there anything at all rather than nothing whatsoever?"

Schmaltz next turns to Descartes' understanding of the dependence of eternal truths on the divine will as their "efficient and total cause." Schmaltz raises a question about the truth that God exists. If this is an eternal truth, it seems to follow that it, too, must depend upon the divine will as its efficient cause. But this seems to conflict with Descartes' doctrine of God as the *causa sui* for whose existence there can be no efficient cause but only a reason. Schmaltz points out that this difficulty assumes that Descartes intends to apply his created truth doctrine to all truths, including the truth that God exists. While acknowledging that certain texts in Descartes can indeed be read in that way, Schmaltz cites other passages that assign a special status to eternal truths about God or about his essence and existence and seem to exclude them from his created truth doctrine, thereby enabling Descartes to avoid this difficulty.

In Chapter 6 ("Being and Being Grounded") Daniel Dahlstrom introduces a discussion of Leibniz's Principle of Sufficient Reason in light of Heidegger's appreciation and critique of the impact of this principle on the modern "technological-scientific construction of the world." According to Heidegger in his *Der Satz vom Grund* of 1957, only by revisiting what Leibniz had in mind when he explicitly formulated this principle can one understand the present age—an age in which the principle of sufficient reason reigns supreme. If Heidegger at times indicates that this unrestricted pursuit of reasons and grounds *(Grund)* is necessary and even promising, more frequently he views it as a threat to another kind of ground *(Boden),* the soil that he regards as essential for human flourishing. The more we search for the grounds and reasons and causes of things in the sciences, the more this vital soil *(Boden)* recedes from our view.

Rather than discard the principle of sufficient reason, however, Heidegger proposes distinguishing two ways of understanding it. On the Leibnizian reading, it is a statement about beings, or whatever is; but on Heidegger's own reading, it is a way of saying what it means to be. In support of his reading, he maintains that certain aspects of being are irreducible to and even "occluded" by Leibniz's understanding of this principle, including the self-sameness and individuality, the historicity and non-dependence, of being. In other words, owing to the modern pursuit of the sufficient reason of beings, one loses sight of being as the ground or reason for beings. Dahlstrom indicates that in his view there is something right and something wrong about Heidegger's position. He finds the issue far more complicated than Heidegger indicates, and proposes to establish what is wrong about Heidegger's reading in order to clarify what is right about it.

Dahlstrom begins by examining Leibniz's own account of this principle and notes an early formulation of it in abbreviated fashion: "nothing is without reason" (ca. 1671), followed by a more qualified version in 1677: "nothing exists for which a sufficient reason of its existence cannot be given." Dahlstrom explains that by "sufficient" in this context Leibniz means the "aggregate of all that is requisite" for something to exist. In a somewhat later presentation (in the 1680s) Leibniz further specifies that the reason for something "must be given" *(principium reddendae rationis)*. Finally, in his *Monadology,* Leibniz combines the just-mentioned specifications by formulating it as the "principle of the sufficient reason that is to be given."

Dahlstrom notes that Leibniz applies this principle in many areas. If we ask him why there is something rather than nothing, he will reply that this is because nothing can exist without a sufficient reason for existing, even though he also holds that nothing within nature contains within itself the sufficient reason for its own existence. "Reason *(ratio)* is why in nature something exists rather than nothing," and this, Leibniz adds, follows from the principle that nothing comes to be without a reason just as, he also remarks, there must be a reason why this exists rather than that.

Dahlstrom points out that in the 1680s Leibniz adds an important qualification to his application of this principle to contingent things. Because a particular contingent thing may depend upon an infinity of other things, only an infinite intellect (God) can grasp the infinite progression required to give the full reason for such a thing. In these cases it is "sufficient for us to know the truth of such things *a posteriori,* that is, through experience," always bearing in mind also, however, that nothing happens without a sufficient reason, and that "that which has the more reason always happens." Leibniz maintains that this universal application of the principle of sufficient reason is not incompatible with the contingency of the world and with God's freedom to create it. God alone is the sufficient reason for the existence of the contingent world, not merely as necessary in himself, however, but by reason of his free choice in producing the world.

As Dahlstrom points out, not everyone agrees that Leibniz has succeeded in leaving a place for contingency in his account, especially so in light of his view that God cannot choose anything but the best possible world. Even so, Dahlstrom notes that in his later writings Leibniz maintains that although the world as produced by God is the most worthy, its being the most worthy is not a necessary truth but one that is contingent. And Dahlstrom emphasizes that Heidegger does not take into account Leibniz's defense of both the contingency of the world and the compatibility of this with the principle of sufficient reason.

Dahlstrom notes that while Heidegger is aware of the frequently repeated criticism that Leibniz misidentifies reasons and causes, Heidegger defends him from this charge by suggesting that the principle of causation is one form of the principle of sufficient reason. But Heidegger does object to the view that the principle of sufficient reason itself is beyond question.

As regards Heidegger's own reading of the principle of sufficient reason, it should not be taken as a statement about beings but rather as a way of saying what it means to be. Understood in this way, it presupposes being as a groundless ground which dispenses itself to us by holding back, by concealing itself in different ways. For Heidegger, being cannot be reduced to a simple presence, since an absence can also be integral to what it means for something to be. He writes that the self-concealing, the withdrawal, "is a manner in which being as being endures, dispenses itself, that is to say, affords itself."

Dahlstrom concludes by pointing out certain shortcomings in Heidegger's understanding of Leibniz's metaphysics. For instance, Leibniz recognizes that God's being is not grounded in something else, but also that there are contingent truths about possible worlds, necessarily known by God, but still contingent. Thus, *pace* Heidegger's claims, Leibniz suggests that contingency and necessity can be brought together in a metaphysical conception of being and, Dahlstrom argues, his account of the principle of sufficient reason does not necessarily eliminate what Heidegger views as the historicity of being. Yet, according to Dahlstrom, Heidegger is right in his reading of the principle of sufficient reason in holding that "being in some sense grounds the beings that are cause and effect, ground and grounded."

In Chapter 7, Holger Zaborowski examines the ultimate why question in the writings of one of the leading representatives of German idealism, F. W. J. Schelling. Zaborowski begins by offering a brief but informative introduction to the origins of this philosophical movement which, beginning in the 1790s shortly after Kant's publication of his third *Critique,* was led by a younger generation of philosophers who viewed themselves as bringing the Kantian project to its fulfillment. They did not follow the letter of his philosophy closely, but were inspired by his spirit, as each of its three leading figures—Fichte, Schelling, and Hegel—attempted to develop a comprehensive and unified philosophical system in an original and distinctive way.

As Zaborowski points out, the main principle for them was the conception of the self as an absolutely free being, the absolutely free Ego. He notes that Schelling follows a trajectory of thought centered around the question of freedom—freedom for the philosopher to think for himself, to be sure, but also freedom as incorporated into the all-embracing system of philosophy he was developing. Schelling strongly rejects the view that a system of philosophy can only be deterministic. And it is within this context that he also raises the ultimate why question. A system of philosophy must deal with this question and think about why there is something rather than nothing. Philosophy, he maintains, should "explain the fact of the world." An appeal to the theological doctrine of creation may explain that God exists and created the world, but this is not sufficient to explain why God created the world and hence why there is something rather than nothing.

In his early writings, Schelling raises and answers the ultimate why question implicitly rather than explicitly. As Zaborowski explains, in developing his early philosophy, Schelling is influenced in various ways by Spinoza, Kant, Fichte, and Plato. While admiring Spinoza's search for an "ultimate point of all knowledge," Schelling finds that in positing God as a necessarily existing substance, Spinoza falls short by denying that God is a free cause. While appreciating Kant's critical philosophy for emphasizing the subject and freedom, in his early period Schelling is not content like Kant to seek for the conditions of possibility (for the world as we perceive and understand it), but rather strives to account for the "conditionedness of the conditioned," thereby raising a particular version of the ultimate why question. To answer this, Schelling moves beyond Kant's critique of metaphysics and turns toward a post-Kantian rational metaphysics that leads him toward the unconditional that conditions all that is conditioned, that is, an absolute basic principle which, much as Fichte does in his *Science of Knowledge,* Schelling identifies as the transcendental Ego that is posited through itself, that is freedom itself, and from which a non-Ego is posited "out of freedom." This, then, is one formulation of his early answer to the ultimate why question. In developing it he is also influenced by his youthful reading of and commentary on Plato's *Timaeus,* especially the part dealing with the role of the Demiurge in the genesis of the world.

Schelling is also interested in overcoming the Cartesian and Kantian "gap" between the subjective and the objective and so eventually seeks to overcome the subjectivism he now finds in Fichte's early idealism as well as in his own. This, he contends, did not account adequately for both the objectivity and subjectivity of nature, and led him to seek for a new and transcendental philosophy of nature in an effort to show how nature can be both product (object/*natura naturata*) and productive (subjective/*natura naturans*). But also he continued to work on his transcendental idealism as well, and produced his book entitled *System of Transcendental Idealism* where, like Kant and Fichte, he accepts knowledge as his starting-point and reasons that "all knowledge is founded on the coincidence of an objective with a subjective." In order to explain this coincidence Schelling now proposes two possible ways, one, the way of the natural sciences and the philosophy of nature, which makes the objective primary and seeks to explain how the subjective coincides with it, and the other the way of transcendental philosophy, which makes the subject primary and asks how the objective coincides with it. As Zaborowski explains, this means that now (around 1800), his answer to the ultimate why question is divided. Just as there are now two basic sciences of philosophy—the philosophy of nature and transcendental philosophy—the ultimate why question has two different answers because there are two primaries or unconditionals, that is, the Ego and nature.

Schelling comes to realize this and begins to develop a philosophy of absolute identity that would overcome the dualism just mentioned by proposing as its basic principle an absolute that lies beyond the distinction of subject and object. But he continues to find it increasingly difficult to answer the ultimate why question, Zaborowski observes, so much so that he eventually supplements what he referred to as his "negative" transcendental philosophy with a "positive" historical philosophy. And this leads him to develop his later answer to the ultimate why question. He now criticizes his earlier philosophy as being merely logical and unhistorical in character and as having not yet taken God into account as its starting point and center. As early as 1806 he had noted, only God or "the All" could offer the answer to the ultimate why question, even though, Zaborowski comments, this answer also reveals Schelling's "somewhat Spinozistic philosophy of identity (be it pantheistic or panentheistic)."

But if his later answer to the why question still focuses on freedom, now it is God's freedom rather than the unconditional transcendental freedom of the Ego. And Schelling now views God against the background of the biblical understanding of him as a historical and living God, whom Schelling describes as "Lord of Being." He is assisted in this by his particular retranslation of Exodus 3:14, in which God describes himself not as "I am who I am" (the traditional translation), but as "I am he who I will be." Schelling takes this as indicating that God is saying "I am who I want to be," thereby indicating that nothing is predetermined about his being; it only depends upon his will. God is free to be a creator or not, and if there is anything at all, this is because of God's free will to create. But Schelling goes even further by asking why there is God, and argues that God freely called his own being into existence, thus developing a "very radical philosophy of divine freedom," as Zaborowski styles it. Hence, if God was free to create or not create, he was also free to be or not to be. He is indeed the "Lord of Being." Hence one must at least grant that Schelling took the ultimate why question very seriously indeed.

In Chapter 8 Edward Halper addresses "The Ultimate Why Question: The Hegelian Option." He notes that this question is usually answered by appealing to a highest cause, a transcendent God, and that in this chapter he wants to contrast this general approach with that offered by Hegel. If the "traditional" account moves to a higher level source or cause, the Hegelian approach emphasizes "interlinked comprehensiveness," as Halper phrases it. Rather than "discover the source of everything, it attempts to explain everything."

Halper cites Plotinus, Aquinas, and Leibniz, among others, as proponents of the traditional account, and notes that these thinkers want to supply for a shortcoming in ancient Greek philosophy, namely, that the ancient philosophers do not raise the ultimate why question. They are content to attempt to explain the way things are. Halper offers Aristotle as an illustration of this with his doctrine of an Unmoved Mover that sustains reproduction (change) but does not account for the intrinsic principles of change (matter and form) nor explain "why what is is, rather than something else," nor "why there is what is rather than nothing at all." Halper finds a similar deficiency in Plato and mentions his account of the role of the Demiurge in the *Timaeus* in the genesis of the world. One might note here, however, as Gerson does in Chapter I, the role that Plato assigns to the Good in the *Republic* in its relationship to the other intelligibles or ideas. In any event, as Halper sums up, the ancient Greeks had no doctrine of *creatio ex nihilo*.

Halper finds that Plotinus recognizes the need for an ultimate cause, and places the One at a higher level than anything else, including Intellect, which the One produces immediately. Halper stresses the point that, in addition to being at a higher level ontically than anything else, the One enjoys agency and so ultimately generates the substance of everything else. Halper then cites as important variations on this approach both Thomas Aquinas and Leibniz. To go beyond Aristotle, Aquinas needed a principle that is generative and, Halper indicates, introduced *esse* as enjoying a higher level of actuality than form. Viewed as an intrinsic principle of finite and caused beings, *esse* is an intrinsic principle that actualizes form (or, in material beings, the matter-form composite essence) and is itself efficiently caused by the First Principle, a creative principle that is itself uncaused and is pure and subsisting Being *(Esse)* or God. As for Leibniz, Halper indicates that he begins with the perfection of the First Cause which, because it is perfect, produces the best possible of its kind. Hence for Leibniz the answer to the ultimate why question is God, but only insofar as he is perfect and hence produces the best possible world.

Halper notes that common to these three thinkers is the need to appeal to a higher level source or cause of the existence of everything else. This source cannot itself be caused by anything else if it is to explain why there is something rather than nothing. But Halper believes that this approach leads to a dilemma. On the one hand, this source must *exist*, must be *one*, and must be *perfect*. This implies that we know something about it. On the other hand, it must not be finite and delimited, as are the things we know, and it must be unlike the things we know. Hence we cannot know this source, maintains Halper. To be the ultimate cause, the first cause must be unlike what it causes and hence, we cannot know it; but if we cannot know it, we cannot appeal to it to account for the detailed characteristics of its effects.

As he turns to Hegel, Halper observes that if it is contradictory to say that there is a cause that accounts for something but that we do not know this cause, Hegel accepts this contradiction. If the cause cannot be determinately thought, in recognizing this, we in some way understand it as indeterminate. For Hegel the problem is to explain how determinacy arises from indeterminacy, and here Halper turns to Hegel's dialectic. For Hegel the first category of his *Science of Logic*—being—is "tantamount to God." But an indeterminate Being cannot cause anything and for Hegel, at the beginning there is only Being and it lacks determination. Hence its determination is Nothing. But insofar as Being is Nothing, the category of Becoming emerges. Halper views this as important since it suggests a way of moving from the cause to what is caused, and in such a way that the content of what is caused "emerges from the character of the cause." Hegel can render the causality of his Being intelligible by having it determine itself.

Halper comments, however, that Hegel's solution brings with it its own difficulties. Being, the cause, cannot be the ultimate cause because it is not transcendent; for in determining itself it transforms itself and in transforming itself it generates another category which, in turn, transforms itself into still another category, and so forth until the final category of the *Logic* is reached—Absolute Idea—which contains within itself all the prior series of transformations. But Absolute Idea acquires another kind of Being that is external to itself and unfolds again through Nature and Spirit, reaching completion with the final category—Philosophy—which contains within itself all that preceded it within the system. While the first cause—Being—is not the ultimate cause for Hegel, he can still offer an answer to the ultimate why question. This comes not at the beginning of the unfolding but at its end with the final category. And so Hegel's ultimate cause is not a transcendent *creator* as in Aquinas or Leibniz, for instance, but it is the *comprehensive creation*. This dialectical unfolding that constitutes the development of Hegel's system is God manifesting himself and indeed it is God thinking himself.

Halper raises what he regards as a serious problem following from Hegel's dialectic. Hegel derives one category from another by showing that it stands in some relation either to itself or to another category; but, Halper notes, this process will succeed only if the category belongs to thought. Here he recalls that Hegel is an idealist, and this leads to another question that appeal to an ultimate cause should enable one to answer: Why is there any thought at all? Halper responds that the ultimate origin of the system cannot be thought since "thought completes itself within the system." Thought still needs to be accounted for. And the well-structured whole needs to be accounted for: Why does it exist rather than nothing? Hence a transcendent cause also seems to be needed.

Halper concludes that an account is needed that is both transcendent (as in the traditional approach) and comprehensive (as in Hegel). He briefly mentions two who have attempted to work out this kind of reconciliation, although obviously in very different ways, that is, Spinoza and Aquinas. But he finds difficulties with each of their solutions. He ultimately concludes, therefore, that while a transcendent cause gives an answer to the existence question, why there is something rather than nothing, it falls short with respect to accounting for the "what" of that which it causes. As regards a satisfactory answer to the ultimate why question, Halper finds philosophy falling short. He concludes by saying that the ultimate cause for our seeking ultimate causes is "the fundamental mystery of world, the world's not being self-sufficient."

In Chapter 9 ("Some Contemporary Theories of Divine Creation"), Robert Neville proposes his own admittedly rough division of conceptions of God into two major different types—those that conceive of God as a determinate entity, and those that conceive of God as the ground-of-being and not as a determinate entity within or alongside the world. While he regards contemporary process theology as a good representative of the first type, he proposes to subdivide the ground-of-being class into "fullness-of-being conceptions and *ex nihilo* conceptions." As examples of fullness-of-being conceptions he cites Neoplatonism, Thomism, and perhaps the Kyoto School of Buddhism. These, he proposes, view God or the Ultimate as beyond finite determinateness and therefore indeterminate by reason of simplicity and by having no contrast term. "As the pure fullness of reality, God is conceived to create the world by some kind of diremption or introduction of negation that finitizes elements of the fullness of being." Neville refers to this as creation by God *(creatio a deo)*. He describes *ex nihilo* conceptions of God as maintaining that God is the creative act that not only gives rise to the world but also thereby gives rise to the divine nature itself as creator. Neville also refers to fullness-of-being conceptions as viewing God as symmetrical, whereas *ex nihilo* conceptions view God as asymmetrical. In this chapter Neville proposes to present process theology's view of God as an example of the determinate-being type, and to criticize it. Then he will bring out the contrast between the fullness-of-being and *ex nihilo* ground-of-being conceptions of God and argue in support of the latter.

As regards process theology's conception of God, Neville begins with Whitehead's conception of God as an everlasting actual entity that "prehends every finite actual entity as soon as it becomes definite and that supplies initial aims to each emerging finite actual occasion." Neville notes that a difficulty was raised concerning Whitehead's view. On this view, God never finishes coming to be and hence is never available as something actual and definite that can be prehended by finite actual entities. Neville notes that as a way of meeting this difficulty Charles Hartshorne offered an alternative conception of God as a society of actual entities, each of which is finite in duration and when definite can be prehended; but Neville comments that this raises another difficulty, namely, that there is nothing to guarantee that a given actual divine entity within the society of divine entities will be succeeded by another divine entity.

Neville next raises an objection to all the process conceptions of God as a determinate entity. He argues that according to process thought any complex thing, be it a single actual entity, or a society of actual entities, or adventitious meetings of trajectories of processes, may be understood by identifying the decision-points involved in its constitution. By a decision-point he understands that point "where an act of creativity adds some novelty that resolves the things prehended into a new definite actual harmony." If each emerging actual entity has its own subjective decision-point, so too each thing prehended has its own objectified decision-point and so forth to infinity. Whitehead referred to this as the "ontological principle." But, comments Neville, according to process philosophy the basic metaphysical situation is God and the world interacting and, since this is a complex metaphysical situation, the ontological principle should oblige one to ask what decision or decisions contributed to the basic complex situation. Even though Whitehead did not raise this question, Neville argues that there should be an ontological decision-point of creativity which constitutes the basic complex metaphysical situation. He argues that this ontological creative act must be singular, eternal, and non-spatial. Neville also argues that the decisive creative act of the basic metaphysical situation may be called ontological, in contrast to decision-points within the metaphysical situation, which may be called cosmological. He also argues that the ontological decision-point has no antecedents and no potentials and hence creates total novelty; it creates *ex nihilo*. Indeed, Neville writes that it is this ontological decision-point that he would call God.

Neville acknowledges that process theologians might respond that the basic metaphysical situation, while complex, is absolutely primary, and thus refuse to raise the ontological question about it. This would be for them not to take seriously the problem of the one and the many, beyond their theory of how emergent entities unify their prehended contents, and therefore not to address the ultimate question of why or how there is anything at all.

Neville next offers what he regards as a stronger argument against process theology, and against all conceptions of God as a determinate being. He asks what is involved in determinateness as such, and he proposes that a thing is determinate when it is this rather than that. He hypothesizes that a thing is a harmony with conditional features and essential features. As regards process conceptions of God, while the primordial nature is the essential element of God, the concrete nature made up of prehensions of finite entities is conditional. But here, argues Neville, one encounters the problem of the one and the many. If a thing is a harmony, as he proposes, each harmony requires a "togetherness of both its essential and conditional features to be itself," and thus there must be some "ontological context" in which the essential features of different harmonies are together in such fashion that it can serve as the ground for the possibility that things can condition one another cosmologically. Neville proposes that the classic idea of creation *ex nihilo* is the ground he is seeking.

With this he turns to the distinction he has drawn under "ground of being theologies" between fullness-of-being and creation *ex nihilo* conceptions of this ultimate ontological ground. He grants that according to fullness-of-being conceptions (Neoplatonic, Thomistic, perhaps Buddhist) the created world "participates" in finite ways in the reality that the "full-being God has." But he finds a major difficulty with such approaches in that, he argues, they cannot explain how God as the fullness of being creates anything determinate. As he puts it: "It would seem that creation would consist in making only negations or limitations so as to break up portions of the fullness of being into finite bits." Any positive finite reality could not be new because it would be a part of the original fullness of being.[2] Only pure negations could be new and, he asks, how could a pure negation be created?

---

2. In the interests of historical accuracy, and bearing in mind Neville's early acknowledgment that perhaps no historical thinker will fit exactly into his classifications, I would like to register a *caveat* about his inclusion of Aquinas under "fullness-of-being" conceptions of

Against this approach he maintains that it is a far simpler hypothesis to propose that divine creating "gives rise to determinate things that have positive being and definite negations or limitations together" and these determinate things include a mixture of being and nonbeing. And so he defends the superiority of creation *ex nihilo* conceptions of God as the ground of being over fullness-of-being conceptions. He concludes by briefly describing different types of piety that may result from the difference between determinate entity conceptions, fullness-of-being conceptions, and creation *ex nihilo* conceptions of God. As regards the ultimate why question, taking this as asking for an account of the "difference between absolutely nothing and the world of somethings," Neville responds that the divine creative act is the answer.

Contrary to the various approaches taken by the majority of the philosophers considered so far in this volume, in Chapter 10 ("Pragmatic Reflections on Final Causality"), Brian Martine proposes to reject the ultimate why question as meaningless if it is understood as asking why there is something rather than absolutely nothing. He takes this question as proposing an alternative to "something" and, because he can find no such alternative in "absolutely nothing," he claims that what was originally formulated as a question proves in fact to be the assertion of something or other. After offering a few remarks about Parmenides and his inconsistency in rejecting the way of becoming and then devoting the final part of his philosophical poem to investigating the world as sub-

God. Aquinas refers to creatures or created essences as participating in *esse* in different ways, two of which in particular must be carefully distinguished. They may be viewed (1) as participating in *esse commune* (the act of existing viewed universally insofar as it is or can be participated in by creatures) and (2) as participating in *esse subsistens* (God) as their uncaused cause by assimilation or imitation. These two usages of *esse* must not be confused or identified. God is not *esse commune* and does not fall under *esse commune*. According to either usage, Aquinas would reject the claim that creation consists "in making only negations or limitations so as to break up portions of the fullness of being into finite bits." Apart from its actual realization in particular creatures, *esse commune* enjoys no preexisting reality in itself outside the intellect and so creation cannot be described as breaking up portions of it into finite bits. Creation is rather the production of the entire being of a creature, including its essence and act of existing, *ex nihilo*—*that is,* from no preexisting subject. Because Aquinas insists that creatures participate in *esse subsistens* by imitation or assimilation as an effect participates in its cause, he emphatically rejects any attempt to say that creation involves breaking up the divine *esse* (*esse subsistens*) into bits or pieces. For discussion and relevant texts in Aquinas see my *The Metaphysical Thought of Thomas Aquinas*, 110–24, and especially pp. 114–16 for a major text from his Commentary on the *De divinis nominibus* of Pseudo-Dionysius, c. V, lect. 2, on the distinction between *esse commune* and God.

ject to change, Martine asks what this "something" presupposed by the ultimate why question could possibly mean. If one replies that this is Being as understood by philosophers, Martine wonders what that means. He reasons that it cannot mean Being in its simple immediacy because such expressions, like others such as "absolutely nothing," prove to mean nothing at all. No term, he reasons, taken out of relation to anything else, can mean anything at all. If someone proposes taking Being as immediate in contrast with mediated Being, one will in fact be thinking of two terms—"immediate" Being and "mediated" Being. Or if one proposes taking Being here as Being *simpliciter* as contrasted with determinate being, then the "something" implied by the ultimate why question must be Determinate Beings, or some things. And then the ultimate why question is reduced to this: "Why is there *this* something rather than some other something?"

But Martine complains that even this restricted version of the why question remains unclear and consequently has been understood in different ways by the ancients and by the moderns. To illustrate the ancient approach, Martine cites Socrates who, while sitting in his cell and awaiting death, points out that the materialists cannot offer an adequate answer to the question "Why is he sitting there?" To explain why this particular state of affairs obtains rather than some other, one must transcend the immediate state of affairs and seek an answer among the forms of justice and goodness, as Plato does in introducing his theory of Ideas. As Martine presents Plato's solution, if we are to reach any understanding of things, we must move beyond our experience of a particular state of affairs and consider it in relationship to other actual and possible states of affairs. That which is common to it and other actual and possible states of affairs can be elevated into beings or meanings (or both) which are held to enjoy a status independent from particular states of affairs. And these may be used to explain why this state of affairs obtains rather than any other.

Martine argues that on this account Ideas such as justice itself and the Good come into view in some way and carry with them the notion of an end that exercises final causality in some manner. Accordingly, Socrates can explain that he is in prison because this is required by justice itself and by his responsibility to act in accord with the form of justice itself. And so Martine reasons that the doctrine of Ideas, and its many descendants, he adds, may be understood as answers to his restricted version of the why question: "Why do particular states of affairs come to be as they are?" They do so by informing themselves with meanings thought to transcend the world of direct experience. Moreover, Martine notes that another problem may be addressed by appealing to Ideas or Forms—the transformation within the practical world of one state of affairs into another may be viewed as a movement toward an end (an Idea) whose influence reaches back through the different states of affairs and renders them purposive.

Martine acknowledges that this is only one way of understanding Plato's explanation of the genesis of the cosmos, but he prefers it because of its relationship to our natural practical experience. He reasons that as human beings we are first driven by ends involved in satisfying the basic needs for human living. As these basic needs are satisfied, the habit of pursuing ends remains with us, and thus it is not surprising that we would subsequently apply this approach to more complex problems and questions. They too should draw their meaning from the ends which are meaningful in themselves.

While granting the attractiveness of such an approach, Martine also comments that many problems arose concerning it, beginning with difficulties raised and addressed by Plato himself in different dialogues. For Martine the greatest difficulty with this approach is this: The various practical ends originally drew their meaning from the particular context in which they were experienced. Once they have been abstracted from that context and are viewed as having some inherent meaning in themselves apart from that context, they become as ineffable as were the originally immediate and ineffable states of affairs they were supposed to explain. Hence, viewed as meanings or beings in themselves, Martine maintains that Plato's Ideas no longer fall within the field of discursive reason. Even if one grants to us some kind of intellectual intuition of the Forms or Ideas, they are still cut off from the practical experience they were intended to explain, and so the "prototype of the many dualisms of the tradition appears."

In examining the possible choices remaining for those who have reached this point in their investigation, Martine notes that someone might simply accept a "diremption between reality and appearance" that cannot be overcome. Or one might reject Parmenides and immerse oneself in the world of movement and becoming, restricting oneself to an effort to understand how things function and are related to one another. Even then, he fears, one may again end with a split between the world we experience and our understanding of it. Nonetheless, Martine concedes, we still find ourselves asking "Why? Why this world rather than some other?" Or, more fundamentally for us, Martine remarks, we ask "Why this course of action rather than some other?"

Martine recommends that we reflect on what prompted us to ask the why question in the first place and to think that there could be a meaning beyond the immediate state of affairs in which we find ourselves in the world of experience. He returns to his original explanation that we first reach for things that we need to survive, and then as our experience broadens, so do our questions. Now we look for reasons to account for our effort to survive and thus for meanings. He does not maintain that we simply invent these meanings. But he insists on a return to the world of practical experience if we are to account for the meaning we attribute to the ends we pursue, and if we are to find any possible answer to the ultimate why question.

Nicholas Rescher begins Chapter 11 by asking whether the real is ultimately rational, intending thereby to ask whether one can ever succeed in explaining the nature of reality as a whole and therefore, I would note, answer the ultimate why question. He presents an argument developed from Kant that purports to show that such a "totalitarian" explanation cannot be given, since it would involve a vitiating regress or a circular accounting for factual conclusions by appealing to factual premises. But, in sharp contrast to Kant (and to Martine), Rescher proposes another approach— to move from "the descriptive/factual to the normative/axiological order of explanation" and thus, by turning to values, to account for reality in terms of what he calls "optimality." He proposes to base this approach on an "axiogenetic optimality principle," meaning thereby that in the "virtual competition" between various possibilities for realization in terms of truth or in terms of existence, "the (or an) optimal possibility wins out." An alternative possibility is optimal when there is no better, although Rescher grants that such a possibility may have equals. Hence things exist, and exist in their given ways because this is for the metaphysically best. And thus a "Law of Optimality" obtains to the effect that value "enjoys an existential bearing, so that it lies in the nature of things that (one of) the best of available alternatives is realized."

Rescher explains that optimalism is a teleological theory, a doctrine of final causes, although not a causal theory in the sense causation is usually understood today, that is, as efficient causation. Optimalism does not regard value as productive, as a kind of efficient cause. Rather it is "eliminative," in that it removes certain theoretical or logical possibilities from the realm of "real possibility." A value offers an explanation, an axiological *reason,* without functioning as an (efficient) *cause* of what it explains. Explanation of why physical objects and events are realized does require appealing to efficient causes, he acknowledges, but laws of nature "do not 'exist' as constituents of the physical realm—they just *obtain.*" Hence they do not require a causal explanation. By eliminating certain possibilities, values offer an explanation as to why something is so, but not an answer in terms of efficient causation.

Rescher is well aware that readers will wonder why anyone should grant that optimalism obtains and that what is truly for the best is actual. He grants that his Law of Optimality is not a logico-conceptually necessary truth and that, from the standpoint of theoretical logic, it is a contingent fact. Yet he reasons that optimalism has an explanation in accord with Leibniz's Principle of Sufficient Reason—"that for every contingent fact there is a reason why it is so and not otherwise." But, argues Rescher, the explanation for the Law of Optimality is to be found within itself. It is for the best that this law itself should obtain! And so "the division between real and merely theoretical possibilities is as it is (i.e., value based) because that itself is for the best."

Rescher argues that optimalism has many theoretical advantages and he cites one. Someone might hold that the existence of a world is a necessary fact, but that its nature is contingent, and so potentially different answers would be required for the questions "Why is there anything at all?" and "Why is the character of existence as it is?" But optimalism will offer a single answer to both questions—simply because "this is for the best."

He also asks whether optimalism is theocentric. In answering the question, he argues that optimalism does not require theism, but that the doctrine is self-supportive and obtains not necessarily because God made it so, but simply because this is for the best. He adds that a question such as "Why is there anything at all?" is a philosophical question and should ideally be answered by philosophical means. At the same time, Rescher comments that axiological explanation is quite congenial to theism.

Nonetheless, Rescher takes care to distinguish his approach from that of Leibniz who, he notes, appealed to God's will to answer the question "Why is it that the value-optimizing world should be the one that actually exists?" Rescher also cautions against concluding that this realization is reality's *purpose*. He argues against personifying nature in such a way that it is thought to act for purposes. No reference to someone's purposes need be involved in an explanation based on values. He distinguishes purpose from order, arguing that "order seeking" in nature does not presuppose one who orders, nor does "value 'seeking' presuppose a valuer." And so he is critical of the traditional argument from design which infers the existence of a creator from the order present in nature. He also distinguishes between purpose and values, arguing that a value can be impersonal, that value explanation need not be purposive, and that a system can be goal-directed through its inherent natural programming. While he acknowledges that axiological explanations do not answer the causal question about how values operate productively so as to bring given laws to actualization, he does not regard this as a fault.

Among other objections which he considers and discusses, perhaps the most crucial has to do with the hesitation of many to accept his claim that the inherently best alternative is the actual one. He argues that "inherently best" should not be understood from the perspective of my interests or desires, or yours, or those of any particular group, or even of humanity in general. The "best" must rather be understood in reference to the condition of existence-as-a-whole. And if one asks, why then is the world not completely perfect, he appeals to the complexity of an object of value. What he has in mind here is a multiplicity of competing values, not all of which can be realized to the maximum degree. The increase of some necessarily entails a decrease of others and so the optimally realizable best will include the optimal balance of these different values. Here Rescher recalls Leibniz's view that this world is not absolutely perfect, but the best that is possible, all things considered. He recognizes that his is an unusual and extraordinary answer to an extraordinary question.

Many different responses to the ultimate why question are represented in this volume, and it is hoped that, after reading them, readers will be in better position to decide which of them they prefer, if any, and whether pure philosophy can ultimately resolve this issue.

Part One

Contributions in Ancient Philosophy

Lloyd P. Gerson

1 ❦ Goodness, Unity, and Creation in the Platonic Tradition

I

By "the Platonic tradition" I mean to indicate certain fundamental principles shared by Plato and by all those who identified themselves as his disciples. From the perspective of the *soi-disants* followers of Plato, he was not the first or the only revealer of the truth; he was, though, the most sublime. Since Platonists regularly appropriated Aristotelian distinctions and arguments for their articulation of Platonism on the grounds that he was himself at heart a Platonist, albeit a dissident one, I will not hesitate to call on the Stagirite as needed.[1]

The Platonic tradition can fairly claim to be the *fons et origo* of reflection on the question "why is there something rather than nothing?" In this regard, Parmenides was thought to lead the way. For Parmenides argued that change, if it is to occur, must involve something coming out of nothing or something disappearing into nothing. But that something should, for example, be in the realm of nothingness, and then appear in the realm of being, is an unintelligible and even implicitly self-contradictory notion. It is worth trying to say exactly why this is so. It is unintelligible to us that something should inhabit the realm of nothingness, for a claim that it does requires one to identify it as such, and therefore, of course, to recognize it as *being* something identifiable. So, the question "why is there something

1. See my *Aristotle and Other Platonists* (Ithaca, NY: Cornell University Press, 2005), especially 24–46, for a sketch of how the Platonic tradition understood the fidelity of Aristotle to the philosophy of his master.

rather than nothing?" if interpreted to mean "why is something that was once nothing something now?" or "why is it that what is nothing now was once something?" is literally an unintelligible one. If, by contrast, we interpret our question as one regarding *relative* non-being—as in "why did this property appear here and now?"—then we have a robust array of tools with which to answer it. We have, that is, an Aristotelian schema of explanation which, for the most part, Platonists were more than willing to employ. On this schema, the explanation for why there is something rather than nothing would properly focus on a *something* as *explanans*. Having arrived at an *explanans* that is both necessary and sufficient, there is nothing left to explain.

But between Parmenides and the Aristotelian articulation of a response to him in terms of relative non-being, Plato interposed a further challenge of his own. His challenge amounted to arguing that the answer to the question "why is there something rather than nothing?" could not be reduced to an explanation of how or why a change occurred. To explain a change was not to explain the being of anything possessing being, particularly the being of changeless things. Some philosophers—especially those in the Peripatetic and Stoic schools—rejected this challenge. They simply denied that there was anything to explain. On the other hand, Platonists fully accepted the legitimacy of the question "why is there something rather than nothing?" where "something" refers to anything that possesses being of any sort, not just changeable being.

The beginning of a response to Plato's challenge is to be found in the dialogues themselves. Plato argues in the *Parmenides*:

If one is, is it possible for it to be and for it not to partake of *ousia* [essence]?—It is not possible—Therefore, the *ousia* of that which is one, since it is, is not identical with that which is one; otherwise, the *ousia* would not be one's *ousia*, nor would that which is one partake of *ousia*, but it would be the same thing to say "one is" and "one is one." However, the hypothesis is not "what follows if one is one," but "what follows if one is." Is this not so?—Of course—Then, the "is" signifies something different from the "one." (142B5–C5, my translation)

The principal point of this passage for our purposes is that Plato seems to have Parmenides offer an argument that being is composite: what has being must partake of *ousia* or essence. In that case, there will be a distinction between that which partakes and that which is partaken of.

It is reasonable to suppose that the *Parmenides* passage provides an analysis of the famous *Republic* passage where it is said that the Idea of the Good is that which provides being *(einai)* and *ousia* to that which is knowable.[2] The Idea of the Good is itself "beyond *ousia*." And so, it would seem, it is "beyond" the being that only comes from participating in *ousia*. And yet, as scholars have noted, this evidently does not mean that the Good is altogether beyond being in any sense. It is, we are informed, "the brightest part of being" (518C9); "the most blessed part of being" (526E3–4); and "the best among beings" (532C5–6).

Two points are sufficiently clear. First, whatever has being partakes of *ousia*. Second, that which provides being to whatever has it is "beyond *ousia*." The compositeness of that which partakes of *ousia* consists in a non-identity between that which partakes in *ousia* and the *ousia* in which it partakes. Crucial to the entire Platonic enterprise is an explanation of this non-identity. In the case of Parmenides' One, we are told that the "is" of it signifies something different from the "one."[3] Presumably, we are meant to be able to generalize from this argument, because Parmenides' One is merely the example chosen to illustrate the distinctions required to rescue the theory of Forms. So, for any x that is f, the "is f" of it signifies something different from the "x."

On the one hand, it is difficult to resist the impression that the compositeness here is that of existence and essence. Nevertheless, there is no hint of how the components of the composite are supposed to be related. Certainly, we are not, for example, given to understand that the compositeness consists in a real minor distinction between essence and existence such that the essence is in potency to the existence that is its actualization. The fact, though, that in the above *Parmenides* passage, the *ousia* of the one and the one itself turn out to be further divisible indefinitely makes it fairly evident that the compositeness is in fact *not* that of essence and existence. So, we are naturally led back to reflection on the claim that whatever is must be composite, that its *ousia* must be nonidentical with it.

The puzzle increases in intensity when we realize that Aristotle argues for the *incompositeness* of primary *ousia*. Its identity with thinking,

2. 509B6–10.
3. Cf. *Sophist* 244B–245E.

far from compelling him to conclude that the thinker is non-identical with its thinking or with that which it thinks, leads him to argue that there is no non-identity within it.[4] So, it seems that he is not prepared to adopt the argument that whatever has *ousia* is non-identical with the *ousia* it has. But the Platonist will surely reply that Aristotle's primary *ousia* does not *have* *ousia;* it *is* *ousia.* And so the dispute becomes not: Is that which has *ousia* non-identical with its *ousia?* but rather: Can primary *ousia* be a first principle of all? The Platonists seem to say no; Aristotle seems to say yes. Note that there is no dispute over whether it is necessary to postulate a first principle, but only over whether or not the first principle is *ousia* or beyond *ousia.*

The Platonic tradition's interpretation of Plato's contribution to the solution to this problem is consistent and clear: *ousia* implies limitedness and the first principle of all must be absolutely unlimited. If Aristotle replies that primary *ousia is* unlimited because it is incomposite, the Platonic tradition holds that an absolutely incomposite first principle is not alone able to account for that for which a principle of *ousia* must account, namely, the diversity of essences in the world. Even supposing the total causal reach of the first principle—a function of its unlimitedness—it cannot be, precisely because of its unlimitedness, the sole principle of limitedness. This conclusion, though, seems to be at odds with the postulation of an absolutely first principle of being. Must not the first principle of all also be the principle of the being of the subordinate principle of limitedness?

This question has been variously understood within the Platonic tradition as: "How can the many arise from the one?" or "How can that which is composite arise from that which is incomposite?" where "arise from" is supposed to indicate a causal relation.[5] Here is a problem about which a philosopher might say, "this obviously works in practice, but it doesn't work in theory." If we are convinced of the need for an absolutely first principle of all, how are we supposed to understand its manifest effects?

---

4. Cf. *Metaphysics* 12.7.1072a31–3; 1072b14ff.; 12.8.1073a30; 12.9.1075a4–10.
5. On the question of how a "many" arises from the One, see Plotinus, *Enneads* III 8 [30] 10. 14–15; III 9 [13] 4; V 1 [10] 6. 4–5; V 2 [11] 1. 3–4; V 3 [49] 15.

II

The answer that the Platonic tradition gives to this question originates, perhaps surprisingly, in one interpretation of Plato's *Symposium*, that of Plotinus. In reporting on Diotima's lessons on the mysteries of love, Socrates gives us her definition of love *(erōs):* "love is [desire for] the possession of the good forever" (206A11–12). And its "work" *(ergon)* is "birth in [the presence of] beauty in the body and the soul" (206B3–8). This birth in beauty, or reproduction, is "what mortals have in place of immortality" (206E7–8). It is the replacement for immortality (207Dff.). Birth in beauty is of two sorts: bodily and spiritual or intellectual (208Eff.). But it is clear that the latter is superior to the former (209C7–D1).

Sometimes, this passage is carelessly interpreted to mean that "birth in beauty" is here being taken to be a *means* to the achievement of immortality. Treating the birth in beauty as an instrument for satisfying the desire for immortality is psychologically lame, to say the least. It is not, in any case, a desire for immortality that motivates the lover, but a desire for the everlasting possession of the good. To the extent that one possesses an image of this good or supposes that one possesses it, one naturally produces. There is much more that needs to be said about this famous text, but the central point for our purposes is that "birth in beauty" is the natural functioning of one in possession of that which is good.

Plotinus stands out among Platonists as absorbed with understanding what Plato has to say about *erōs*. It is not merely that Plotinus wrote a treatise (III 5 [50]) devoted to the topic, but that he endeavored to integrate the concept of *erōs* fully into Platonic metaphysics and psychology. Most remarkably, he employed Plato's concept of *erōs* in his own characterization of the One or the Good, the first principle of all, as "love of itself."[6] This is remarkable because, as we know, *erōs* in the *Symposium* at any rate is a concept from which connotations of "lack" or "deficiency" are seemingly inseparable. Yet the absolutely first principle of all is without limitation or imperfection of any kind. How can this be? Why does Plotinus take from Plato the appropriateness of applying the concept of *erōs* to the One?

6. VI 8 [39] 15. 1–2. See the penetrating study of Agnès Pigler, *Plotin. Une métaphysique de l'amour: L'amour comme structure du monde intelligible* (Paris: Vrin, 2002).

This claim is, in effect, an abductive inference or *quia* proof from the claim that goodness is essentially self-diffusive.[7] And the proof that goodness is essentially self-diffusive relies upon the self-evident multiplicity of intelligible forms in the universe. That the knowledge of intelligible reality necessarily produces true virtue is one expression of the necessary production of intelligible form from the Good. The Good must love itself if in the achievement of its desire it necessarily produces. Since it necessarily produces, and since production is the *ergon* of love of the Good, the perfect self-possession of the Good that is present in the first principle of all must result from its self-love.

The self-love of the first principle is expressed by Plotinus as a sort of gloss on the fact that the first principle is "self-caused" *(aition heautou)*.[8] It is inferred that the extraordinary phrase "self-caused," which appears here for the first time in the history of philosophy so far as we know, applies to the One owing to its absolute simplicity and, hence, its uniqueness. Therefore, anything other than the first principle is not self-caused. Whatever has its causality outside of it is, then, the product or work of the self-love of the One. Since love is always for the Good, the products of the One's self-love are not loved by it.[9] But at the same time, production by the One insures that whatever is capable of desire loves the One or the Good.

The self-causality of the One is also, remarkably, described as "[making] itself from nothing *(oudenos)*."[10] Since there are no real distinctions whatsoever within the One, its being and its activity are indistinguishable. Its being is the activity of self-love. What, then, is the difference between the making that belongs to the One's "self-making" and the making that belongs to the One's products? Stated otherwise, how can the self-making of the absolutely simple first principle of all result in something *other than* that first principle? What is not the One is also not made from nothing; nor is it identical with the One. So, what does its causal dependence consist in?

The formally precise way in which Plotinus answers these questions

7. On the history of this idea see Klaus Kremer, "Bonum est diffusivum sui: Ein Beitrag zum Verhältnis von Neuplatonismus und Christentum," in *Aufstieg und Niedergang der Römischen Welt* (ANRW), ed. W. Haase and H. Temporini, Pt. II, vol. 36.2 (Berlin: Walter de Gruyter, 1987), 994–1032.

8. VI 8 [39] 14. 41.   9. V 5 [32] 12. 40–49.

10. VI 8 [39] 7. 54; cf. 15. 9.

is to say that the One is "virtually all things" *(dunamis pantōn)*.[11] Scholars and exegetes who translate *dunamis* as "potency" or even as "power" really do get off on the wrong foot. It is obvious why there cannot be any potency attributable to the One; it is somewhat less obvious, though equally certain, that there can be no power in the One either, if by "power" we just mean *active* potency. What Plotinus wants to say about the One is that it is everything that exists, but in the way, roughly, that "white" light is all the colors of the spectrum or in the way that a function is all of its substitution instances. And just as the dichotomy transcendent/immanent is inappropriate in explaining the connection between white light and the spectrum, so it is inappropriate in explaining the causal connection between the One and everything else.

If the virtuality of the One were "static" as is the virtuality of a function in relation to its values, then to say that the One is virtually all things would hardly serve as an answer to the question of how a "many" is supposed to *arise* from the One. But the virtuality that the One is is an activity *(energeia)*.[12] It is an activity that is "beyond," that is, logically and ontologically prior to the activity of primary *ousia* or Intellect.[13] It is tempting from a later perspective to identify this activity as *ipsum esse*. Indeed, Plotinus does even say that the One "gives itself existence" *(hupostēsas hauto)*, and that all things derive their existence from it.[14] There are two grounds, however, for hesitation. First, if the One is virtually all things, then *ipsum esse* is virtually all things. Yet it is not insofar as the One is *esse* that it is virtually all things, but rather insofar as it is one. Second, if the One is *ipsum esse,* then its causal activity would consist in the endowment of all that is with existence. There can be no intermediaries or instrumentality in the endowment of existence. Yet all things depend on the One through intermediaries.[15] Even Intellect depends on the transcendent activity of the One by the instrumentality of the One's "external" activity.[16] If we choose to reserve the word "cre-

11. V 1 [10] 7. 9; V 3 [49] 15. 31; V 4 [7] 2. 38; VI 9 [9] 5. 36–37.

12. VI 8 [39] 16. 16; VI 8 [39] 20. 15.

13. VI 7 [38] 17. 11.

14. VI 8 [39] 16, 15; cf. V 4 [7] 1. 38; cf. VI 9 [9] 1.1. The One is said to be the efficient cause of the being of everything else: cf. V 3 [49] 15.12–13; 28; 17. 10–14; VI 4 [22]10; VI 7 [38] 23. 22–24.

15. VI 7 [38] 42. 23; cf. VI 9 [9] 1. 23.

16. V 1 [10] 6. 30–39; IV 8 [6] 6. 8–12; V 4 [7] 1. 27–34; 2. 28–39; VI 8 [39] 18. 51–52.

ation" for direct existential causal dependence, then the One is only a self-creator.[17]

Within such a metaphysical framework, the self-diffusion of the Good is the *only* possible answer to the question "why is there something rather than nothing?" The necessary self-diffusion of the One consists in its being "ungrudging" *(aphthonos)*, which is only conceptually distinct from the property of having self-love.[18] But the claim that goodness is self-diffusive is no answer to our question if goodness is not identified with an absolutely unique first principle of all, a first principle that explains the being of everything else.

III

Although Plotinus alludes to many arguments for the existence of the One, his central argument for such a principle seems to be the one found in his treatise "How That Which Is after the First Comes from the First, and on the One" (V 4 [7]).[19] Here is the argument:

There must be something simple before everything, and this must be different from all things which are after it, existing by itself, not mixed with the things which come from it, and yet being able to be present to these things in a different way, being itself really one, and not with its being as different from its oneness. It is false even to say of it that it is one, and there is no *logos* or knowledge of it; it is in fact "beyond being"; for if it is not simple, outside of all coincidence and composition, and really one, it could not be a first principle. And it is the most self-sufficient, by being simple and by being the first of all. For that which is not the first needs that which is before it, and that which is not simple is in need of the simple [parts] in it in order that it can come from them. Such a [first principle] must be one alone; for if there were another of the same kind, both would be one. (V 4 [7] 1. 5–17, my translation)

Plotinus seems to be arguing here for two conclusions: (1) every composite must be accounted for by that which is incomposite or absolutely simple and (2) there can be only one absolutely simple thing. We can bet-

17. See my "Plotinus' Metaphysics: Creation or Emanation?" *Review of Metaphysics* 46 (1993): 559–74 for further discussion.

18. V 4 [7] 1. 35–9.

19. See, for other arguments or allusions to other arguments, I 3 [20] 1. 4–5; II 9 [33] 1. 11–16; III 8 [30] 9. 19–32; 10. 31–35; 11. 8–11.

ter understand the reasoning for (1) if we concentrate first on the reasoning for (2). Assume that there were more than one absolutely simple thing. Then, there would have to be something that each one had that made it at least numerically different from the other, say, for example, a unique position. But that which made it different would have to be really (not merely conceptually) distinct from that which made it to be the one thing it is. That which had the position would be really distinct from the position itself. But then something which had a position and so was distinct from it would not be absolutely simple. So, that which is absolutely simple must be absolutely unique. Only the first principle of all is unqualifiedly self-identical; the self-identity had by anything else is necessarily qualified. This argument suggests the meaning of "composite" that Plotinus has in mind when he argues for (1). A composite is anything that is distinct from any property it has. What we might call a "minimally composite individual" is one with one and only one property from which it is itself distinct. Compositeness is then equivalent to qualified self-identity.

The simplicity of the first principle is explicitly said to consist in the fact that there is no difference between its "being" (*ōn*) and its "oneness" *(hen)*. From this it follows that the complexity possessed by everything else is at least a complexity consisting of a distinction between being and oneness. The argument alludes to the passage in *Parmenides* mentioned in the first section of the paper where Plato distinguishes between that which is one and the *ousia* in which it must partake. The passage also makes explicit that the name "One" does not indicate that this principle is oneness; rather, it indicates that it is unique.

The minimal complexity of every being other than the One consists in that being's partaking in *ousia*. To be is to be *something or other*. Being requires identity and identity requires distinguishability. For us even to conceive of something is for us to suppose that it has an *ousia* in virtue of which we can identify it and re-identify it. But if that which exists has an *ousia*, it cannot be identified *with* that *ousia*, even though it must be identified *by* it. To identify something with its *ousia* is to commit oneself to the false view that no two things can have that identical *ousia*. If it turns out that only an absolutely simple first principle can explain the being of anything which partakes of *ousia*, then the only viable option for one wanting to deny such a principle is to claim that there is nothing which is distinct from its *ousia* or, what amounts to the same thing, that no two things can partake in the identical *ousia*. This is the position of radical nominalism, and it is committed to maintaining that there cannot even be two things which are the same just insofar as they partake in the identical *ousia* oneness. Indeed, it is not even clear that radical nominalism is not reducible to hyper-radical nominalism, according to which the putative one and only one thing that exists is incapable of being identified owing to the fact that it is incapable of being re-identified. For to re-identify it over time is to pick out one or more features that are the same across time, features that this one thing possesses. In addition, if we pick out the features of our universe at a certain time, the mere possibility that there should be another universe possessing these features depends on our distinguishing the *ousia* of our universe from the *ousia* of the other.

In any case, it is fair to say that Plotinus is not particularly interested in the nominalist challenge. So, he does assume that the relevant minimal complexity exists and he holds that it can be explained only by the absolutely simple. Plotinus criticizes Aristotle, not for disagreeing with this point, but for concluding that thinking is absolutely simple. It is, once again, tempting to suppose that the relevant complexity is a composition of act and potency and that the reason the complex needs to be explained by the simple is that potency is always a function of act, but that the act of such a composite does not explain itself; it is always a received act. This, again, cannot be quite right, because the *ousia* in which the minimally complex partakes is not received from outside. This minimally complex, that is, Intellect, does indeed receive from the One that by which Intellect "defines" itself, that is, that by which it produces *ousia*.[20] What Intellect receives is a *dunamis* for self-definition. I have already argued that when Plotinus says that the One is *dunamis pantōn*, a power is not being indicated, at least if "power" indicates any potency whatever. Here, however, no such restriction is necessary. Intellect, as the "external" activity of the One, really does have the "power" of self-definition, and in the actualization of this power, Intellect becomes the intelligible world.

For Plotinus, a proof of the existence of an absolutely simple first principle of all could in fact start anywhere with any complex entity, but if it does not start with Intellect, that proof must pass through Intellect.

This is a direct consequence of the instrumentality of Intellect in the One's causal activity. To reach Intellect "from below" as it were, one must merely acknowledge that understanding is other than sense-perception. Within the entire Platonic tradition, understanding is not something that sense-perception alone allows us to attain. The central Platonic text is *Timaeus* 51D3–52A4, where it is argued that if understanding *(noēsis)* exists, then Forms exist, because understanding is not of sensibles. What understanding is of is *ousia;* hence, if *ousia* is always partaken of, whatever has *ousia* is composite in the way that Plato and Plotinus argue. That *ousia* can be without being partaken of is denied by both. What possesses *ousia* and what is constituted by minimal complexity is Intellect. So, a proof for the existence of the One, more remote from the proof from compositeness, but clearer to us, is available beginning with the premise that understanding is real and different from sense-perception.

Understanding is, roughly, the cognition of material identity or, more exactly, the cognition of two objects that are the same (and therefore numerically different) owing to their real or ultimate identity. Every equation in mathematics or in the sciences, other than expressions of formal identity, represents a claim of cognition of this type. Similarly, the cognition of instances of the application of a rule evinces understanding. When, in the series, 1, 1, 2, 3, 5, 8, 13, . . . , we cognize the rule of which each successive number is an application, we manifest understanding. It should be added—though it is not our direct concern here—that the following of the rule, which a computer is perfectly capable of doing, is not equivalent to the cognition of the rule.

Understanding is not possible if *ousia* does not exist or if it has no being. But the being of *ousia* is irreducibly complex. For example, what we understand when we understand the *ousia* that makes all odd numbers the same is different from what we understand when we understand the *ousia* that makes all even numbers the same. The being of *ousia* is not equivalent to an instance of that *ousia*. Plotinus follows Aristotle exactly in maintaining that the being of *ousia*—primary *ousia,* as Aristotle calls it—is the being of a separated Intellect. For Plotinus, if there were not such an Intellect, cognitively identical with the full array of intelligible entities, it would not, for example, be true that oddness and evenness are generically one. Intellect is virtually all that it thinks. But the identity of Intellect and that which is leaves a residual complexity, as we have seen.

Intellect and *ousia* are themselves expressions of or are the same insofar as they manifest the first principle of all. This first principle, which is virtually Intellect and the intelligibles, cannot, of course, have the complexity of *ousia* or Intellect.

The identification of the first principle of all, the One, with the Good follows from the three claims that (1) everything seeks its own good and (2) the good for anything consists in the fulfillment of or achievement of its nature, that is, its *ousia* and (3) the One is virtually all *ousia,* and so, is virtually the Good of everything that is. The self-diffusiveness of goodness is, then, the self-diffusiveness of the Good itself. Eventually, any question regarding the "cause of being" *(aition tou einai)* of anything needs to be referred to the self-causing first principle of all. But owing to the fact that this first principle is "beyond *ousia,*" the "why" question about being is not to be answered by a direct causal link to the first principle; the causality must go through the instrumentality of Intellect and the intelligibles with which Intellect is identical.

It goes without saying, I think, that the Platonic tradition wants to insist both that this sort of explanation for the being of anything does not preclude or preempt causality within nature *and* that natural causality does not make the Platonic explanation otiose or redundant. Illustrative of this point, I would like now to turn in the last section of the paper, to say a kind word about intelligent design, albeit not exactly the sort that is prominent in contemporary debates.

IV

Plato's Demiurge and, perhaps somewhat more contentiously, Aristotle's Prime Unmoved Mover, are postulates of Intelligent Design Theory. So is Plotinus' One-Good. Under the rubric "Intelligent Design Theory" I mean to include any theory that starts with the rejection of any other theory that holds that the cosmos and everything in it can be completely explained without the causality of Intellect. Evolutionary Theory is the leading anti intelligent design theory. The evolutionary theorist who grants that evolutionary explanations are incapable of explaining why there is something rather than nothing might justly insist that in this regard she is in no worse position than her opponent.

Contemporary intelligent design theorists seem to me to make the mistake of challenging evolutionary theorists only after having accepted the assumption of their opponents that makes their own challenge hollow. I mean the assumption that individual biological entities strive for survival by reproduction. If one grants this assumption, one need only add the well-documented mechanisms of natural selection in order to complete the explanatory picture. We might think that evolutionary theory does not in fact provide a satisfactory explanation for complexity; but neither does intelligent design theory. More to the point, reproduction as a survival mechanism is, to say the least, questionable. Indeed, it is easy to show that the survival of the individual is nowhere in nature aided by reproduction. In reply, the evolutionist will surely want to say that it is not the survival of the individual but the survival of the species that is facilitated by reproduction. Why all the behavior of a living thing, apart from its reproductive activity, is geared toward individual survival is never explained. It is here that the miracle occurs. Grant this miracle and no further intelligence is required.

The most sophisticated contemporary versions of evolutionary theory try to minimize the miraculous by locating the impetus for survival at the genetic level. According to this view, a gene is defined as any portion of chromosomal material that potentially lasts for enough generations to serve as a unit of natural selection. Animals, we are told, are just the survival mechanisms for genes. A gene is not just one portion of DNA; it is all the replicas of a portion of DNA everywhere. What do genes do? They try to become more numerous in the gene pool. That is, their survival is their reproduction.

The elision of survival with reproduction is the device for minimizing the miraculous. If survival is just some x striving to be what it is, there is no mystery; we simply have a thing with an *ousia* striving to fulfill its own nature. But I suspect that the elision of survival with reproduction is in fact an incoherent idea. For there to be survival, there must be living things that are aiming to survive. A gene is not a living thing. But even if we grant that it is a living thing, the survival of *that* living thing is not facilitated by its reproducing another living thing. If it is replied that what survives is not the individual living thing, but the genetic "blueprint," then it needs to be pointed out that it is not then the gene that is trying to survive. And it needs to be asked why the gene is trying to have its blueprint carry on.

It should by now be apparent that the Platonic answer to the question of why things reproduce is that goodness is self-diffusive. As goodness diffuses from the first principle, it employs Intellect and its intelligible entities instrumentally to produce all that there is or can be. Because the Good is what all things are virtually, in fulfilling their natures, they achieve the Good each in its own way.[21] In surviving, they strive to achieve the Good; in reproducing, they emulate the Good. As Plotinus argues, "there was certainly nothing that prevented anything whatever from having a share in the nature of that which is good, insofar as each thing is capable of participating in it."[22] There is in every nature, says Plotinus, the capacity to produce that which "comes after it" and to unfold itself "as a seed." The production is the natural result of participating in the Good. This Good explains the being of as many things as there are; the instrumentality of Intellect and all the intelligibles with which it is identical explains the complex natures of these many things.

This is probably not the sort of intelligent design theory that, say, the members of the Discovery Institute have in mind. For them, intelligent design of this type is here bought at too high a price. On the other hand, intelligent design of *any* sort is anathema to the theorists of evolution. Surely, in accounting for the fecundity of being, they would want to insist, like Mae West, that goodness has nothing to do with it. By contrast, the Platonic tradition maintains that goodness has everything to do with it.

21. Plotinus, *Ennead* VI 7 [38] 27.
22. IV 8 [6] 6. 16–18.

2 ∽ The Question of Being, Non-Being, and "Creation *ex Nihilo*" in Chinese Philosophy

Some commentators on Chinese philosophy maintain the position that in classical Chinese philosophy there is no question about being. Yu Jiyuan asserts that Aristotle's examination of the question of being is linked to predication.[1] That the Chinese language lacks the pertinent subject-predicate grammar of Greek leads Yu to deny that the question of being exists for classical Chinese philosophy. Yu says, "it is the absence of predication in Chinese that is responsible for the absence of the question of being in Chinese philosophy" (440). Similarly, David Hall appeals to Angus Graham's contrast between *you* (sometimes translated "being," but more literally "having") and *wu* (translated "not to be," more literally "not to be around") to show that the *you/wu* distinction "suggests contrast rather than contradiction."[2] Accordingly, Hall maintains that the Chinese language is an "aesthetic" and "correlative" language that does not deal with Being or not-being per se, so that any dialectic between being and not-being will "not be easily discoverable in the Chi-

I am most grateful to Msgr. Wippel for his helpful changes and comments in editing this chapter. My thanks also go to the participants of the 2006 Metaphysical Society of America Meeting at the Catholic University of America. Their questions and comments inspired me to develop an earlier version of this essay.

1. See his "The Language of Being: Between Aristotle and Chinese Philosophy," *International Philosophical Quarterly* 39 (1999): 439–54.

2. See his "On Looking Up 'Dialectics' in a Chinese Dictionary," in *Being and Dialectic: Metaphysics and Culture,* ed. William Desmond and Joseph Grange (Albany: State University of New York Press, 2000), 197–212, esp. 201.

nese tradition" (208).[3] Hall explains (277) that the Chinese way of catego-
rizing things is analogical, and thus is dependent on the particularities
of things, rather than logical, or dependent on the "logical essences" or
"natural kinds" of things. Since Hall believes that logical thinking is required for questioning about being, and because Chinese reasoning is
analogical rather than logical, he maintains that the Chinese never asked
"The Question of Being."

In contrast, other commentators claim that there is a problem about
being and non-being in classical Chinese thought.[4] Robert Neville, for
example, finds a "structural parallel" to the Western model of what he
calls "creation *ex nihilo*" in Chinese philosophy despite the absence of
such language therein.[5] Specifically, Neville holds that any radical contingency, and hence any determinate being, must come from nothing.
This nothing which gives rise to the created world for Neville is "a creative nothing, not mere nothing in itself."[6] Finding a similar assertion
of the origins of being in non-being in Chinese thinkers like Laozi and
Zhoudunyi,[7] Neville thinks that being was and is a question for Chinese
philosophers.[8]

3. See also Hall, "The Culture of Metaphysics: On Saving Neville's Project (from Neville),"
in *Interpreting Neville*, ed. J. Harley Chapman and Nancy K. Frankenberry (Albany: State University of New York, 1999).

4. See Tu Weiming, "The Continuity of Being: Chinese Visions of Nature," in *On Nature*,
ed. Leroy S. Rouner (Notre Dame, IN: University of Notre Dame Press, 1984), 113–29. Tu explains that "[a]ncient Chinese thinkers were intensely interested in the creation of the world
. . . [the] real issue is not the presence or absence of creation myths, but the underlying assumption of the cosmos: whether it is continuous or discontinuous with its creator" (113). Also
see Cheng Chungying, "Reality and Divinity in Chinese Philosophy," in *A Companion to World
Philosophies*, ed. Eliot Deutsch and Ron Bontekoe (Oxford: Blackwell Publishers Inc., 1997),
185–200. Cheng tells us that the process of generation through the 64 hexagrams depicted in
the *I Ching* gives us a "cosmogonical picture of the rise and development of reality as a world
of things" (185). Cheng characterizes the process of generation as the *dao* and the sustaining
source of the generation as *taiji*. He says, "It is this theory of *taiji* and *dao* that represents the
main stream of metaphysical thinking in the 3,200-year history of Chinese philosophy" (185).

5. See Robert C. Neville, "From Nothing to Being: The Notion of Creation in Chinese and
Western Thought," *Philosophy East & West* 30 (1980): 21–34.

6. Ibid.

7. Even though I use the Pinyin system, I will retain the Wade Giles system when quoting
from commentators who use it.

8. As John H. Berthrong, *Concerning Creativity: A Comparison of Chu Hsi, Whitehead, and
Neville* (Albany: State University of New York, 1998), puts it: "Here in the work of the North-
ern Sung master Chou Tun-I (1017–1073), Neville finds a doctrine of the ontological grounding
of the Neo-Confucian cosmology. Neville argues that we can read the opening line of Chou's
famous and terse 'An Explanation of the Diagram of the Supreme Ultimate' as expressing this

Despite my agreement with commentators who think that the question of being and non-being is found in Chinese philosophy, I am skeptical about Neville's "creation *ex nihilo*" in Chinese philosophy analysis.[9] In the present text I expound the two ways in which I find Neville's account of creation *ex nihilo* in Chinese philosophy to be flawed. First, although Neville's account fits certain aspects of Chinese philosophy well, there are other aspects which his creation hypothesis does not seem to fit. And second, it is not clear that the Chinese thinkers are responding to the same issue of creation *ex nihilo* as the Western thinkers. For instance, Tu Weiming in his "The Continuity of Being: Chinese Visions of Nature" expresses skepticism about the existence of conceptions of creation *ex nihilo* in the Chinese traditions. He says, "It is precisely because [the Chinese] perceive the cosmos as the unfolding of continuous creativity that [they] cannot entertain 'conceptions of creation *ex nihilo* by the hand of God, or through the will of God, and all other such mechanistic, teleological, and theistic cosmologies.'"[10]

Neville's creation hypothesis maintains that "determinate beings come from nothing."[11] Something determinate "is determinate with respect to some other determinate things" (22). A determinate thing then has features which relate to and contrast with other things, making it complex. This complex nature is a harmony of its component features. To the question, why is there such harmony, Neville replies, "Harmonious determinate things must be contingent upon a ground or they would not exist at all" (22). He calls this "ontological contingency," in contrast with "cosmological contingency," which characterizes the "interrelations and harmonies of determinate things" (22). Whereas cosmological causation

'asymmetrical ontological grounding' (*Behind the Masks of God: An Essay toward Comparative Theology* [Albany: State University of New York Press, 1991], 77). Neville takes the relationship of the Uncontrived Ultimate *(wu-chi)* and the Supreme Ultimate *(t'ai-chi)* to express the Neo-Confucian understanding of the relationship of the ontological ground of being and the beings themselves as cosmologically conditioned" (88–89). This same understanding of an ontological ground is applied to Zhuxi when Berthrong says: "Neville asserts that 'Chu Hsi, after Chou, gave a profoundly ontological rendition of the harmony or mind of Heaven and Earth'" (*BMG,* 79). There is no higher philosophic praise within the Nevillian corpus than to acknowledge such a vision on Chu's part (89).

9. See Carl Vaught, "Being, Nonbeing, and Creation *Ex Nihilo*" in *Interpreting Neville,* for his criticisms of Neville's creation *ex nihilo* thesis from within the Western tradition, 154–56.

10. "The Continuity of Being," 114.

11. "From Nothing," 21. In-text page numbers in the present paragraph refer to this article.

stems from determinate or "partially determinate" things in the world, ontological causation is "that causation of the world by what cannot itself be determinate" (22). Neville calls this indeterminate ground the "nothing" (21–22). The nothing in itself, apart from its relation to the beings that come from it, is not something about which we can speak or think, because speech or thought is necessarily directed at something rather than nothing. As he puts it in *Behind the Masks of God* (1991), "In fact, as source of all norms and beings, transcending both, God is hardly distinguished from non-being, the abyss from which all things emerge."[12] In his 1980 article "From Nothing to Being," Neville says, with respect to nothing, that "In itself it cannot be spoken of because speaking and thinking presuppose that there is no 'nothing' which is in itself, while assuming the 'something' about which speech or thought is directed."[13] Hence, it is only in relation to, and in the context of, the beings that come from it that this nothing is "creative" and has the character of being the "source" of the world.

Neville's nothing is the ground which does not in turn need a ground, because of its indeterminacy. "[T]here is an asymmetry in the existential status of things. The things together are dependent on ontological creation for their very being" but not vice versa. He continues by saying, "although what they are depends on their immanent context."[14] *Ex nihilo* creativity that grounds the contingent world is "undefined, unconstrained, and unreal,"[15] transcending the world's limits. Accordingly, *ex nihilo* creativity must be transcendent, for if it were to be in the world, it would have been determinate and hence would have required a prior context, which context in turn would have to have been provided by the act of ontological creativity. Whereas determinate things need ontological creativity to exist, God does not need determinate things.

Neville compares his "creative nothing" with the Chinese views of creation exemplified by Laozi's Daoism, Confucius's and Mencius's Confucianism, and Zhoudunyi's and Zhuxi's Neo-Confucianism. He finds among these Chinese thinkers a notion similar to his notion of ontological creativity and its characteristic asymmetry.[16] In fact, he finds

---

12. *Behind the Masks*, 54.   13. "From Nothing," 22–23.
14. *Behind the Masks*, 74.   15. Ibid.
16. See David Hall's "The Culture of Metaphysics: On Saving Neville's Project (from Neville)" in *Interpreting Neville*, 273, for his argument against Neville's characterization of asym-

his views to be better illustrated in the Chinese traditions than in the Western. As he puts it, "My argument has been that both the category of ontological creativity and the categories of the primary cosmology are illustrated by the Chinese philosophic-religious tradition. They are illustrated there perhaps even more clearly than in the Western traditions that gave rise to my terminology."[17]

Neville understands Westerners and Chinese to be responding to the same question concerning change. He explains that, for the Chinese, the process of change does not simply consist in an alternation of the opposite material forces of *yin* and *yang*. Rather, a more "primordial meaning" of *yin* is the situation from which things arise and to which they return for replenishment (54). Similarly, *yang*'s more primordial meaning refers to its extension beyond the situation of *yin*, "particularly with [its] making something new" (54). Nevertheless, *yang*'s extension has a limit, violation of which will lead to competition between the two or the destruction of *yang*. According to Neville's understanding, *yang* must return to its source in *yin* for its own renewal. Also in this understanding, *yin* and *yang*'s movements illustrate cosmological causation, since *yang*'s creativity arises out of *yin* rather than out of nothing. Neville puts the distinction between *yin* and *yang* as follows:

The basic distinction . . . is the fundamental cosmological one that change, or we may say creativity, involves a pulsation away from the given source and a contraction back to it. *Yang* may be the production of novelty, but its very being arises out of *yin* and finds its fulfillment in returning to *yin*. Creativity is not an act making something out of nothing, . . . but the very being of process weaving novelties out of matrices filled with incipiencies and then reconstituting itself as at one with its sources. (54)

Beneath what Neville calls the "horizontal," cosmological genesis of things, he finds a "vertical," ontological creativity which enables cosmological genesis; whereas *yin* and *yang* process is the *dao*, they arise from the

---

metry in the Chinese. He says, "The key feature of Neville's formulation as it applies to the Chinese sensibility is that of the asymmetry of *ground* and *determinate things*." Hall goes on to argue, against Neville: "The disposition of the Chinese from the beginning to the present is highly inhospitable to asymmetrical relations of any kind. It is true that every relation is hierarchical, but the terms of the hierarchy are always in transition."

17. *Behind the Masks*, 83. In-text page numbers in the next several paragraphs will refer to this work.

"true *Dao*." The relation between these two *daos*, like Neville's relation between the ontological source and determinate things, is asymmetrical: one creates and the other is created. Applying his creation hypothesis sketched out earlier to the vertical *Dao* and the horizontal *dao*, Neville says,

> The true *Dao* is that which gives rise to the horizontal *dao* of *yin-yang* process. Only the determinate *dao* is nameable, and the true *Dao* giving rise to it is not quite determinate and hence not nameable. . . . The relation is asymmetrical: the unnameable *Dao* creates and the named *dao* is created. *Nothing can be said of the former except in reference to the latter.* At best, the unnameable *Dao* is pregnant, containing the incipient beginnings of determinate *yin-yang* changes but always hidden within and behind the visible alterations. (55; my emphasis)

Neville finds the ontological ground in Confucianism by pointing to the incipience of determinate states in Mencius's four beginnings, in Confucius's harmony of Heaven and Earth, and in Zhuxi's harmony or mind of Heaven and Earth. Although none of these thinkers explicitly discusses "the ontological ground actively creating the immanently defined state of affairs," Neville asserts that "[the ontological ground] is indeed the incipience of that determinate state and is thus in asymmetrical relation to it" (75). Any state of affairs depends on "an ontologically more basic state in which the former was incipient" (75). Neville finds his asymmetry of ontological creation and the determinate things in Zhoudunyi's ultimate of non-being and great ultimate. Zhoudunyi's ultimate of non-being enables the great ultimate, which in turn generates the *yin* and the *yang*, which generate the five elements, which in turn bring about the movement of the seasons and other natural changes. For Neville, the ontological ground for the Chinese "has no character except the incipience of, or *readiness to give rise to,* the immanently defined state" (75).

The source, in each (i.e., Confucians, Daoists, and Neo-Confucians), seems to be unconstrained, to transcend world limitations, and to be asymmetrically related to determinate beings.[18] What Neville calls the "ontological ground" is the reason why there is something rather than nothing, and so it seems that the Chinese are indeed responding to the same issues as Neville's creation *ex nihilo*. It is not clear, however, that

---

18. Berthrong says of the Supreme Ultimate and the Way or Dao, for instance, that "They are not the concrete things or events, rather, they are the sources or lures for the possibility that events can achieve actuality in becoming what they should be" (*Concerning Creativity*, 120).

the Chinese would agree with some of Neville's characterizations of this ontological creativity, and so we may question also whether the Chinese are concerned with Neville's creative nothing. It is entirely possible for similar answers to be given by thinkers asking rather different questions.

In what follows, I contrast Neville and the Chinese on their respective views on the source by focusing on three discussions: (1) their characterizations of the source; (2) their explanations concerning how their respective sources relate to harmony and value; and (3) their characterizations of spontaneous activity in change.

I

As for the first issue, Neville's characterizations of his ontological ground as indeterminate and characterless in itself does not fit the Chinese sources. Neville maintains that nothing can be said about the source except in reference to its creations. This position does not fit the Chinese sources because of many claims made about them without reference to their effects. For instance, Laozi characterizes the Dao/Way as "confused," yet "perfect." It is:

> Still and indistinct, it stands alone and unchanging.
> The Way models itself on what is natural *(ziran).*[19]
> Turning back is how the Way moves.
> Weakness is how the Way operates.[20]

Finally, the Way is expansive (ch. 34), forever nameless (ch. 32), vague and elusive (ch. 21). These characterizations do not refer to the Way's being the cause of Heaven and Earth and the myriad things. Although I would agree that Laozi's Dao also has the characteristic of indeterminacy Neville emphasizes, Laozi also offers determinate statements about the Dao quite independently of its creations.[21]

19. *The Daodejing of Laozi,* trans. P. J. Ivanhoe (Indianapolis-Cambridge: Hackett, 2003), ch. 25.

20. Ibid., ch. 40.

21. Cheng Chungying also recognizes this more balanced approach to Laozi's Dao when he says, "As *dao* is a power creative of all things as well as the process of creative production, it has both the activity of *wu* [i.e., no-thing] and the activity of *yu* [or *you*, i.e., having-things], just as all things have both the *yin* (emptying) and *yang* (substantiating) functions" ("Reality and Divinity," 191).

Similarly, here are some of Zhuxi's assertions about principle and the great ultimate: "Principle itself has neither physical form nor body"[22] and "Principle is one."[23] "The Great Ultimate is nothing other than principle,"[24] and "considered in the state before activity begins, this state is nothing but tranquility."[25] Zhuxi's principle is incorporeal, one, the great ultimate which is tranquil, and the principle of the highest good. Again, these are characterizations of the source independent of its effects and so do not exemplify Neville's characterless *ex nihilo* creativity.

Zhuxi's principle, moreover, is only the cause of something's nature, whilst material force *(qi)* is in turn needed before something can have a physical form. Zhuxi says, "Principle has never been separated from material force," yet the former exists before physical form and hence is without it, whilst material force exists after physical form and hence is with it.[26] Since Zhuxi's principle needs material force for creation, it is not quite sufficient to be Neville's ground. John Berthrong makes a similar point regarding Zhuxi's principle when he says, "*Li* are formal principles that have being or true actuality when they are actualized in some concrete event or entity—although they lack pure activity without recourse to the other elements of Chu Hsi's system." Again, Berthrong says of Zhuxi that "without objects or events there would be no principles to investigate or understand, hence nothing for the mind to consider."[27] Unlike Neville's creation *ex nihilo*, Zhuxi's principle needs a prior context in order to create.[28]

Claiming Chinese adherence to the proposition "the indeterminate in itself is not an object of knowledge,"[29] Neville says: "There are not nu-

22. 49:3a–b, Wing-Tsit Chan, *A Sourcebook in Chinese Philosophy* (Princeton: Princeton University Press, 1963), 635.

23. 42:2b, Chan, 612.

24. 49.8b, Chan, 638.

25. "The Great Ultimate has neither spatial restriction nor physical form or body. . . ." (49:11a–b, Chan, 639). Also: "The Great Ultimate is simply the principle of the highest good" (49:11b, Chan, 640).

26. 49.1a–b, Chan, 634.

27. *Concerning Creativity*, 121 and 122.

28. Berthrong would agree that Zhuxi lacks a transcendent God that precedes material things, for he says, "There is no possibility for something utterly transcendent entering into the process qua the natural process of growth, because there is nothing that is transcendent from some kind of relationship to everything else" (ibid., 125). Again, Berthrong says, "There is no actual entity, such as Whitehead's God, which has a mental pole prior to the physical pole."

29. *Behind the Masks*, 74–75. Neville cites Plato's Form of the Good in the *Republic* and

merically two *Daos,* since the eternal has no being or determinateness separate from the named *Dao.*"[30] If Chinese thought is in agreement, then we will not find claims about knowing the Dao; such claims, however, are to be found, some of them emphatic:

> Knowing *(zhi)* harmony *(he)* is called constancy *(chang).*
> Knowing *(zhi)* constancy *(chang)* is called enlightenment *(ming).*[31]

Harmony *(he)* is the Way, for Laozi says: "The Way of Heaven takes from what has excess and augments what is deficient,"[32] and "The Way modifies things by blending their *yin* and *yang* to produce a harmony."[33] Laozi's Way is knowable, and such knowledge is significant. Laozi says that the sages "know without going abroad"[34] and "The ability to know the ancient beginnings . . . is called the thread of the Way."[35] Despite passages putting down knowledge,[36] Laozi distinguishes knowledge of the Way from conventional knowledge of facts. He approves of the former and criticizes the latter. He says, "Those who know are not full of knowledge; Those full of knowledge do not know."[37]

Aristotle's Prime Mover as examples of the transcendent ground which is totally indeterminate and unknowable. Though a case can be made for the Platonic Form of the Good's being unknowable in the *Republic,* the same cannot be said about Aristotle's Prime Mover. After all, as a primary substance in the *Metaphysics,* Aristotle's Prime Mover satisfies the criteria for substance in Book Zeta, one of which is knowability. More specifically, in *Met.* VII, c. 1, Aristotle says, "Now 'primary' has several meanings; but nevertheless substance is primary in all senses, both in definition and in knowledge and in time. For none of the other categories can exist separately, but substance alone . . . " (1028a31–35). See *Aristotle. Metaphysics Books I–IX,* trans. Hugh Tredennick, Loeb Classical Library (Cambridge, Mass.: Harvard University Press, 2003).

30. *Behind the Masks,* 75.
31. *Daodejing,* ch. 55. *Ming* also means clarity or brightness. *Ming* is etymologically composed of the radicals for sun *(ri)* and moon *(yue),* emphasizing the brilliance of such a state.
32. Ibid., ch. 77.
33. Ibid., ch. 42. It causes the myriad creatures: "It blunts their sharpness; Untangles their tangles; Softens their glare; (and) merges with their dust" (ch. 4; see also ch. 29). Additionally, since the word for constancy *(chang)* is the same word for the constancy of Dao in chapter 1 of the *Daodejing,* it is also possible to read the knowledge of this constancy as relating to the constancy of Dao in ch. 55. (See also ch. 16 where the line "Knowing constancy is called enlightenment" was used to refer to things returning to their root, which is their destiny, and the return to one's destiny is also called "constancy.")
34. Ch. 47.
35. Ch. 14.
36. Chs. 10, 3, 27, 65 in the *Daodejing.*
37. Ch. 81. Cheng Chungying, "Reality and Divinity in Chinese Philosophy," would agree that Laozi regards the Dao as knowable. Cheng says, "According to the Daoist, any human being can come to an intimate knowledge and understanding of the *dao* so long as he reduces

Similarly, Zhuxi's principle must be knowable, because principle is the substance of Heaven with which Heaven endows all things.[38] However, Berthrong reminds us that Zhuxi's principle in itself is not creative. It "only became a lively principle within the medium of the heart-mind as the seat of the human person."[39] Thus, man's knowledge of principle is crucial for its functioning. This principle, according to Zhuxi, is eternal, and what man cultivates is this original principle, which cannot be changed even if man were to be evil.[40] To know principle, one needs to return to the self and discover it in one's own nature and function.[41] Zhuxi says, "If I investigate principle to the utmost and fully develop my nature, then what I have received is wholly Heaven's moral character, and what Heaven has endowed in me is wholly Heaven's principle."[42] Zhuxi's remark that knowledge starts with the self illustrates the accessibility of knowledge.[43]

II

How does Neville's account of value and harmony in the source compare with Chinese accounts? They differ in that the Chinese sources are the sources of value, whereas Neville's harmony is the source of order and goodness but also of chaos, and "harmony" represents a "value" that can be good or bad.[44] For Neville, every identifiable thing is a harmo-

---

his desires, knowledge and actions to a state of oneness. (See chapter 39)" (192). Again, Cheng says, "Not only can man observe the *dao* both outside of himself and within his own person, and thus come to an understanding of it, he can also cultivate the *dao* (participating in it or imitating it) in order to achieve a desirable and ideal state of life" (193).

38. 42:1b–2b, Chan, 612. As such, everything that is created consists of the Heaven-endowed nature that is principle (42:5a, Chan, 613–14). See 42:13a–b, Chan, 617 for the principles in all men.

39. *Concerning Creativity*, 134.

40. 67:16b–18a, Chan, 599. See also Chan, 597, and 508–9, nos. 30 and 32, for Zhangzai's account of the persistence of this Heaven-endowed nature.

41. 42:13a–b, Chan, 617.

42. 42:3a–b, Chan, 613. See also p. 509 for Zhangzai's similar account of how knowledge leads to the principle of nature.

43. Berthrong supports the knowability of Zhuxi's principle when he says, "it is important to note that the direction of the analysis is always from the concrete mind-heart to the principles involved and not vice versa" (*Concerning Creativity*, 134).

44. As Robert S. Corrington says of Neville's position on harmony in his "Neville's 'Naturalism' and the Location of God," *American Journal of Theology and Philosophy* 18 (1997): 257–80, "We are cautioned, however, not to assume that the word 'harmony' always denotes a stability or a peaceful process of regular change. Harmonies can be profoundly displeasing and

ny. A thing could mean "substance, event, change, situation, condition, whatever."[45] Mixtures of components which make up things are ordered by patterns that result in harmonies. These patterns are not "necessarily static but might be patterns of change,"[46] and not all harmonies are good (61). Conflict and strife are not opposed to harmony but are required and justified, either to loosen existing harmonies or to bring about harmonies. The question of when conflict or strife is called for is a matter for "independent normative assessment" (61). Because harmonies result from conditional features, Neville thinks that what harmonies the world has, and what orders it ought to have, are not to be determined by metaphysics but, rather, empirically and by independent normative analyses (62–63). He writes: "Reference to divine creation, however, is never helpful in answering the question why an entity is this way rather than that, for the question always refers either to determining conditions or to the specifics of the entity's own spontaneity." God is the ground of both order and chaos, and is the source of value, but he does not dictate what ought to exist.[47] Nor is God good or valuable in himself, since "only created determinate harmonious things are valuable" and also because we cannot say anything about God in himself independently of his relations with his creations.[48]

Laozi's Dao as harmony is nothing like Neville's ground.[49] Laozi's

---

need not reflect anything congenial to human aspiration or desire. In this sense, the concept of harmony is morally neutral" (p. 269).

45. *Behind the Masks*, 61.

46. Ibid., 61. Neville says: "[a] harmony is a mixture of components and patterns, requiring each and giving each equal importance."

47. "From Nothing," 23, 24. Contrasting Whitehead and Neville's use of "forms," Corrington explains why God does not dictate the orders in the world for Neville: "The future is tied to form and different forms entail different values. 'It is the forms in things that make the difference in value.' Yet we must always ask: just where are the forms? Whitehead would have us believe that they are resident in the primordial mind of God, waiting to be sent out as tantalizing lures to hungry actual occasions. Neville . . . prefers to let the future have its own distinctive features. Hence, forms are not mental quasi-actualizations in a divine mind, but realities awaiting actualization via the other modes of time. 'Far better to say that form is the essential feature of the future and that determinate forms are the ways the future is made determinate by concrete actualities in the past and by the shifting decisions of present moments.' Actualities and decisions work together to render certain forms actual to the things of the world. These forms are located in a kind of cosmic 'would be' that is not a form-bank so much as a potential for actualization." See "Neville's Naturalism," 266–67.

48. "From Nothing," 23, 22.

49. Laozi's harmony/Dao blends the *yin* and the *yang*, and balances excess and deficiency.

Dao is the norm of harmony, which is necessarily good and the way to achieve value. Neville's conflict-strife-ridden harmony contrasts with Laozi's "smooth and easy" harmony. Laozi stresses nonaction or effortless action (*wuwei*, chs. 2, 63) and what's natural (*ziran*, chs. 23, 25, 17, 15) so that any action that involves conflict or strife such as war (ch. 31), or active attempts (ch. 48), or intrusiveness (ch. 57), is not in accord with the Dao. As Laozi puts it,

> Follow no activity and gain the world . . .
> The more taboos and prohibitions there are in the world, the poorer
>   the people.
> The more sharp implements the people have, the more benighted the state.
> The more clever and skillful the people, the more strange and perverse
>   things arise.
> The more clear the laws and edicts, the more thieves and robbers. (ch. 57)[50]

Similarly, Zhuxi's principle is the measure of harmony and goodness, which is necessarily good in itself. He says, "What exists before physical form is the one principle harmonious and undifferentiated, and is invariably good."[51] For Zhuxi, cultivating the same mind of Heaven and Earth, which produces things according to moral principles, is the way to the norm. Just as the mind of Heaven and Earth produces things infinitely with the principle of origination, the human mind loves people and benefits things with the principle of *ren*.[52] *Ren* is the highest Confucian virtue, wherein one extends one's love for one's family to the rest of the world and cosmos. We see in the area of values and harmony, then, this further difference between Chinese thought and Neville's "ontological creativity": that Zhuxi's harmonies are metaphysically determined, but Neville's harmonies are determined by independent normative analyses.[53]

50. See also *Daodejing*, ch. 53.
51. 67:16b–18a, Chan, 597.
52. *A Treatise on Ren*, Chan, 594–95. See my *Remastering Morals with Aristotle and Confucius* (Cambridge: Cambridge University Press, 2007), chapter 1, for a detailed discussion of *ren*. As Berthrong puts it, "There are ample indications that Chu Hsi understands an axiological unity to be the essential cosmological feature of principle. . . . For Chu Hsi, there is a vision of the perfect mode of action and society that is definitely coherent, even harmonious" (*Concerning Creativity*, 125).
53. See my "Harmony and the Mean in the *Nicomachean Ethics* and the *Zhongyong*," *Dao: A Journal of Comparative Philosophy* 3 (2004): 253–80, for how the *zhong* (equilibrium or mean

III

Let us, finally, consider Neville's view that every change requires spontaneity and novelty. Spontaneous changes, he says in "From Nothing to Being," "always involve a harmonious relation between *yin* and *yang* elements such that there is an ordered relation between them—*yin* is the source of *yang*" (26). Past states of affairs constitute the "material and the limiting conditions" in the emergence of the new (26). Spontaneity consists in the "self-constitution" of a new entity which "has feelings" for the past and conforms to past conditions. What is new is that the new entity "fully embraces the past, the *yin* elements, and transforms them" (27). "The novelty derives from the fact that they [i.e., the past] can be embraced in unexpected ways" (27). Despite the new entity's spontaneity or self-constitution, it is still related to the past and hence to "previous instances of divine creation" (27). Any "spontaneous activity of emergence or change reflects the ontological grounding of the change in the creator."[54] Hence, any spontaneous activity is also grounded in creation *ex nihilo*.

Applying this to followers of Daoism, Neville maintains that they give priority to the past, from which the present arises. They favor an "inclusive harmony" over an "intensive" or "limited" harmony (28). He holds that the Confucians, by contrast, give priority to the present. Although the past provides the ritual proprieties *(li)* dictating the harmonious norm, their emphasis on "personal investment," while realizing harmony, makes their emphasis the present (30). Confucianism's focus is on "special obligations to create the human world with its *unique values*" (31; my emphasis). Neville understands the Confucian's loyalty to the past, as in filial piety and ancestor worship, to be for "the present making of a man; ancestors are cultivated to secure their present cooperation" (31). Just as he criticizes the Daoists for not having a justification for preferring the past in their pursuit of harmony, he criticizes the Confucians for running the risk of confusing their creativity with creation *ex nihilo*. Since Confucian norms are made by human art and are thus sus-

---

state that is prior to joy, anger, sorrow and pleasure), in the Confucian text the *Zhongyong*, is the ground of harmony and the norm for human action and all things under Heaven.

54. Ibid. There would not be a past from which this new entity emerged were it not for other determinate beings in the past.

ceptible to being appearances of morality rather than real morality (30, 32), failure to recognize their limitation,[55] says Neville, could lead to the problem of "pride."[56]

I do not think that the Confucians are liable to confuse their creativity with creation *ex nihilo,* because their aim is not to "create the human world with its unique values."[57] If Confucians are not primarily creators of their norms and values, then they do not risk creating moral values that do not take into consideration a more objective source, nor do they risk being prideful. Confucians, as Neville explains, emphasize "personal investment" when performing rituals so that they are not just mindlessly going through the motions, but rather are sincere in their actions.[58] But this does not mean that Confucians aim to create unique values. The Confucian values of filial piety toward parents, being trustworthy in speech, being generous and doing one's best, are not unique (in the sense that they are novel) just because one invests oneself when performing these virtuous actions. Rather, Confucius maintains that these values are the same as those of the Zhou dynasty.[59]

One's personal investment, far from embracing the past rituals in "unexpected ways," embraces them in just the right ways, that is, in the expected ways. For instance, one is expected to mourn three years for one's parent's death and to do so sincerely. Investing oneself wholeheartedly does not create a unique value but recreates the same value that all filial persons in mourning share. Nor is it present-centered, as in Neville's description of ancestors being worshipped "to secure their present cooperation."[60] Such an aim would violate the Confucian gentleman's virtue of appropriateness *(yi)* wherein he focuses on doing what is right in all situations rather than on securing his personal gain (*Analects* 4.16). Confucians are keen on cultivating themselves by following the past rituals, not on creating novel values. Confucius repeatedly stresses the importance of

55. As contrasted with ontological creation, which does not have the same shortcomings since it is immediate and spontaneous.

56. "From Nothing," 32.

57. Ibid., 31.

58. See my "The Moral Self in Confucius and Aristotle," *International Philosophical Quarterly* 43 (2003): 439–62, on the necessity of personal investment in actions for the Confucians.

59. *Analects* 3.14. *The Analects of Confucius: A Philosophical Translation,* trans. with an introduction by Roger T. Ames and Henry Rosemont, Jr. (New York: Ballantine Books, 1998).

60. "From Nothing," 31.

learning (17.8), especially by studying the *Odes* (16.13, 17.9), and he professes that he is a follower of the ancients rather than a maker of new paths.[61]

A second point, not unrelated to the first, concerns Neville's views about the source of the Confucians' ritual principles. He thinks that these Confucian rituals as norms are man-made and conventional, and that appearances of morality may thus be mistaken for real morality. He also thinks that, in their failure to recognize the possibility of this error, Confucians may be guilty of pride. (He finds adherents to an explicit creation *ex nihilo* view to be more attuned to this problem.) We need only look, however, to Zhuxi or Mencius to see that rituals are founded on metaphysical principles governing human nature rather than on mere conventions. Because the human mind is exactly the same as the mind of Heaven and Earth, containing exactly the same principles, what we do to cultivate this original principle is not a matter of arbitrary, man-made conventions. Rather, the rituals for cultivation are bound up with the way we are and with the way the natural world around us is.

This is also the point of Confucius's discussion about when one is to bow—on entering the hall or after ascending it.[62] In spite of the convention of bowing after one ascends the hall, Confucius recommends bowing upon entrance. Presumably, Confucius's recommendation is based on the fact that conventions are not simply arbitrary but rather are governed by our nature as well as by the harmony that governs human relationships and the whole cosmos. Consequently, Confucius recommends controverting a current convention if practicing it would not lead to the desired outcome, say, of reverence. Human fabrication alone, then, is not the source of Confucian rituals. Rather, different Confucians appeal to different sources, all of which are objective from their own standpoints. For example, Confucius himself appeals to Heaven *(tian),* Mencius appeals to the four sprouts of virtue, Zhuxi appeals to principle, and the Confucian text of *Zhongyong* appeals to the *zhong* (equilibrium or mean).[63] If Confucian rituals are governed by metaphysics, then it is not clear that they are especially prone to the problem of pride.

---

61. *Analects* 7.1. A similar point about the conservative nature of the Neo-Confucians is made by Berthrong when he says, "In many respects, the Neo-Confucians were more rabbinic in style, valuing commentary, exegesis, and explication of the classics above transitory individual creativity in terms of novel literary publications" (*Concerning Creativity,* 116).

62. *Analects* 9.3.

63. See my "Ritual and Realism in Early Chinese Science," *Journal of Chinese Philosophy* 29

IV

Our comparisons between Neville and the Chinese, with respect to their understandings of the origins of beings and the ways these beings change, have shown that the Chinese are also concerned with the question of being, non-being, and creation *ex nihilo,* albeit in ways that are quite different from Neville's way of understanding these concepts. I agree with Neville's identification of an ontological ground of creation in the Chinese thinkers beyond the cosmological processes of change, which they also possess. I agree also that this ontological ground is, for the most part, asymmetrically related to the determinate things, as Neville maintains. Nevertheless, there seem to be at least two cases in which the Chinese understanding of the relation between the source and the determinate things manifests symmetry. Zhuxi's understanding of principle provides an example of the relation between the ground and determinate things being symmetrical, because Zhuxi's principle *(li)* needs material force *(qi)* before something can have a physical form. Mencius's conception of the four sprouts, too, can be considered an instance of symmetrical relation between the source and determinate things. This is because Mencius's four sprouts are born into each human being. It can be argued that these sprouts need the physical being in order to exist and to have the potential to be actualized. These exceptions aside, though, the sources are, as Neville maintains, asymmetrically related to the determinate beings; this is true for Zhoudunyi's ultimate of non-being, for the Confucian *Zhongyong's* equilibrium *(zhong),* and for Laozi's *Dao.* The sources of these other Chinese thinkers are prior in time, in being, in knowledge, in cause, and prior ethically, to the determinate things they cause, whereas for Zhuxi and Mencius, their sources are only conceptually and ethically prior to the determinate things they cause.

In spite of the fact that in so many of the Chinese thinkers the relation between the ontological ground and determinate things it causes is asymmetrical, their views need not be instances of Neville's understanding of the ground as a nothing that creates. Recall two of the differences

---

(2002): 501–23 and "Categories and Commensurability in Confucius and Aristotle: A Response to MacIntyre," in *Categories: Historical and Systematic Essays,* ed. Michael Gorman and Jonathan J. Sanford (Washington, D.C.: The Catholic University of America Press, 2004), 58–77, for extended discussions of the closeness of rituals and reality for the Confucians.

we have seen above: (1) the unknowability of Neville's ontological ground as contrasted with to the knowability of the Chinese sources; (2) the fact that the Chinese sources are the metaphysical norms for harmony and goodness (e.g., rituals) of determinate things, while Neville's ontological ground is neither a metaphysical norm for harmony nor a norm for the values of contingent things.

More importantly, Neville's conception of the Nothing is quite different from the Nothing in the Chinese sources. Whereas Neville's ground is an indeterminate Nothing about which nothing can be said apart from its relation to the beings it causes, these Chinese sources are quite determinate in their own ways, though not in the ways that contingent things are. This explains why so many of these Chinese sources are said to be non-being *(wu)*—that is, they are not being in the sense that they are any of the particular beings in the world, but rather, they are the standards that define the limits of determinate beings. Take for instance, the *Zhongyong*, I.4:

Prior *(wei)* to the happening *(fa)* of joy, anger, sorrow and pleasure is called *zhong* (equilibrium/mean). When these feelings have happened and they are regulated according to *zhong* it is called *he* (harmony). *Zhong* is the basis of all under Heaven *(tian)* and *he* is the way *(dao)* of all under Heaven.

Not only is the equilibrium *(zhong)* in this passage the cause of all beings under Heaven and all actions, but also it delimits the nature of things and the goal of actions. Since the *zhong* is the state that exists prior to things and actions in the world, it is not any particular thing, and hence can be understood as nothing. Yet, the Confucian *zhong* is not the same as Neville's nothing, because it is determinate and very definite things are said about it in the *Zhongyong*. We saw above in note 25 that Zhuxi's Great Ultimate is said to have neither spatial nor physical form, nor is it a body, but it is the principle of the highest good. Again, because this Great Ultimate is neither spatial nor physical, it is not a thing. But because it is the principle of things and their goodness, it is not an absolute nothing in itself, like Neville's Nothing. The same is true of Zhoudunyi's ultimate of non-being and Laozi's *Dao,* for each of these is a source which is not any particular thing, and yet each has definite characteristics in itself, as we saw earlier.

It is true also that not all of the Chinese sources transcend this world as Neville's ontological ground does. Again, Zhuxi's correlativity of principle *(li)* and material force *(qi)* is an example of a ground that does not transcend this world. Mencius's four sprouts, being innate in each human being, clearly do not transcend the world. In contrast to Mencius's and Zhuxi's sources, though, Zhoudunyi's ultimate of nonbeing and the Confucian equilibrium *(zhong)* do seem to be sources that transcend the changeable things in this world. Given these differences, however, among and within the Chinese traditions, it seems they cannot all represent the kind of ontological creativity Neville proposes.

These comparisons between the Chinese sources and Neville's ontological ground do reveal that these Chinese thinkers also are grappling with a question about why there is something (i.e., the contingent beings in this world) rather than nothing (as the Chinese understand "nothing"). Our comparison between Neville and the Chinese thinkers also shows that the Chinese are concerned with how the sources are related to the beings in this world—causally, in time, in knowledge, and ethically. Put otherwise, they too are interested in explaining why the beings in this world undergo the changes they do (both naturally and morally). But whereas for the Chinese the changes of the things in this world are directly related to the sources, in that the sources dictate the metaphysical norms for beings and their values, Neville's contingent things and ontological ground are not so directly related, inasmuch as he separates the determinations and values of things from the ontological Nothing and instead relates these contingencies directly to each other. Hence, even though the Chinese too are concerned with their own sense of "creation *ex nihilo*," their understanding of it is radically different from Neville's sense of creation *ex nihilo*.

Appendix

I differ also from commentators like David Hall and Chang Tung-sun (whom Hall quotes in "The Way and the Truth," in *A Companion to World Philosophies* [hereafter CWP], ed. Eliot Deutsch and Ron Bontekoe [Oxford: Blackwell Publishers, 1997], 214–24), who contrast the Chinese way of knowing, which they characterize as a kind of 'knowing-how', with the ancient Greek way of knowing, which they characterize as a kind of 'knowing-that'. See also "The Culture of Metaphysics," where Hall cites with approval Angus Graham's assertion that "the Chinese have no concept of truth" (p. 207). Unlike Hall and Chang, a number of the Confucians and Neo-

Confucians who are more metaphysically minded would want us to know the metaphysical principle(s) dictating the way of things, including human beings; for knowing what we are will also allow us to know how to cultivate or attain this way. Zhuxi, for example, would hold that we need to know the mind of Heaven and Earth, which mind contains the same principles that are in us, in order to know how to cultivate ourselves and hence to act correctly. Daniel K. Gardner claims that we are to turn to the canonical texts of the Confucian canon for Zhuxi when we are seeking the principle. Gardner says, "It is here, in the canonical tradition, then, that principle is most accessible, that one can hope to arrive at a penetrating understanding of the true nature of things" (p. 109). See his "Attentiveness and Meditative Reading in Cheng-Zhu Neo-Confucianism," in *Confucian Spirituality*, vol. 2, ed. Tu Weiming and Mary Evelyn Tucker (New York: The Crossroad Publishing Company, 2004), 99–119.

See also Shun Kwong-Loi, "Ideas of the Good in Chinese Philosophy," in CWP, 139–47, where he explains Guoxiang's (a Neo-Daoist, d. 312) view of "letting everything follow its own nature without intervention" (145). Because different things are endowed with different natures, "different human beings may have different natures suited to fulfilling different roles in society" (145). Hence rituals governing human relations are based on such differences in nature. Both Gardner and Shun then, would agree with me that the Chinese also emphasize a kind of 'knowing that' which is not incompatible with 'knowing how' to cultivate oneself or act appropriately.

Part Two

Contributions in Medieval Philosophy

3 ∾ The Ultimate Why Question

Avicenna on Why God Is Absolutely Necessary

The question "Why is there anything at all rather than absolutely nothing?" was not a question medieval Arabic-speaking philosophers were prone to raise, at least not in this exact wording. Instead, they were more concerned with the related question, "Why is there a world rather than no world at all?" or more exactly, "Why does the world have the particular features that it has?" Certainly in the classical and medieval periods the standard answer to this latter question was simply, in one form or another, 'God.' Plato invoked the need for a demiurge to explain the orderly existence of our world; Aristotle argued that there must be an unmoved mover to explain the manifest motion in the world; and Neoplatonists later appealed to the One to explain the unified existence of the world. What is common to all of these thinkers is that they began with what might be called a 'physical fact', that is to say, some particular feature about the way the world actually is, whether it be its order, motion, unification or the like, and then they invoked God as the required cause of these physical facts. Since all these proofs for the existence of God begin with what I am calling a 'physical fact' about the world, one might call them 'physical' arguments for the existence of God.

The medieval Arabic philosopher Ibn Sīnā (980–1037), the Latin Avicenna, found the use of 'physical' arguments to prove the existence of God wanting and complained that what was needed was a 'metaphysical' proof for the existence of God.[1] I understand his complaint to be that

---

1. See *Commentary on Lambda,* in *Arisṭū ʿinda l-ʿArab,* ed. ʾA. Badawi (Cairo: Maktabat an-nahḍa al-miṣrīya, 1947), 23–24; *Taʿlīqāt,* ed. ʾA. Badawi (Cairo: Maktabat-al-ʿArabīya,

'physical' arguments for the existence of God prove only the conditional necessity of God: *since* some physical fact exists, *then* God exists. If that physical feature of the world had counterfactually not existed, and some physically different world existed, then a necessary premise of the proof would be lacking and so that particular argument would fail to prove the existence of God. In contrast, a 'metaphysical' argument, or so I contend, would prove the absolute necessity of God regardless of any physical facts or specific features about the way the world actually is, as such a 'metaphysical argument' would show that if anything exists, no matter how it might exist, then God necessarily exists. For Avicenna such an argument must begin from an analysis of existence itself, or being *qua* being, and more precisely the irreducible modal structure of existence.[2]

In this study I want to consider Avicenna's 'metaphysical' argument for the existence of God and the modal metaphysics that underpins it, but I also want to consider how Avicenna's modal metaphysics provided him with the means to argue for another historically important philosophical thesis, namely, the eternity of the world. Avicenna's argument for the existence of God attempts to show that if anything exists, then a Necessary Being, namely God, must exist; his proof for the eternity of the world attempts to show that if it is even possible that the world exists, then the world must be eternal. What is of particular interest about Avicenna's proof for the eternity of the world, I shall argue, is that, when it is coupled with his proof for the existence of God, the result is an even stronger proof for the existence of God, namely, one that shows that if anything whatsoever is simply possible, then necessarily God exists. In other words, in response to the 'ultimate why question,' "Why is there anything at all rather than absolutely nothing?" Avicenna's answer comes down to "Because something is possible."

1973), 62; and the distinction was implied though not explicitly made at *al-Ishārāt wa-t-tanbīhāt*, ed. J. Forget (Leiden: E. J. Brill, 1892), *namaṭ* 4, *faṣl* 29, 146–47. For a discussion of the historical context for this distinction see Dimitri Gutas, *Avicenna and the Aristotelian Tradition: Introduction to Reading Avicenna's Philosophical Works* (Leiden: E. J. Brill, 1988), 261–65.

2. For an excellent study of the historical context for Avicenna's doctrines of existence as well as the necessary and possible existents see Robert Wisnovsky, *Avicenna's Metaphysics in Context* (Ithaca, NY: Cornell University Press, 2003), part II.

I

Let us then begin with Avicenna's analysis of existence and his modal metaphysics. Book I, chapter 5 of the *Metaphysics* of his *Shifā'* is dedicated to an indication that something exists *(mawjūd)* and what the divisions of existence *(wujūd)* are. That something exists and that there is existence, he begins, is the first thing impressed upon the soul and simply cannot be doubted.[3] Trying to demonstrate that there is existence or that something exists, he argues, is a fool's errand, since every demonstration proceeds from things better known than and prior to the conclusion.[4] Thus if one assumed that there were anything better known than and prior to existence itself, one would be committed to the *existence* of that thing itself, and so would have to assume *its existence,* the very thing that one was attempting to demonstrate. In short, for Avicenna, any proof that there is existence must be inherently circular.

Such a claim I take to be clear enough and in need of little defense. Avicenna goes on, however, to add that since the necessary *(wājib wujūd)* and the possible *(mumkin wujūd)* are the primary divisions of existence, they too must have the same epistemic status as existence, namely, any attempts to prove that or what the necessary and possible are will be inherently circular.[5] The claim that necessity and possibility have, as it were, the same epistemic status as existence should give one reason to pause; for it is not immediately obvious how necessity and possibility, even if they are existence's primary divisions, are on a par with existence when it comes to being 'better known than' and 'prior to' anything else whatsoever; for it certainly seems that while one is immediately aware of existence, in some way or another, one is not immediately aware of necessity and possibility.

Avicenna freely concedes that certain physical facts about the world

3. *Shifā', al-Ilāhīyāt* (henceforth *Metaphysics*), I.5, 22.11–12; references to the *Metaphysics* are to the Cairo edition found in *The Metaphysics of* The Healing, trans. (with Arabic edition) M. E. Marmura, Islamic Translation Series (Provo, UT: Brigham Young University Press, 2005). Also see *Najāt, Ilāhīyāt,* ed. M. T. Danish pazhuh (Tehran: Danishgah-i Tihran, 1985/6), I.4, 396. All translations are my own.

4. For a discussion of Avicenna on the primacy of existence see Michael E. Marmura, "Avicenna on Primary Concepts in the *Metaphysics* of the *Shifā',*" in *Probing in Islamic Philosophy* (Binghamton, NY: Global Academic Publishing, 2005), 149–69 (henceforth *Probing*).

5. *Metaphysics,* I.5, 27.32–28.27.

68   *Jon McGinnis*

draw one's attention to existence in a way that they do not draw one's attention to necessity and possibility.[6] Part of the reason for this fact is that, to use an Aristotelian distinction that Avicenna himself appropriates, physical facts, namely, things perceived by the senses, might be 'better known' and 'prior' *relative to us,* but they are not 'better known' and 'prior' *absolutely* or *by nature* to the necessary and the possible, or so Avicenna believed.[7] In other words, we often are better acquainted with certain effects while being wholly oblivious to the causes of those effects, even though the causes are better known and prior by nature or absolutely.

The reason that Avicenna believes that the necessary and possible are on a par with existence is that one's conceptualizing *(taṣawwur)*—and so one's knowing—necessity and possibility are exactly like conceptualizing and knowing existence; for in all of these cases there is nothing more basic by which one could explain or define the notion in question. Thus the very status Avicenna observed about existence, he also would observe about modal terms:

Virtually everything that has reached you from the ancients concerning how to explain [the 'necessary', 'possible' and 'impossible'] requires [you do so] circularly. That is because . . . when you want to define the possible, you take either the necessary or the impossible in its definition, and there is no other way but that. [Similarly] when you want to define the necessary you take either the possible or impossible in its definition.[8]

For Avicenna, then, any explanation of what necessity and possibility are must be inherently circular, and it is just in this respect that necessity and possibility are like existence. There is something ultimately basic about them. There simply is nothing better known or prior to them by which one could define or demonstrate these modalities. Moreover, because any attempt to define or demonstrate these modal concepts is ultimately circular, Avicenna maintains that they have the same status as existence with respect to being primary, albeit as the primary divisions of existence itself.

Here a somewhat extended digression seems warranted; for Avicen-

6. Ibid., 28.28–32.

7. Avicenna treats at length the distinction between "better known and prior by nature" and "better known and prior to us" at *Shifāʾ, al-Burhān,* ed. ʿA. Badawi (Cairo: Association of Authorship, Translation and Publication Press, 1966), I.10, and again at *Shifāʾ, aṭ-Ṭabīʿīyā,* ed. S. Zayed (Cairo: General Egyptian Book Organization, 1983), I.1 (henceforth *Physics*).

8. *Metaphysics,* I.5, 27.19–28.3.

na rests the primacy of necessity and possibility on the basis that they can be defined only circularly, and yet it is not clear that this is the case. Certainly if one considers only the 'definitions' of 'necessity' and 'possibility' found in book *Delta* of Aristotle's *Metaphysics* these concepts are explained in terms of one another; for there Aristotle does define the 'possible' *(dunaton)* as that which is not necessary *(anangkē)*,[9] while he defines the necessary as that which cannot be otherwise *(mē endechomenon)*,[10] where 'can' and 'possible' are logically equivalent.[11]

Still this is not the only way that Aristotle defined these terms. Indeed, implicitly in his logical works and explicitly in the *De caelo* Aristotle explains 'necessity', 'possibility', and 'impossibility' in terms of a temporal frequency model of modalities.[12] On this model, if something exists for all time, it is necessary; if it exists at some time, but not at another time, it is possible; and if it exists at no time ever, it is impossible. Now what is interesting about analyzing modalities in terms of temporal frequency is that this model apparently reduces modalities to non-modal elements, namely, temporal elements. Such an account of modalities obviously raises a problem for Avicenna's 'circularity thesis.' Moreover, not only was the temporal frequency model of modalities arguably the best-known means of defining modal concepts by both Greek-speaking and early Arabic-speaking philosophers, but also it is the very one that Avicenna himself used to explain necessity and possibility in his logical works.[13] Consequently, since Avicenna is aware of the temporal frequency model and even uses it himself, he owes his reader an account of how temporal fre-

9. Aristotle, *Metaphysics*, V, 12, 1019b27–29.

10. Ibid., V 5, 1015a34.

11. Cf. *De Interpretatione*, 13, 22a15–16.

12. See *De Interpretatione*, 9, 19a1–4, 32–36; 23a2–3, and *De caelo* I 11, 281a1–6; I 12, 281a28–30. For a discussion of Aristotle's modal concepts, see Sarah Waterlow, *Passage and Possibility: A Study of Aristotle's Modal Concepts* (Oxford: Clarendon Press, 1982).

13. Within the Arabic-speaking logical tradition prior to Avicenna see Yaḥyā ibn ʿAdī, "Establishing the Nature of the Possible," edited and translated by Carl Ehrig-Eggert, "Yaḥyā ibn ʿAdī: über den Nachweis der Natur des Möglichen," in *Zeitschrift für Geschichte der arabisch-islamischen Wissenschaften* 5 (1989): 283–97, [Arabic] 63–97, esp. 78–80. Interestingly, during his discussion of *De Interpretatione* 9, al-Fārābī suggests that in certain contexts modalities might be taken as self-evident without appeal to temporal frequencies. As for Avicenna, one can see his use of the temporal frequency model of modalities at *Shifāʾ*, *al-Qiyās*, ed. S. Zayed (Cairo: Wizārat-al maʿārif, 1964), I.4, and *Al-Ishārāt wa-t-tanbihāt, nahj* 4; also see Tony Street, "Fakhraddin ar-Razi's Critique of Avicennan Logic," in *Logik und Theologie: Das Organon im arabischen und im lateinischen Mittelalter*, ed. U. Rudolph and D. Perler (Leiden: E. J. Brill, 2005), § 2 for a discussion of temporal frequency in Avicenna's logic.

quencies presuppose modal concepts; yet in his *Metaphysics* there is no mention of this model at all. Thus not only does it seem that Avicenna was being disingenuous when he said that necessity and possibility can be defined only circularly, but also his general argument for the primacy of these concepts seems jeopardized.

Although one cannot help but feel that Avicenna is being less than forthright at this point, he does provide sufficient material to piece together a general argument showing that defining modalities in terms of temporal frequency ultimately does involve a circular definition, albeit this material comes not from his *Metaphysics* but from his *Physics*. In that work, Avicenna, following Aristotle, defines time in terms of motion, namely, as "the number of motion when it is differentiated into prior and posterior."[14] Unlike Aristotle, however, before Avicenna defines *what* time is, he provides an explicit proof *that* time is.[15] We can set aside the details of his proof for the reality of time, since what is interesting about it is that it is argued in terms of a varying 'possibility' *(imkān)*, which belongs to motion, to traverse greater and lesser distances. Avicenna, then, ultimately identifies this *possibility* to traverse greater and lesser distances with time.[16] In other words, on Avicenna's analysis of time, time is understood first and primarily in terms of the modal notion of possibility, and then only secondarily in terms of the motion in which that possibility resides. In short, if Avicenna's analysis of time is correct, one comes to know time only if one already knows what possibility is. Consequently, any attempts to define or explain possibility and the other modalities in terms of temporal frequency, and so in terms of time, would in fact, on Avicenna's analysis of time, implicitly presuppose a modal notion, again namely, possibility. Certainly, relative to ourselves, we may come to know that there is time before we know that there is possibility and what possibility is, but considered absolutely or by nature, if Avicenna's analysis of time is correct, possibility is 'better known than' and 'prior to' time. Even if this argument is not Avicenna's own as it applies to the circularity of defining modal notions in terms of temporal frequency, it certainly is Avicennan in spirit.

14. *Physics*, II.11, 157.6.
15. See my *Avicenna* (Oxford & New York: Oxford University Press, 2010), 71–75, for a discussion of Avicenna's proof.
16. *Physics*, II.11, 155.4–156.17.

Thus, to return to the original aim, for Avicenna necessity and possibility stand alongside existence as its primary divisions. They, like existence itself, simply cannot be defined or explained in terms of something more basic. Still, Avicenna did believe that one could provide descriptions of the necessary and possible, or in other words, criteria for identifying them, even if these descriptions or criteria are in terms of things less evident in themselves than necessity and possibility.[17] Again, as we have already seen, however, Avicenna could and happily did concede that sensible things are 'better known' and 'prior' relative to us, even though necessity and possibility are 'better known' and 'prior' absolutely or by nature.

Thus Avicenna describes the 'necessary in itself' as that mode of being that is in itself wholly determinate and as such is in no need of a cause to explain its existing at all. In fact, should the necessary in itself exist, there would be no conditions whatsoever under which it could fail to exist. Conversely, Avicenna describes the 'possible in itself' as that mode of being that is indeterminate between existence and non-existence, in which case either the presence of a cause selectively determines that it exists or the absence of a cause selectively determines that it does not exist. Again, these claims are not intended to be definitions of the modal terms they describe, but just descriptions. As such they provide one simply with criteria for identifying and so determining what would count as falling under one or the other of existence's divisions.

For the sake of completeness, I should add that Avicenna made one further division of existence, which, as it were, is a hybrid of the necessary in itself and the possible in itself. This further division is that which is possible in itself, but necessary through another, namely, it exists necessarily as a result of a cause. In effect, this last division, namely, the possible in itself, but necessary through another, corresponds with any created thing's actual or determinate existence.[18] With this final division Avicenna's analysis of existence is complete.

17. Avicenna's criteria for identifying the necessary and the possible in itself, as well as the possible in itself, but necessary through another, can be found at *Metaphysics* I.6 29.32–32.6 and *Najāt, Ilāhīyāt*, II.1. George F. Hourani has collected together and translated a number of the most important passages in which Avicenna discusses descriptions of the necessary and possible in "Ibn Sīnā on Necessary and Possible Existence," *Philosophical Forum* 4 (1972): 74–86.

18. *Metaphysics*, I.6, 31.27–32.6; *Najāt, Ilāhīyāt*, II.3, 548–49.

II

Bearing in mind the primacy of the necessary and the possible in Avicenna's thought, as well as their descriptions, I want to turn to Avicenna's argument for a Necessary Existent or God as he presents it in his smaller encyclopedic work, the *Najāt*, or the Latin *Metaphysices compendium*.[19] Here, as in the *Shifā'*, Avicenna takes it as beyond doubt that something exists and that the necessary and the possible are the primary divisions of existence. Using this division of existence as his starting point, Avicenna argues that there must be a Necessary Existent as follows: if, on the one hand, the existence that immediately presents itself to us is necessary, there is a Necessary Existent. On the other hand, if the existence of which we are immediately aware is only possible existence, then, given the description of the possible, it must have a cause. At this point, rather than denying the impossibility of an infinite causal chain, as virtually all earlier physical arguments for the existence of God had done, Avicenna asks his reader to consider the totality *(jumla)* of all the possible things that exist at some given moment, regardless of whether that totality is finite or infinite.[20] He next observes that the existence of this totality itself must be either necessary in itself or possible in itself, given again that these are the two primary divisions of existence and that the totality itself exists.

On the one hand, the totality cannot be something necessary in itself,

19. *Najāt, Ilāhīyāt*, II.12, 566–68; for a translation of the text see Jon McGinnis and David C. Reisman, *Classical Arabic Philosophy: An Anthology of Sources* (Indianapolis: Hackett Publishing Co., 2007), 214–15. As for the occurrence of this proof in the *Shifā'*, see Michael E. Marmura, "Avicenna's Proof from Contingency for God's Existence in the *Metaphysics* of the *Shifā'*," in *Probing*, 131–48.

20. It has been noted that one thing that sets apart Avicenna's proof for the existence of a Necessary Existent from other proofs for the existence of 'God' is that it does not require the premise that an actual infinite is impossible: see Herbert A. Davidson, *Proofs for Eternity, Creation and the Existence of God in Medieval Islamic and Jewish Philosophy* (New York: Oxford University Press, 1987), 300–302 (henceforth *Proofs*); and Toby Mayer, "Ibn Sīnā's 'Burhān al-Siddīqīn,'" *Journal of Islamic Studies* 12 (2001): 18–39, esp. 25–35. Almost certainly one of the primary motivations for this new type of argument is the fact that earlier in the *Physics* of the *Najāt (aṭ-Ṭabī'īyāt*, IV.7, 244–52, esp. 246), Avicenna permits the possibility of 'non-positional' actual infinities, as for instance an infinite number of immortal human souls; see Michael E. Marmura, "Avicenna and the Problem of the Infinite Number of Souls," in *Probing*, 171–79. Consequently, if the present argument simply assumed that there could not be an actually infinite number of (non-linearly) essentially ordered causes, Avicenna would have been guilty of special pleading.

argues Avicenna; for the existence of a totality subsists only through the existence of its members, in which case that which is purportedly necessary in itself would be necessary through another, namely, its members, but this is a contradiction.[21] Moreover, it is impossible that there should be any conditions under which the necessary in itself should fail to exist; for this is one of the very criteria by which one identifies necessary existence. If, however, all the members of the totality exist only possibly in themselves, and things that exist possibly in themselves can fail to exist, then, if each of the members of the totality failed to exist, the totality itself would fail to exist. In other words, there is at least one condition under which the totality of all possible things could fail to exist, namely, if all of its members failed to exist. Again, however, there is no condition under which the necessary in itself could fail to exist, should it exist. Consequently, the totality of things possible in themselves cannot exist necessarily in itself.

"On the other hand," Avicenna continues, "if the totality is something existing possibly in itself, then in order for the totality to exist it needs something that provides existence [that is, causes it to exist], which will be either external or internal to the totality."[22] If it is something existing internal to the totality, it itself would be one of the members of the totality and as such that member cannot exist necessarily, since the assumption is that the totality includes only things possible in themselves. Thus if the cause of the totality's existence were internal and necessary in itself, there would be a contradiction.

Furthermore, the cause of the totality's existence cannot be something internal and possible in itself; for since anything internal is part of the totality itself, it would be the cause of its own existence. In that case, one and the same thing would be both a cause and an effect in the very same respect, which Avicenna himself takes to be absurd. Still, it would seem that Avicenna was aware that the denial of self-causation with respect to existence is too 'physically' robust a claim for his metaphysical argument. Thus, per impossibile, he granted for the sake of argument that something could cause its own existence; however, in that case one must still concede that this member is sufficient to necessitate its own ex-

---

21. At *Najāt, Ilāhīyāt*, II.4–5, 549–52 Avicenna argues extensively that the necessary in itself cannot have parts, since this would in fact make the necessary in itself necessary through another.

22. *Najāt, Ilāhīyāt*, II.12, 567–68.

istence, in which case it exists necessarily through itself. Again, however, the assumption is that the totality includes only things possible in themselves, and so again there would be a contradiction, namely, something is both necessary in itself and possible in itself.

Thus one is left only with the option that the totality is possible in itself and the cause of its existence is something external to the totality. Again, this external thing cannot be something possible in itself; for everything existing possibly in itself is included within the totality. Consequently, this external cause of the existence of all things possible in themselves must fall within existence's other division, namely, the necessary in itself. Therefore, concludes Avicenna, this external cause is something that exists necessarily in itself, and so there must be a Necessary Existent. Q.E.D.

The first thing to observe about this argument is that if one sets aside the modal metaphysics underlying it, then the argument is extremely modest in the premises it requires. Avicenna assumes something about sets or totalities, namely that they subsist through their members, but such a claim seems to be almost true by definition. At one point he takes self-causation to be absurd, but, as he quickly notes, the argument does not absolutely require this premise. Thus, as far as I can see, the most ontologically or physically robust claim assumed by the argument is simply that something exists.[23] It is irrelevant to Avicenna's argument whether

---

23. This fact, in addition to the fact that the argument is driven by Avicenna's modal metaphysics, has led to a debate in the secondary literature as to whether the argument should be classified as an 'ontological argument', a 'cosmological argument', or some hybrid of the two. Perhaps the strongest supporter of the ontological reading is Parvis Morewedge, "A Third Version of the Ontological Argument in the Ibn Sinian Metaphysics," in *Islamic Philosophical Theology*, ed. P. Morewedge (Albany: State University of New York Press, 1979), 188–222; on the other side is Herbert A. Davidson, *Proofs*, 298–308. Others who see both an ontological and a cosmological element are S. A. Johnson, "*Ibn Sīnā's* 'Fourth Ontological Argument for God's Existence,'" *Muslim World* 74 (1984): 161–71, and Toby Mayer, "Ibn Sīnā's 'Burhan al-Siddīqīn.'" My own view is that, strictly speaking, Avicenna's argument is not an ontological one. The hallmark of ontological-style arguments is that they assume only a priori premises, and so have no recourse to empirical experience. Now although Avicenna thinks that existence is one of the primary intelligibles, and so one would never remember a time when one did not know existence, it does not follow that such a conception is innate or a priori; rather, for Avicenna, existence is the very first thing we experience and so the very first thing impressed on the intellect. Thus it seems that the argument is not strictly speaking an ontological-type argument at all, since nothing is taken as a priori. Of course, if one means by 'ontological' merely that Avicenna's argument refers solely to existence or being as such without making reference to any physical facts about existence, then in this qualified sense his argument is an ontological one.

the existence is chaotic or ordered, as is assumed by Plato's argument for a demiurge; whether the existence is undergoing motion or not, as in Aristotle's argument for an unmoved mover; or whether the existence is unified or wholly multiple, as certain Neoplatonists assumed when arguing for the One. In short, based on the existence of anything however it might exist and his analysis of existence, Avicenna can show that there must be a Necessary Existent. In other words, the world could have been wholly different than it is—indeed a world that we might not even be able to conceive—but provided that something exists, there will necessarily be God.

III

We have now considered Avicenna's analysis of the modal structure of existence and his 'metaphysical' as opposed to 'physical' proof for the existence of God. In the remainder of this study, I want to consider how Avicenna uses his modal metaphysics to argue for the eternity of the world.[24] In its simplest form, the structure of Avicenna's argument is that if it is ever possible that the world exists, that is to say, if it is possible that something other than God exists, then the world must have existed eternally. Since the world obviously exists now, its existence was possible. Thus the world must have existed eternally.

That the world exists now cannot be gainsaid. The inference from the world's existence to its prior possible existence requires only the weak and intuitively plausible modal commitment that if x is now, then x was possible. Avicenna further justifies this modal commitment by arguing that if there had been no prior possibility of x's existence, then the present existence of x would have been initially impossible; but if x had been impossible, then it would not exist right now.[25]

---

24. Herbert A. Davidson provides an exhaustive list of arguments for the eternity of the world found among medieval Islamic and Jewish philosophers in *Proofs*, 9–48; proof *(b)*, 16–17, is a condensed version of the argument that I shall present here. Also, that this argument had wide currency during the Middle Ages is witnessed by the fact that both Moses Maimonides (*Guide of the Perplexed*, book II, ch. 14) and Thomas Aquinas (*Summa theologiae* I, q. 46, a. 1, obj. 1) considered it one of the strongest arguments for the world's eternity. For a general discussion of Avicenna's arguments for the eternity of the world (although interestingly *not* the argument presented here), see Rahim Acar, *Talking about God and Talking about Creation: Avicenna's and Thomas Aquinas' Positions* (Leiden: E. J. Brill, 2005), pt. 2, esp. ch. 4.

25. *Metaphysics*, IV.2, 140.7–11; *Najāt, Ilāhīyāt*, I.17, 534; and *Physics*, III.11, 232.15–233.3.

The premise that clearly is in need of justification is that if the world's existence is possible, then the world must have existed eternally. Avicenna's defense of this premise is complex, but considering it in some detail, I believe, will be fruitful. The general strategy of his argument is to identify, as it were, the ontological basis for the possibility of anything that comes to be, namely, the possibility associated with those things that at one time did not exist—such as myself prior to 1965—and then later do exist.[26] Thus he begins: if possibility exists, and again this is beyond doubt for him, then it is either (1) a substance in its own right, that is to say, it is some self-subsisting thing, or (2) it inheres in a substrate and subsists through that substrate. Option (2), namely that possibility inheres in a substrate, can be divided into two further options, namely that the possible in itself might exist either (2a) in a material substrate or (2b) in an immaterial substrate, such as either a created intellect or God Himself.

Avicenna denies that possibility is a substance in its own right (option 1), for in that case, possibilities would not be able to stand in the proper relation with other substances. Thus he writes:

If [possibility] *(jawāz)* were subsisting in itself, neither in a substrate *(maḥall)* nor in a subject, then as such it would not be something related; however, as possible existence it is related to something and intellectually understood by the relation. So it is not a substance subsisting essentially. Perhaps instead it is a certain relation or accident belonging to a substance. Now it cannot be a substance that has a relation, because that relation is associated with something assumed to be non-existent. Also it is impossible that that relation is simply a certain association, however it might chance to be; rather, it is a determinate association, wherein the association is determinate only in that it is possible. Therefore, possibility is itself the relation, not some substance to which the relation is attached, in which case the sum of the two would be possibility.[27]

---

26. Here it is worth noting that while I shall speak simply of the possible and the possible in itself, I mean specifically the possibility of those things that come to exist after having not existed. In this respect, the present account is limited in that it does not address the possibility of sempiternal beings such as angels, for while according to Avicenna, there is no time that angels have not existed, their existence is nonetheless wholly dependent upon God. Thus for Avicenna angels are beings that are merely possible in themselves even though they have always existed.

27. *Physics,* III.11, 233.3–11.

Avicenna's general point, as I understand it, is that if possibility were a substance in its own right, then it could never properly be related to other substances in the requisite way that possibilities are so associated with substances. Neither here nor in other parallel passages does he explain exactly what possibility's proper relation to substances is;[28] however, my suspicion is that, for Avicenna, what it is to be a certain substance is in a very real sense determined precisely by the range of possibilities that belong to that substance. In this respect, then, the range of possibilities that belong to a substance must be related to it essentially, whereas any two distinct substances can only ever be related to each other accidentally. So if possibility were a substance, the range of possibilities that belong to a substance would be accidental to it, just as the clothes I am wearing (one substance) are accidental to me (another substance). It certainly seems false that the range of things I can do, for instance, are accidental to me; for in a real sense what defines me as the sort of substance I am, namely, human, is determined by what I as a human can do.[29]

Thus it would seem that possibility must exist in a substrate. Now if that substrate is immaterial, it might be either a created intellect, such as the human soul or an angel, or a wholly uncreated immaterial being, namely, God. The substrate for the possibility of what comes to be cannot be a created, immaterial substrate; for insofar as such a substrate is created, the possibility of its existence is ontologically prior to (even though not necessarily temporally prior to) the actually existing created thing; however, if this created immaterial substrate is to provide the ontological basis for possibility, its actually existing would be ontologically prior to possibility itself, in which case, points out Avicenna, there is a contradiction—the created immaterial substrate is both ontologically prior to and ontologically posterior to the possible.[30]

As for the suggestion that a wholly uncreated, immaterial being, namely, God, is the ultimate ontological basis for the possibility of what comes to be, there is for Avicenna a sense in which this is correct and a sense in which it is incorrect. At the end of this paper I shall return to the sense in which this claim is correct, but for now it is enough to recall

28. *Metaphysics*, IV.2, 140.11–14 and *Najāt, Ilāhīyāt*, I.17, 535–36.
29. This point is somewhat suggested when Avicenna writes: "those [created] essences are that which in themselves are what is possible of existence" (*Metaphysics*, VIII.4, 276.26–30).
30. Cf. *Physics*, II.12, 160.13–16.

that for Avicenna the Necessary Existent is the ultimate explanation and cause for the actual and determinate existence of anything that is merely possible in itself.

As for the present context, namely, whether God can be the substrate in which the possibility inheres and has its subsistence, Avicenna finds the claim wholly untenable.[31] He offers a number of arguments against this thesis, each depending upon one of the various ways one might consider that God is the ultimate basis or explanation of the possible in itself. Two such arguments that I shall consider correspond with two common accounts of how possibility might be referred back to God. One is that *possibilia* refer to ideas in the mind of God, in which case these ideas represent the exemplars of all that can possibly be; the other is that the possibility of something's existing resides in God's power to create that thing, and so all things falling within the range of God's omnipotent power are possible and otherwise they are impossible. In general terms, Avicenna would argue that populating the divine mind with *possibilia* or multiple ideas jeopardizes the divine simplicity, whereas referring possibility back to God's power without some independent account of possibility strips the notion of omnipotence of any significance.

Against the first suggestion, namely, that the possible in itself is referred back to the divine understanding, Avicenna's critique begins by observing that God's understanding is simple and not made up of multiple ideas.

[W]hen it is said that understanding *('aql)* belongs to the First [Cause, that is, God], it is said according to simple intention (which I explained in the *Psychology*) and that there is not in it a variety of various ordered forms . . . ; for it belongs to that [Cause, that is, God] to understand things all at once as one, without either being multiplied by them in His substance or conceptualizing them by their forms' being in His essence.[32]

In other words, for Avicenna there simply are not multiple ideas in the mind of God by which he knows things; rather, God knows directly only

31. Although Avicenna addressed, on an ad hoc basis, the suggestion that God might be a substrate of possibility Moses Maimonides, clearly working within the *falsafa* tradition itself, took any position that makes God a substratum to be manifestly absurd, since it jeopardizes divine simplicity, for God would then be a composite of the substratum and that which inheres in the substratum; see *Guide for the Perplexed*, book I, ch. 52.

32. *Metaphysics*, VIII.7, 291.6–9; also see *Najāt, Ilāhīyāt*, II.18–19, 593–99.

his simple essence and everything else only inasmuch as he knows that essence.[33] Avicenna's reason is that if the Necessary in Itself, that is God, were to understand multiple things, and not merely Itself alone, then the divine understanding, which in a very real sense is identical with the Necessary in Itself, would be constituted by or subsist through these multiple ideas. Now inasmuch as a unity made up of multiple elements subsists only through those elements as its cause, so likewise the Necessary in Itself would be caused, which is absurd. The same point, stated slightly differently, is that for Avicenna whatever has multiple parts requires a cause in order to make those parts a unified existent. Thus, since there can be no cause for the existence of the divine mind, it cannot have multiple parts, in this case, multiple ideas.[34]

Therefore, on the one hand, the plurality of possibilities that exist in the world cannot refer back to a plurality of ideas or exemplars in the mind of the Necessary in Itself; for there absolutely is no plurality in the Necessary in Itself. On the other hand, if the possible in itself were referred back to the absolutely simple understanding of the Necessary in Itself, and that understanding is to remain simple, then the possible in itself would have to be identical with that understanding; but that would be to make the Necessary in Itself possible in itself, which is a contradiction. In short, for Avicenna, since the Necessary in Itself is absolutely simple, the possible in itself cannot be referred back to the divine understanding.

Avicenna likewise argues against locating the foundation for possibility solely in divine causal power. The suggestion would be that something is possible only because it is within God's power to cause it to be.[35]

---

33. For differing approaches to Avicenna's conception of divine knowledge, and particularly how the Necessary Existent knows things other than himself, see the following: Michael E. Marmura, "Some Aspects of Avicenna's Theory of God's Knowledge of Particulars," in *Probing*, 71–95; Rahim Acar, "Reconsidering Avicenna's Position on God's Knowledge of Particulars," in *Interpreting Avicenna: Science and Philosophy in Medieval Islam*, ed. J. McGinnis (Leiden: E. J. Brill, 2004), 142–56; and Peter Adamson, "On Knowledge of Particulars," *Proceedings of the Aristotelian Society* 105 (2005): 273–94.

34. *Metaphysics*, VIII.4, 273–78, provides an extended discussion of why the Necessary Existent cannot be a composite, whether of quantitative parts or merely conceptual parts, such as ideas constituting the divine mind, which in fact is essentially the Necessary Existent; for these parts would be causes of the Necessary Existent, but the Necessary Existent is in no way caused.

35. The following authors all attribute this conception of possibility to Avicenna: Gerard Smith, "Avicenna and the Possibles," *New Scholasticism* 17 (1943): 340–57; Beatrice Zedler,

Avicenna rejects this suggestion since, if possibility is understood to be through an agent's power rather than through some independent account of possibility, then both the terms 'power' *(qudra)* and 'possibility' *(imkān)* become vacuous.

[Possibility] is not the power of the one who has power over it, otherwise when by replacement it is said that it is not an object of power because it is not possible in itself, it would have been said that it is not an object of power because it is not an object of power, or it is not possible in itself because it is not possible in itself. Clearly, this possibility is different than the one who has power over it . . . .[36]

In other words, if possibility referred to nothing more than the power of the agent to do or make something, then to say, "Something is possible if it falls within the agent's power" simply means, "Something falls within the agent's power, if it falls within the agent's power." Consequently, should one say that God is 'omnipotent' and so can do whatever is possible, one actually would be saying that God can do whatever God can do. Clearly, however, everything can do what it can do, and so everything would be omnipotent on this account of possibility. For Avicenna, then, what is needed is an independent understanding and grounding of the possible in itself, if God's power over all possible things is not to be trivial.

Before completing Avicenna's proof for the eternity of the world, let us quickly assess the argument to this point. Again, Avicenna's primary aim is to justify the claim that if the existence of the world was ever possible, then the world is eternal. In order to prove this claim, he has one consider the ways in which possibility might be said to exist. Avicenna notes that possibility might be understood to exist either as a substance in its own right or in a substrate. He quickly denies that it exists as a substance, and so concludes that possibility must exist in a substrate. He goes on to catalogue the various types of substrates in which it might

---

"Another Look at Avicenna," *New Scholasticism* 50 (1976): 504–21 and "Why Are the Possibles Possible," *New Scholasticism* 55 (1981): 113–30; and James Ross, "Aquinas's Exemplarism; Aquinas's Voluntarism," *American Catholic Philosophical Quarterly* 64 (1990): 171–98. For reasons quite similar to Avicenna's, Lawrence Dewan ("St. Thomas and the Possibles," *New Scholasticism* 53 [1979]: 76–85) rejects this conception of possibility in Aquinas in favor of concept compatibility.

36. *Al-Ishārāt wa-t-tanbīhāt, namaṭ 5, faṣl 6,* 152; also see *Metaphysics,* IV.2, 139.11–140.12, and *Najāt, Ilāhīyāt,* I.17, 534–35.

inhere. These could be either material or immaterial; if possibility were to inhere in an immaterial substrate, that substrate might either be created, such as the human intellect or one of the separate intellects, or not be created, in which case it would be God. We have just seen a series of arguments that Avicenna provided against the inhering of the possible in itself in an immaterial substrate.

Avicenna concludes this extended argument by asserting that the ultimate substrate for the possibility of whatever comes to exist after having not existed must be matter.

> We ourselves call the possibility of existence the potentiality of existence, and we call what bears *(ḥāmil)* the potentiality of existence in which there is the potentiality of the existence of the thing 'subject', 'prime matter', 'matter' and the like, on account of many different considerations.[37] Thus, whatever comes into existence is preceded by matter.[38]

Of course the reason why, for Avicenna, whatever comes to exist is preceded by matter is precisely because, for him, the existence of anything that comes to exist is preceded by the possibility of its existence, and, as has just been argued, there would be no possibility if there were no matter *qua* subject in which that possibility inheres.[39]

---

37. At *Physics*, I.2, 14.14–15.5 Avicenna lists the various considerations: "This matter, inasmuch as it potentially receives a form or forms, is called its 'prime matter'; and, inasmuch as it actually bears a form, it is called in this [book] its 'subject'. (The sense of 'subject' here is not the sense of 'subject' we used in Logic, namely, as part of the description of substance; for prime matter [15] is not a subject in that sense at all.) Next, in as much as it is common to all forms, it is called 'matter' and 'stuff' [lit. 'clay']. It is also called an 'element' because it is resolved into [elements] through a process of analysis, and so it is the simple part receptive of the form as part of the whole composite, and likewise for whatever is analogous. It is also called a 'constituent' because the composition begins from it in this very sense, and likewise for whatever is analogous. It is as though when one begins from it, it is called a 'constituent', whereas when one begins from the composite and ends at it, then it is called an 'element', since the element is the simplest part of the composite."

38. *Metaphysics*, IV.2, 140.15–17; also see *Najāt, Ilāhīyāt*, I.17, 536.

39. For treatments of Avicenna's theory of matter see Arthur Hyman, "Aristotle's 'First Matter' and Avicenna's and Averroes' 'Corporeal Form,'" in *Essays in Medieval Jewish and Islamic Philosophy*, ed. A. Hyman (New York: KTAV Publishing House, 1977), 335–406; Elisabeth Buschmann, *Untersuchungen zum Problem der Materie bei Avicenna* (Frankfurt am Main: Peter Lang, 1979); Abraham D. Stone, "Simplicius and Avicenna on the Essential Corporeity of Material Substance," in *Aspects of Avicenna*, ed. R. Wisnovsky (Princeton, NJ: Markus Wiener Publishers, 2001), 73–130; and Jon McGinnis, "The Avicennan Sources for Aquinas on Being: Supplemental Remarks to Brian Davies' 'Kenny on Aquinas on Being,'" *Modern Schoolman* 82 (2005): 131–42, esp. 135–37.

Consequently, for Avicenna it is simply absurd to claim that God created matter, and so the world, at some first moment in time before which it did not exist. This is because if only what is possible can be created, and matter is supposed to be created after not existing, then the possibility of creating the matter must have existed prior to the matter; but again for Avicenna, this possibility requires the existence of matter as the substrate in which it inheres. In short, to claim that the possibility of creating matter existed prior to the matter is tantamount to saying that the possibility of creating possibility existed prior to possibility, which indeed is absurd. In summary, given that the existence of the world has always been possible, matter must have existed eternally, and thus something other than God exists eternally.

We have just seen that God cannot be the ultimate ontological basis of the possible in itself, inasmuch as one might consider God to be a substrate for the possible in itself or one might think that in some way God creates possibilities *ex nihilo;* for in a very real sense, for Avicenna possibilities are simply given. Still, there is a sense in which, for Avicenna, God is the ultimate cause for the actual existence of the possible in itself, namely, inasmuch as God ultimately actualizes and makes determinate the existence of anything possible in itself.

One of the more interesting features of Avicenna's claim here is that if matter were not eternally being actualized and so made determinate, matter, indeed the possibility for whatever comes to be, would have not existed, and as such the very existence of the world would have been impossible. The reason is that, for Avicenna, matter is wholly indeterminate with respect to existence, where again the indeterminacy of existence is one of Avicenna's preferred descriptions of possibility. Now Avicenna did not believe that anything ever actually exists as wholly indeterminate, as for example existing all at once indeterminately as a possible platypus, plankton, platinum and everything else.[40] Matter actually exists only insofar as it is specified to a particular kind by a cause, and we have already seen that for Avicenna the Necessary in Itself is the ultimate cause for any determinate or actual existence. Consequently, if the Necessary in Itself did not ultimately cause the determinate actual existence

40. See Jon McGinnis, "The Avicennan Sources for Aquinas on Being" and "A Penetrating Question in the History of Ideas: Space, Dimensionality and Interpenetration in the Thought of Avicenna," *Arabic Sciences and Philosophy* 16 (2006): 47–69, esp. 59–62.

of the possible in itself, then, since nothing exists indeterminately, nothing would have been possible in itself and everything, other than God, would have been impossible. Simply stated, for Avicenna, either the existence of the world is eternal or its existence would have been impossible; nevertheless, the actual existence of the world wholly is dependent upon God as its cause.

I conclude, now, with one brief final observation about the relation between Avicenna's arguments for the Necessary in Itself and the eternity of the world. I noted about Avicenna's argument for the Necessary in Itself that its only existential commitment was that something actually exists. What we have seen in the course of Avicenna's argument for the eternity of the world is that if anything that comes to be is even possible, then matter must exist as the substrate in which that possibility inheres. If we now couple these two conclusions, we see that Avicenna's two arguments jointly show that the mere possible existence of the world entails that God necessarily exist; for if there is that possibility, then the matter in which the possibility inheres must exist; but according to Avicenna's argument for the Necessary in Itself, if anything exists, then God necessarily exists. In short, if anything, whatever it might be, is possible, God must exist.

Returning to the central question of this volume, "Why is there anything at all rather than absolutely nothing?" we can state that for Avicenna the answer is simply: because something is possible.

John F. Wippel

4 ∽ Thomas Aquinas on the Ultimate Why Question

Why Is There Anything at All Rather than Nothing Whatsoever?

Let me begin by acknowledging that I have not found Aquinas raising this question in these exact words. But it is interesting to note that a contemporary of his who was teaching in the Faculty of Arts at the University of Paris, the so-called Latin Averroist, Siger of Brabant, did address the question in these terms. He did so either during or immediately after Thomas's second teaching period at the University of Paris, which ended in 1272. Siger considers this issue in two of the four surviving versions of his *Quaestiones in Metaphysicam* (ca. 1272–75), which in fact are *reportationes,* that is, student reports of his lectures on Aristotle's *Metaphysics.* While commenting on Aristotle's *Metaphysics* Bk. IV, chapters 1–2, Siger recalls Aristotle's claim that there is a science that studies being as being and the properties that pertain to it per se. Moreover, Siger notes that, according to Aristotle, it belongs to this science to inquire after the first principles and causes of being insofar as it is being.[1]

Siger is aware that this remark might seem to contradict a position he

This chapter is an expanded version of the Presidential Address to the Annual Meeting of the Metaphysical Society of America given on March 11, 2006, at the Catholic University of America.

1. See the Munich version, in *Siger de Brabant. Quaestiones in Metaphysicam* (Munich and Vienna versions), ed. William Dunphy (Louvain-la-Neuve: Éditions de l'Institut Supérieur de Philosophie, 1981), 168–69.

himself had defended earlier in the "Introduction" to his Commentary on Bk. 1. There, at question 2, he had stated that there can be no principle and cause of being as being, for such a principle would then be a cause and principle of itself. This also implies that for Siger the First Principle or Cause—God—falls under being as being, the subject of metaphysics.[2] Yet, as Siger now notes, in *Metaphysics* IV, c. 1, Aristotle himself clearly does refer to the need to inquire after the principles and causes of being as being in this science.[3]

Siger proposes to resolve this apparent conflict in the following way. When Aristotle refers to principles and causes of being as being, he does not intend to speak of being in the absolute or unqualified sense, for this would imply that every being has a cause. That in turn, Siger comments, would imply that no being would have a cause, presumably because if there were no uncaused cause, there would be no caused causes, and hence no effects whatsoever. Siger continues, however, by saying that Aristotle really intends to speak of causes of every *caused* being when he refers to the need to search for the principles and causes of being as being.[4]

Moreover, Siger comments, not every being has a cause of its existence, nor does every question about existence admit of an answer in terms of a causal explanation. Thus, he continues: "If it is asked why there is something rather than nothing," we may take this question in either of two ways. If we restrict the question to things that are themselves caused, we may respond that this is ultimately because there is some immobile *Primum Movens* and some immutable First (that is, Uncaused) cause for every caused being. But if we take the question as applying to the totality of beings and ask why there is something rather than nothing, a causal answer cannot be given. For this would be to ask why God himself exists rather than not, and this question cannot be answered by citing some cause. Siger therefore obviously does not admit the possibility that God could be the efficient cause of his own existence. Rather, he

2. *Quaestiones in Metaphysicam* (Munich version), 37.

3. Ibid. (Munich version), 169.

4. Ibid. See especially: "Et est hic intelligendum quod non intendit Philosophus per principia et causas entis secundum quod ens, quod ens absolute dictum habeat causas et principia, ita quod causam habeat eius in eo quod ens, quia tunc omne ens haberet causam; quod enim convenit enti in eo quod ens, cuilibet enti convenit quia inest per se et universaliter; si autem omne ens haberet causas, tunc nullum ens haberet causas; non enim esset aliqua causa prima et si non esset prima, nec aliqua aliarum."

concludes, not every question and not every being admits of a causal explanation.[5]

Lying behind Siger's consideration of and answer to this issue is Avicenna's discussion of the subject of metaphysics in the Latin translation of his *Liber de Philosophia Prima* I, chapters 1–2. In chapter 1 Avicenna considers at some length and rejects the view that God (or God's existence, according to the Marmura translation) is the subject of metaphysics ("first philosophy" or "divine science"). God's existence must be examined in this science, whereas a science must grant the existence of its own subject and investigate the properties of that subject. Since no science can establish the existence of its own subject, God cannot be the subject of metaphysics.[6] In chapter 2 Avicenna concludes that its subject is being as being (or the "existent" insofar as it is existent, according to a more literal translation from the Arabic). He comments that there is no cause or principle for all beings, because such an entity would then be a principle (or cause) of itself. Here, too, the implication is that for Avicenna God falls under being as being, the subject of metaphysics, just as Siger was later to hold. According to Avicenna, therefore, being taken absolutely does not have a cause or principle, but particular beings do. So this science will seek after the principles (and causes) of some beings, but not of being taken absolutely.[7]

5. Ibid., 169:60–170:71: "Sed intendit Philosophus per causas et principia entis inquantum ens, causas simpliciter et per se entis causati, non causas secundum accidens, sed causas per se entitatis eorum quae causam habent illius. Non enim omne ens entitatis suae causam habet nec omnis quaestio quaerens de esse habet causam. Si enim quaeratur quare magis est aliquid in rerum natura quam nihil, in rebus causatis loquendo, contingit respondere quia est aliquod Primum Movens immobile et Prima Causa intransmutabilis. Si vero quaeratur de tota universitate entium quare magis est in eis aliquid quam nihil, non contingit dare causam, quia idem est quaerere hoc et quaerere quare magis est Deus quam non est, et hoc non habet causam. Unde non omnis quaestio habet causam nec etiam omne ens." For essentially the same position see the Cambridge version in *Siger de Brabant. Quaestiones in Metaphysicam*, ed. Armand Maurer (Louvain-la-Neuve: Éditions de l'Institut Supérieur de Philosophie, 1983), 135–36. Note that there Siger asks specifically: "Utrum entis secundum quod ens sint causae et principia" (135).

6. Avicenna, *Liber de Philosophia Prima sive Scientia Divina I–IV*, ed. Simone Van Riet (Louvain-Leiden: Brill, 1977), 4–5. For an English translation see *The Metaphysics of the Healing*, trans. Michael Marmura (Provo: Brigham Young University Press, 2005), 3–4.

7. Ibid., c. 2 (Van Riet ed., 12–14, especially 14:58–63); Marmura translation, 9–10, 10–11, par. 15.

I

With this background in mind, we turn to Thomas Aquinas. Before Siger's consideration of this in his *Quaestiones in Metaphysicam,* Thomas had already addressed the issue of the subject of metaphysics and the closely related question about the relationship between being as being, on the one hand, and divine being, on the other, first in his Commentary on the *De Trinitate* of Boethius (ca. 1258–59), and then again in the Prooemium to his own Commentary on the *Metaphysics* (ca. 1272–73). For Thomas, as for Avicenna and Siger, the subject of metaphysics is certainly not God or divine being. Its subject is being as being.[8] Moreover, at least on my reading, metaphysics does not presuppose prior knowledge of God's existence, as it would have to do if God were its subject, and as Averroes had maintained.[9] Rather, it pertains to a science to arrive at knowledge of the causes and principles of its subject. This, says Thomas, is the end or goal of its investigation. In this case, therefore, it belongs to metaphysics to arrive at knowledge of the cause or principle of being as being (its subject), that is to say, at knowledge of God. Consideration of God enters into metaphysics only indirectly, in one's search for the cause or principle of what does fall under its subject.[10] This, then, is how Aquinas manages to unite into one science Aristotle's science of being as being as presented in *Metaphysics* IV, cc. 1–2, and his "divine science" presented in *Metaphysics* VI, c. 1, which might otherwise seem to be di-

8. See Thomas Aquinas, *Super Boetium De Trinitate,* q. 5, a. 4 (ed. Leonina, Vol. 50, 153–54, esp. p. 153, lines 82–87 = Leon. 50.153:82–87). See also 154:157–162: "[U]nde et huiusmodi res divinae non tractantur a philosophis nisi prout sunt rerum omnium principia, et ideo pertractantur in illa doctrina in qua ponuntur ea quae sunt communia omnibus entibus, quae habet subiectum ens in quantum est ens." Also see his *In duodecim Libros Metaphysicorum Aristotelis Expositio* (Rome-Turin: Marietti, 1950), *Prooemium,* 1–2, where he refers to the subject of metaphysics as *ens commune,* or being as taken universally.

9. For more on this see my *The Metaphysical Thought of Thomas Aquinas: From Finite Being to Uncreated Being* (Washington, D.C.: The Catholic University of America Press, 2000), 14–22.

10. See *Super Boetium De Trinitate,* q. 5, a. 4 (Leon. 50.153:82–87): "Sciendum si quidem est quod quaecumque scientia considerat aliquod genus subiectum, oportet quod consideret principia illius generis, cum scientia non perficiatur nisi per cognitionem principiorum, ut patet per Philosophum in principio Physicorum." Also see *In Met., Prooemium,* 1–2: "Eiusdem autem scientiae est considerare causas proprias alicuius generis et genus ipsum: sicut naturalis considerat principia corporis naturalis. Unde oportet quod ad eamdem scientiam pertineat considerare substantias separatas, et ens commune, quod est genus, cuius sunt praedictae substantiae communes et universales causae." Also see the text cited in note 11.

rected only to a particular kind of being, divine being, rather than to being taken universally or as being.[11]

More importantly for our immediate purpose, however, unlike Avicenna, unlike Siger, and unlike practically all of his contemporaries, Aquinas denies that God or divine being is even included under the subject of metaphysics, that is to say, under being as being or under what he sometimes refers to as being in general *(ens commune)*.[12] This position, I would speculate, is closely connected with another of Aquinas's distinctive and controverted positions, his denial that in this life human beings can arrive at quidditative knowledge of God.[13]

In any event, Aquinas's denial that God falls under the notion of being that serves as the subject of metaphysics makes it fairly easy for us to see how he would overcome the difficulty addressed by Siger with respect to the ultimate why question. If we ask Thomas why is there something rather than nothing whatsoever, he would distinguish different meanings for the term "something" before replying. If by "something" we mean whatever falls under the subject of metaphysics (being as being), Thomas would argue that any such entity must ultimately consist of an essence and a distinct act of existing. Therefore it must depend upon something else for its existence, or be efficiently caused. Therefore, if, as he claims, recourse to an infinite regress of caused causes of existence adequately explains nothing, any such being must ultimately depend upon an uncaused cause of existence. As will be seen below, this reasoning appears most explicitly in what is, in my judgment, his most metaphysical argument for God's existence, that found in his *De ente et essentia*, c. 4.[14]

11. See *In Met.*, Prooemium, 2: "Ex quo apparet, quod quamvis ista scientia praedicta tria consideret [first causes, being taken universally, separate substances], non tamen consideret quodlibet eorum ut subiectum, sed ipsum solum ens commune. Hoc enim est subiectum in scientia, cuius causas et passiones quaerimus, non autem ipsae causae alicuius generis quaesiti. Nam cognitio causarum alicuius generis, est finis ad quem consideratio scientiae pertingit."

12. *Super Boetium De Trinitate*, q. 5, a. 4 (Leon. 50.154). *In Met.*, Prooemium, 2; *In Librum B. Dionysii De Divinis Nominibus Expositio*, V, 2, ed. Ceslaus Pera (Turin-Rome: Marietti, 1950), 245, n. 660, where he compares God and *esse commune*.

13. Unaided reason can successfully demonstrate that God exists and can indicate what God is not; but unaided reason cannot deliver any kind of quidditative knowledge of God to us in this life. See, for instance, *Summa contra Gentiles*, Bk. I [hereafter SCG I], c. 30. For other passages and for discussion see my *The Metaphysical Thought of Thomas Aquinas*, c. 13, section 1.

14. For his *De ente et essentia*, c. 4 see Leon. 43.376 and following. For discussion see my *The Metaphysical Thought*, c. 5, 137–50.

On the other hand, if we take the term "something" as it appears in the ultimate why question more broadly, so as to include not only all that falls under being as being but even the cause or principle of the same, Aquinas would agree with Siger of Brabant's response. No causal explanation can be given for this since God himself has no cause. He is the uncaused cause. Aquinas would never entertain the thought that God could be regarded as an (efficient) cause of his own existence. He explicitly rejects as self-contradictory the suggestion that anything might efficiently cause its own existence, for instance in *De ente*, c. 4.[15]

Nonetheless, there are other aspects to Aquinas's consideration of our question. Suppose for the sake of this discussion we grant him that he and others have succeeded in demonstrating philosophically that an uncaused cause of existence does exist, and that it is the ultimate causal explanation for the existence of all caused being. Having established this philosophically to his own satisfaction, Aquinas finds it necessary to determine why God has created anything at all rather than nothing whatsoever. He also asks why God created this universe rather than some other possible universe. Since his discussion of the second issue presupposes his answer to the first and more fundamental question, I will concentrate on that question and will raise three questions concerning it: (1) According to Aquinas, why did God create anything at all? (2) In addressing this question, does he offer a causal explanation for God's decision to create, or perhaps something else? (3) What would Aquinas say if we were to raise the ultimate why question about God himself and ask Thomas why does God exist rather than not exist?

II

In taking up the first question (Why did God create rather than not create anything at all?), I would like to begin by briefly considering Aquinas's understanding of the term "nothing" *(nihil)*. It is well known that he defends the view that God is a creative principle and that he produces the world "from nothing" *(ex nihilo)*. Thomas explains that by "nothing" we should not understand any kind of preexisting subject or sub-

---

15. Leon. 43.377:131–135: "Non autem potest esse quod ipsum esse sit causatum ab ipsa forma vel quidditate rei, dico sicut a causa efficiente, quia sic aliqua res esset sui ipsius causa et aliqua res se ipsam in esse produceret: quod est impossibile."

stratum from which things might be produced. By using the expression "from nothing" Thomas simply means that what is created is not produced from something, that is, from any kind of preexisting subject. For instance, in *Summa theologiae* [= ST] I, q. 45, a. 1, he explicitly asks whether to create is to make something from nothing *(Utrum creare sit ex nihilo aliquid facere)*. In contrast with any kind of production by generation, he argues that in the case of the emanation of the whole of [created] being from the First Principle, it is impossible for any kind of being to be presupposed. "Nothing" simply means *nullum ens*, no being whatsoever. To create is to produce something from no preexisting subject, hence from nothing.[16]

In the following article 2 he argues that it is necessary to hold that all things are created by God from nothing, that is, not from something. For if God could not create without presupposing some preexisting subject, that subject would not be caused by him. But Thomas notes that in q. 44, aa. 1–2 he has already shown that there is no particular being which is not caused by God, who is the universal cause of the whole of being *(totius esse)*, meaning, of course, the whole of finite or caused being.[17]

In other contexts Thomas also asks whether God could reduce something to nothing, that is to say, whether God could annihilate something. In ST I, q. 104, a. 3, for instance, he observes that some held that God produced things necessarily by reason of his nature. If this were true, counters Thomas, God could not reduce something to nothing. But he maintains that the fact that God communicates existence to creatures depends upon the divine will. Moreover, God conserves things in exis-

---

16. In addition to this meaning of being produced "from nothing," Thomas had also identified a second meaning in his Commentary on II *Sentences*, d. 1, q. 1, a. 2. Nonexistence is prior to existence in a created thing in the sense that if the creature were simply left to itself without being caused by God, it would not exist. The priority involved in this usage is a priority of nature, but not necessarily one of time. See *Scriptum super Libros Sententiarum*, vol. 2, ed. P. Mandonnet (Paris: Lethielleux, 1929), 2, 18.

17. Here (in q. 44, a. 1) Thomas bases his argument on his earlier proof in q. 3, a. 4 that God is *esse subsistens* and that there can be only one instance of this (see q. 7, a. 1, ad 3). This is because subsisting *esse* is not received in any subject, and it is thereby distinguished from all other instances of *esse*, which are multiplied in accord with distinct principles or subjects that receive it. Therefore all things other than God are not identical with their *esse* but only participate in it. Hence things that are diversified according to their different degrees of participation in *esse* are caused by one first being which exists most perfectly. Also see q. 44, a. 1, ad 1, where he writes: "quia ex hoc quod aliquid per participationem est ens, sequitur quod sit causatum ab alio" (Leon. 4.455).

tence by continuously communicating existence to them. Therefore, just as before things existed God was able not to communicate existence to them, so too, after they have been made he could cease giving them existence. They would then simply cease to exist; and this would be for God to reduce them to nothing, or to annihilate them. Nonetheless, in the immediately following article he also argues that in fact God will not do this because the divine power and goodness are better manifested by the fact that he keeps things in existence. In *De potentia*, q. 5, a. 4 he argues that no intrinsic contradiction is involved in holding that it is possible for creatures not to exist. This is because a creature's essence is not identical with its *esse* (act of existing).[18]

At the same time, Thomas's appeal to the goodness of God as an explanation for the fact that he willed to produce created beings has led some authors to criticize his argumentation as either insufficient or inconsistent. Norman Kretzmann, for instance, acknowledges that Aquinas successfully establishes the presence of intellect and of will in God, and grants that he is consistent in maintaining that, just as the divine essence is the only adequate object of the divine intellect, so too the divine goodness is the only adequate object of God's willing. Kretzmann insists, however, that this is not enough to justify Aquinas's claim that God freely decided to create the universe rather than not create it. Kretzmann does grant that, given the divine decision to create, Thomas has successfully shown that God is free to create this universe or any other possible universe.[19]

As evidence for his claim that Aquinas should not have maintained that God is free to create or not to create, Kretzmann notes that Thomas often cites with approval a Neoplatonic philosophical axiom to the effect that the good is diffusive of itself *(bonum est diffusivum sui)*. Since God is all good and therefore naturally and necessarily wills his own goodness, he naturally and necessarily must will the goodness of things other than himself. Therefore, Thomas should have concluded that God had to create.[20]

In his *Great Chain of Being*, written more than sixty years before

18. See *Quaestiones disputatae De potentia*, ed. Paul M. Pession (Turin-Rome: Marietti, 1965), 136: "Creaturas autem simpliciter non esse, non est in se impossibile quasi contradictionem implicans. . . . Et hoc ideo est, quia non sunt suum esse . . . ."

19. Norman Kretzmann, *The Metaphysics of Theism: Aquinas's Natural Theology in Summa contra Gentiles I* (Oxford: Clarendon Press, 1997), cc. 6–7.

20. Ibid., 217–25. Also see his "Goodness, Knowledge, and Indeterminacy in the Philosophy of Thomas Aquinas," *Journal of Philosophy: Supplement* 80, n. 10 (1983): 631–49; *The Meta-*

Kretzmann's *The Metaphysics of Theism,* Arthur Lovejoy had argued that
not only is inconsistency on this issue present in Aquinas and in other
medieval Christian theologians, but it can be traced back to the classical
period of Greek philosophy. Thus Lovejoy finds in Plato two conflicting
views of the supreme ontological principle for all of reality. On the one
side, there is the otherworldly view best captured by Plato's description
of the Good in *Republic* VI and VII, which is so transcendent, so beyond being and essence, that it would seem that our physical world is not
needed, and which Lovejoy identifies as the equivalent of Plato's God. On
the other side there is the Demiurge of the *Timaeus* who was responsible
for forming the sensible universe as it actually is because "he was good,
and in one that is good no envy of anything else ever arises. Being devoid
of envy, then, he desired that everything should be so far as possible like
himself."[21] While recognizing that this next step is open to considerable
dispute, Lovejoy judged it more likely that Plato did identify the Good of
the *Republic* with the Demiurge of the *Timaeus.* Consequently, he finds
Plato attributing to one and the same entity the self-sufficiency and transcendence of the Good of the *Republic* and the desire to communicate its
goodness of the Demiurge of the *Timaeus.* And thus, Lovejoy maintains,
the view that the good is diffusive of itself, if not in so many words, in
fact appears for the first time in the history of philosophy, thereby giving rise to an internal conflict that would trouble Western philosophy
for much of its subsequent history. Moreover, on Lovejoy's account, the
fecundity on the part of the Good does not result from free choice, but is
necessary. It must produce things like itself insofar as it can.[22]

As for the medieval period, Lovejoy quotes a key text from the *Divine
Names* of Pseudo-Dionysius:

The Good by being extends its goodness to all things. For as our sun, not by
choosing or taking thought but by merely being, enlightens all things, so the
Good ... by its mere existence sends forth upon all things the beams of its
goodness.[23]

---

physics of Creation: Aquinas's Natural Theology in Summa contra Gentiles II (Oxford: Clarendon Press, 1999), 120–26, 132–36.

21. Lovejoy, *The Great Chain of Being* (Cambridge, Mass.: Harvard University Press, 1936,
repr. 1964), 47. See *Timaeus* 29E–30A.

22. As quoted by Lovejoy, *The Great Chain of Being,* 50–54.

23. Lovejoy, *The Great Chain of Being,* p. 68, translating from *De divinis Nominibus,* c. IV, 1

One can easily understand why Lovejoy (and others) might take this text as implying necessary creation on the part of God.[24] Such a reading is strengthened by the analogy the author draws with the sun. Just as the sun, without choosing or thinking but simply by existing illuminates all things, so the Good, by merely existing, sends forth "the beams of its goodness."

In his Commentary on the *Divine Names*, however, Aquinas himself does not read the text this way. He notes that the point of the analogy with the sun is to show that, just as it extends its beams to all visible things, God extends goodness to all other things that share in goodness. In other words, according to Aquinas, the analogy holds only for one side—the universal communication by God of his goodness to all good things. It does not hold for the other side, the necessary and automatic diffusion of the rays of the sun to visible things.[25]

As we turn to Aquinas's texts themselves, I will assume for the sake of this discussion a number of items which he accepts as already established on philosophical grounds before he takes up this question. He himself follows this order in his synthetic treatments of this issue in *Summa contra Gentiles* [= SCG I and II, and in ST I. Thus he claims to have already demonstrated the existence of God in SCG I, cc. 13 and 15, and in ST I, q. 2, a. 3. Moreover, he has also argued on philosophical grounds that God is all-perfect (SCG I, c. 28; ST I, q. 4), that he is perfectly good (SCG I, c. 37, and c. 30; ST I, q. 6), that he is infinite (SCG I, c. 43; ST I, q. 7, a. 1), and subsequently that intellect and will are present in him. If I may fill this in briefly, Aquinas holds that we can by reasoning from effect to cause know that God is, and that by denying of him anything that implies imperfection, we can also discover what God is not. But, as noted above, we cannot know what God is.[26] And so, by following the way of negation, in SCG I, cc. 15–27, Aquinas develops a number of appropriate names for

(Patrologiae cursus completus, Series Graeca, ed. J. P. Migne, vol. 3 [Paris, 1857], col. 693). See *Pseudo-Dionysius: The Complete Works* (New York: Paulist Press, 1987), for Colm Luibheid's translation of this text, 71–72.

24. See Fran O'Rourke, *Pseudo-Dionysius and the Metaphysics of Aquinas* (Leiden: Brill, 1992), 242; John D. Jones, "An Absolutely Simple God? Reading Pseudo-Dionysius Areopagite," *The Thomist* 69 (2005): 403–4.

25. *In De divinis nominibus* c. 4, 1 (lect. 1, nn. 270–271). Also see *De potentia*, q. 3, a. 15, obj. 1 and ad 1.

26. See SCG I, c. 30, for instance, and my *The Metaphysical Thought of Thomas Aquinas*, 502–43.

God which are negative in content; then, also by using the way of negation, he applies the names, concluding for instance that God is simple
(that is, not composed in any way), and immutable (that is, not subject to
change of any kind), and so forth. Subsequently, however, and this point
should not be overlooked, he also applies certain other names to God
which appear to be positive in content, for instance, good, intelligent, et
cetera, even though such names can be predicated of him only analogically. So true is this that in later discussion he argues that such names
can be predicated of God substantially *(substantialiter)*.[27]

The turning point in this development in SCG I occurs in Aquinas's
discussion of divine perfection in c. 28. He begins his effort to prove that
God is perfect, still using the way of negation. A being is perfect in every respect if no excellence of any kind is lacking to it. But this is true of
God. For instance, in his first argument Thomas reasons that the excellence of a thing pertains to that thing in accord with the mode whereby
it enjoys *esse,* that is, the act of existing. Insofar as a thing's act of existing is limited to a greater or lesser mode of excellence, that thing is more
or less perfect. If there is something to which the total power of existing
(virtus essendi) pertains, no excellence that can belong to any thing *(res)*
is lacking to it. God possesses the act of existing according to the total
power of existing, because his essence is identical with his act of existing. Therefore no excellence that can pertain to any being is lacking to
him, and so he is all perfect. What is striking about this argument is the
fact that, by negating any kind of limitation or imperfection of God—in
other words, by negating any such negation—Aquinas ends with a very
important positive conclusion: God is all perfect.[28]

Pursuant to this, in c. 29 Thomas argues that because every effect
must in some way be like its cause, the form of an effect must in some
way be present in the cause that produces it (formally or at least virtually, I would add), even though the cause may greatly surpass the effect in
excellence and perfection. Thus, in c. 30 Aquinas maintains that names
such as goodness, wisdom, being *(esse)*, which signify perfection without
any limit whatsoever, may be applied to creatures and to God as their

27. See *De potentia,* q. 7, a. 5; ST I, q. 13, a. 2. See my *The Metaphysical Thought,* 523–27, 537–39 for discussion.

28. See also the second argument, in which Thomas establishes divine perfection by eliminating any *non esse* from God.

cause, but only with certain restrictions. The creaturely way in which they signify *(modus significandi)* must be denied of them when they are applied to God, and what they signify *(res significata)* can be said of God only analogically.

Most important for our discussion is Aquinas's account of divine goodness. For Thomas, the good is a transcendental, that is to say, a property or characteristic of being that is as general or universal in extension as being itself *(ens)*. Here I have in mind ontological goodness, not moral goodness. As a transcendental, the good is really identical and convertible with being, but differs from it conceptually. Being is known as good when it is explicitly recognized as an object of will or of appetite, as something that is desirable in itself.[29] Thomas also insists that the good is perfective with respect to something else insofar as it serves as an end for that which is perfected by it. Thus, he observes, those who correctly define the good include in its meaning a relationship to an end.[30]

Thomas's response to an objection in *De veritate*, q. 21, a. 1 is interesting. Objection 4 argues from Pseudo-Dionysius that the good is diffusive of itself and of being, and therefore that something is good by reason of the fact that it is diffusive. But to diffuse implies action. Aquinas acknowledges that, if taken strictly, the word "diffuse" seems to imply the action of an efficient cause. But when taken broadly it can refer to any kind of causality. Thus, as used by Dionysius in this context, it does not imply efficient causality but final causality.[31] As we shall see, this is an important part of Thomas's defense of God's freedom to create or not. As for the point that God is good, in SCG I, c. 37 Aquinas maintains that this follows from the fact that God is all perfect, which he has established in c. 28. He argues in similar fashion in ST I, q. 6, a. 3, in order to conclude that God alone is good of his essence.

Following this, in both SCG I and ST I, Thomas offers philosophical argumentation to show that intellect is present in God. For instance, in

---

29. See *De veritate*, q. 1, a. 1; q. 21, aa. 1–2; ST I, q. 5.

30. *De veritate*, q. 21, a. 1 (Leon. 22.3.594:201–209). Note: "et inde est quod omnes recte diffinientes bonum ponunt in ratione eius aliquid quod pertinet ad habitudinem finis." For a fuller presentation and discussion of much of what follows in the remainder of this section and which I summarize here, see my "Thomas Aquinas on God's Freedom to Create or Not," c. 9 in my *Metaphysical Themes in Thomas Aquinas II* (Washington, D.C.: The Catholic University of America Press, 2007), 224–37.

31. *De veritate*, q. 21, a. 1, ad 4, Leon. 22.3.594:251–269.

SCG I, c. 44, he offers a series of arguments for this, one of which is based on divine perfection. Among all perfections, the most powerful *(potissima)* is for something to be intellective. By means of intellection such a thing is, in a certain sense, all things since by knowing all things it possesses their perfection in some way (that is, cognitively). After discussing various aspects of divine knowledge in the following chapters, in c. 72 Thomas takes up the issue of the divine will. In the first of a series of arguments for will in God, he reasons from the fact that God is intelligent to the conclusion that he wills. Aquinas assumes that the proper object of will is an object understood as good by intellect. Insofar as something is understood as good (or desirable), it is something that is willed. Therefore one who understands a being as good is one who wills. Because God is perfectly intelligent, he understands being as good. Therefore he wills. What is an object of divine appetite or divine will is loved, not as something that God lacks and wants, but as something in which he takes delight.[32]

In c. 73 Aquinas maintains that God's will is identical with his essence. He reasons to this conclusion because of God's perfection and simplicity. For instance, just as the divine act of understanding *(intelligere)* must be identical with the divine being *(esse)*, so too, the divine willing *(velle)* must be identical with the divine being. Hence the divine will itself is also identical with the divine being or, as he puts it in his second argument, with the divine essence itself. There can be no real composition in God of being or essence and operation as, according to Thomas, there is in created agents.

In c. 74 he argues that the principal object of the divine will is the divine essence itself. For instance, he recalls from c. 72 that a good that is understood by intellect is an object of will. But the primary object of God's understanding is the divine essence itself. Therefore the divine essence is also the primary object of the divine will. Moreover, if God were to will something other than himself as the primary object of his willing, such a thing would cause God's act of willing. But his willing is identical with his being *(esse)*. Thus something else would cause his *esse* (see the third argument: *"Praeterea"*).

Next, in c. 75 Thomas reasons that by willing himself, God also wills

---

32. As Thomas sometimes puts this, as something which he loves. See the conclusion of Thomas's third argument. On this see Kretzmann, *The Metaphysics of Theism,* 203–6.

other things. For instance, he first argues, it belongs to one who wills an end in primary fashion to will those things which are ordered to that end by reason of that end. But God himself is the ultimate end for all things. Therefore, since he wills his own being (literally, wills himself to be), he also wills other things which are ordered to himself as to their end.

Again *("Item")* Thomas reasons that everyone desires the perfection of that which he wills and loves for its own sake, and wills for it always to be improved and multiplied insofar as this is possible. God wills and loves his essence for its own sake. But his essence cannot be increased or multiplied in itself, but can only be multiplied by means of his likeness which is participated in by many things. Therefore, God wills a multitude of things by reason of the fact that he wills and loves his own essence and perfection.[33]

And still again (*"Item 2"*) Aquinas reasons that to the extent that something possesses more perfect power, to that extent does its causality extend to more things. The causality of an end consists in the fact that other things are desired on account of it. Therefore, the more perfect an end is and the more intensively it is willed, the more things are willed by reason of that end. Since the divine essence is most perfect both in goodness and as an end, it will extend *(diffundet)* its causality to many things to the maximum degree. Hence a multiplicity of things are perfectly willed by God in accord with the fullness of his power.[34]

In light of these and similar arguments in c. 75, Aquinas does present a very strong case to prove that God wills to diffuse his perfection to other things, since he is the ultimate final cause of everything else. But, one may ask, does it not follow from this that he is thereby falling into a necessitarian position, as both Lovejoy and Kretzmann maintain? Before responding to this difficulty, Thomas adds another point in c. 76: it is by one act of willing that God wills himself and other things. This statement

33. See Lovejoy, *The Great Chain of Being*, 73–74. As Thomas puts this in another context (SCG II, c. 35, ad 7), it was fitting for the divine will to produce creatures as participating in his goodness so that by likeness they may represent the divine goodness: "Sic igitur divinae voluntati conveniens fuit in suae bonitatis participationem creaturam producere, ut sua similitudine divinam bonitatem repraesentaret" (Editio Leonina manualis [Rome, 1934], 125).

34. See Kretzmann, "A General Problem of Creation: Why Would God Create Anything at All?" in *Being and Goodness*, ed. Scott MacDonald (Ithaca: Cornell University Press, 1991), 222. He views this passage in particular as implying a Platonic-necessitarian tendency in Thomas. See also his *The Metaphysics of Theism*, 217–20.

should cause little surprise, since, as we have seen, Thomas cannot admit any real distinction between God's essence, his will, and his act of willing; yet it does seem to make his effort to defend God's freedom to create more difficult.

Seemingly causing still more difficulty for Thomas is his view in c. 80 that God necessarily wills his own being *(esse)* and his own goodness. As he explains, this follows from his earlier proof in c. 74 that God wills his own *esse* and goodness as the primary object of his willing, and as he now notes in c. 80, this willing in turn is the reason for his willing other things.[35] In addition, Thomas now reasons that it is not possible for God not to will something actually, for otherwise he would do so only potentially. This must be rejected, because his act of willing is identical with his being. Hence he necessarily wills his own *esse* and his own goodness.[36]

And so, in c. 81 Aquinas realizes that the conclusion he had reached in c. 80—that God necessarily wills his own goodness—might seem to some to imply, as in fact it does for Kretzmann—that God creates other things necessarily. For Thomas has maintained in c. 75 that by willing his own goodness, God wills other things. He has also maintained that God necessarily wills his own goodness. Therefore, it might seem, he necessarily wills other things.[37]

Thomas replies that the divine will is directed to other things insofar as they are ordered to his own goodness as their end. But a will is not ordered necessarily to things which are directed to an end if that end can be perfectly realized without them. Because the divine goodness is fully realized without the existence of anything else and receives no increase in perfection from the fact that other things exist, it is not necessary for the divine will to create anything else, even though God necessarily wills himself.[38]

Thomas's third argument in this chapter is very different but is worth mentioning. By willing his own goodness, God wills other things to ex-

35. SCG I, c. 80: "Ostensum est enim supra quod Deus vult suum esse et suam bonitatem ut principale obiectum, quod est sibi ratio volendi alia" (Ed. Leonina manualis, p. 74). For c. 74 see ibid., 70–71.

36. Ed. Leon. manualis, 74.

37. Ed. Leon. manualis, 75.

38. Ibid. Also see SCG II, c. 31, as part of Thomas's argumentation to show that it is not necessary for creatures to have always existed.

ist insofar as they participate in his goodness. Because the divine goodness is infinite, it can be participated in in an infinity of ways and in ways
which have not yet been actually realized. If it were true that, because
God necessarily wills his own goodness, he necessarily wills those things
that participate in it, he would have to will an infinity of creatures which
would participate in his goodness in an infinity of ways. But, says Thomas, this is clearly false, presumably because he finds it contrary to the *de
facto* situation.[39]

Thomas had already made this point in *De veritate,* q. 23, a. 4. There,
too, he observes that the fact that God necessarily wills his own goodness does not imply that he necessarily wills things other than himself.
If that which is ordered to an end is perfectly proportioned to that end in
such fashion that the end cannot be attained without it, then if the end
is necessarily willed, so are the means. But since no effect can be equal
to the divine power, nothing that is ordered to God is adequately proportioned to or equal to the divine end. This is so because no creature is
perfectly like God. No matter how excellent the manner in which some
creature is ordered to God and in some way is like him, it is possible for
another creature to be ordered to him and to represent his goodness in
equally excellent fashion or, I would add to Thomas's reasoning, even in
more excellent fashion. For no matter how perfect any creature may be, it
will always be finite and therefore never equal to the intensively infinite
divine perfection.[40]

If this argument seems to show that there is no necessity for God to
produce any given creature rather than some other, what about God's
freedom not to create anything at all? In the text from the *De veritate,*
Thomas now explicitly addresses this issue: There is no necessity for God
to produce the whole of creation, that is, to create at all. The divine goodness is so perfect in itself that, even if no creature whatsoever existed,
God's goodness would still be completely perfect in itself. As Thomas
succinctly puts it, the divine goodness is not the kind of end that is produced or results *from* those things that are ordered to it. Rather it is the
kind of end *by which* those things which are ordered to it are themselves
produced and perfected.[41]

39. Ed. Leon. manualis, 75.   40. Leon. 22.3.662:197–663:221.
41. *De veritate,* q. 23, a. 4, Leon. 22.3.663:229–232.

Underlying Thomas's defense of God's freedom (1) to create or not to create, and (2) to create this creature rather than that, is the lack of proportion, the lack of any kind of equality, between the goodness and perfection of any creature or any number of creatures whether actual or possible, on the one side, and God's infinite goodness and perfection, on the other. Here Aquinas has in mind what we may call intensive infinity as distinguished from any kind of extensive infinity based on quantity, such as the numerical multiplication to infinity of finite goods or finitely perfect beings. According to Thomas, no addition can be made to that which is intensively infinite in goodness and perfection. Therefore, even if no creature whatsoever existed, the divine goodness would still be completely and infinitely perfect in itself.

III

In light of Thomas's discussion, we may now turn to the second main question raised above: Does anything cause God to will to create other beings? In SCG I, c. 86 Thomas replies that a *ratio* (a reason or explanation) can be given for God's willing other things. Again Thomas points out that God wills his own goodness as an end and all other things as ordered to it. Therefore his goodness is the reason *(ratio)* why he wills such things. Indeed, in c. 80 he had already referred to God's *esse* and his goodness as the primary object of his will and hence as his reason for willing other things.[42] And in *De veritate*, q. 23, a. 4 he had also made this point and had observed that just as the divine essence is the reason *(ratio)* for God's knowledge of other things, so is the divine goodness the reason for his will's willing all things.[43] But now in SCG I, c. 87, he argues that while there is a reason for God's willing of things other than himself, it does not follow from this that something must be a cause of this, thereby introducing an interesting distinction between a *ratio* and a cause.[44] Moreover, by identifying a reason though not a cause for God's

42. Ed. Leon. manualis, 74. See n. 35 above.
43. See Leon. 22.3.662:184–188: "Unde ea quae circa creaturas vult sunt quasi eius volita secundaria quae propter suam bonitatem vult, ut divina bonitas ita sit eius voluntati ratio volendi omnia, sicut sua essentia est ei ratio omnia cognoscendi." Cf. ST I, q. 19, a. 2, ad 2: "Et sic, sicut alia a se intelligit intelligendo essentiam suam, ita alia a se vult, volendo bonitatem suam" (Leon. 4.233).
44. Ed. Leon. manualis, 79.

willing things other than himself, Thomas avoids falling into any kind of blind divine voluntarism in his account.

At this point it may be helpful to see how Thomas develops this distinction between a reason and a cause within this context. To return to c. 86, there he writes that an end is the reason *(ratio)* for willing those things which are ordered to that end. But God wills his goodness as an end, and wills other things insofar as they are ordered to that end. Thus his goodness is the reason (note that he does not say the "cause") why he wills other things that differ from him. In a second argument *("Rursus"),* Thomas argues that a particular good is ordered to the good of a whole as to its end, just as the imperfect is ordered to the perfect. Certain things fall under the divine will insofar as they are ordered to the good. Therefore, the good of the universe is the reason *(ratio)* why God wills each particular good in the universe.[45]

A third argument *("Item")* brings out more explicitly Thomas's understanding of the term "reason" within this context. He recalls from c. 83 that if God wills something, it follows necessarily that he wills what is required for it. But what imposes necessity upon another thing is the reason why that thing exists. Therefore the reason why God wills the things that are required for each thing is so that every such thing may exist. Then Thomas spells out different ways in which reasons may be assigned for God's willing. God wills man to have reason in order for man to exist. He wills man to exist in order for the universe to be complete. And he wills the good of the universe because this befits his own goodness. But these three kinds of reasons involve different relationships. Thus the divine goodness does not depend upon the perfection or completeness of the universe, nor does the perfection of the universe add anything to God's goodness. The perfection of the universe depends necessarily upon certain particular goods which are its essential parts, and depends in non-necessary fashion upon others which are not essential to the universe, but which may add some goodness or beauty to it. A particular good depends necessarily upon those things which are absolutely presupposed for it, although it may also contain others which only serve to embellish it. Therefore, the reason or *ratio* for the divine will in some cases includes only what is fitting, that is, what befits the divine good-

45. SCG I, c. 86, Ed. Leon. manualis, 79.

ness. Presumably Thomas here has in mind God's reason for creating a universe. In some cases the reason includes usefulness, presumably of one particular good for another to be realized. In some cases it includes necessity *ex suppositione,* presumably for the realization of another good under the supposition that that good is willed. But a reason for the divine will includes absolute necessity only when it wills itself. In other words, Thomas continues to hold that while God freely wills all other things, he necessarily wills himself.[46]

In c. 87 he maintains that while a reason can be assigned for the divine will, this does not imply that something actually causes it to will. Because of some difficulty in interpreting this text, however, I will number the sentences as I quote it here in translation:

(1) Although some reason *(ratio)* can be assigned for the divine will, it does not follow that something is the cause of this will. (2) For a will, the end is the cause of its willing. (3) But the end of the divine will is its goodness. (4) Therefore, for God it (the divine goodness) is the cause of his willing, which is identical with his willing. (5) But of other things willed by God, none is a cause of willing for God.[47]

Proposition 1 simply asserts Thomas's purpose—to show that while some reason can be assigned for God's willing, this does not imply that something causes it. One wonders whether here Thomas is speaking only of God's willing other things, or also of his willing himself. Proposition 2 states that the end is the cause of a will's willing. One wonders whether this applies only to finite agents accessible to us, that is, human beings, or also to God. Proposition 3 simply recalls that the end of God's willing is his own goodness. But proposition 4 concludes from this that the divine goodness is therefore a cause for God's willing, but also adds that it is in fact identical with his very act of willing. The latter part of this proposition follows from God's simplicity. But the first part, while it is consistent with propositions 2 and 3, seems to clash with proposition 1, which warned the reader that while there is a reason for God's willing, it does not follow from this that something is a cause of it.

---

46. Ibid.

47. SCG I, c. 87, Ed. Leon. manualis, 79. "(1) Quamvis autem aliqua ratio divinae voluntati assignari possit, non tamen sequitur quod voluntatis eius sit aliquid causa. (2) Voluntati enim causa volendi est finis. (3) Finis autem divinae voluntatis est sua bonitas. (4) Ipsa igitur est Deo causa volendi, quae est etiam ipsum velle. (5) Aliorum autem a Deo volitorum nullum est Deo causa volendi." Translation mine.

One way of interpreting this is to conclude that Thomas intends to show that there is indeed a reason (or reasons) for God's willing things other than himself, and that none of these is a cause for God's willing them. According to proposition 4, however, there is a cause for God's willing himself, namely his own goodness which, we are reminded, is identical with his act of willing. Yet since it is difficult to understand how anything in God, including his willing, can be caused, especially since it is identical with his being, Sylvester of Ferrara suggests that after proposition 4 we should insert the following: "Therefore neither is (divine) goodness itself really the cause of the act of willing, since nothing is a cause of itself." He also suggests that in proposition 4, when Thomas refers to the divine goodness as causing God's willing, he is speaking according to our human mode of understanding, but realizes that in reality there can be no cause of God's willing.[48] Whether one prefers such an explanation or thinks that Thomas really did regard the divine goodness as a (final) cause of God's willing when God wills himself, Thomas has proposed a number of examples of *rationes* or reasons in c. 86 which are not causes of God's willing other things. This suffices to bring out the point that a reason for God's willing does not have to be a cause of the same. And this distinction will serve us well in the final section of this paper.

Before turning to that, however, I should note that in c. 88 Thomas wants to show that free choice *(liberum arbitrium)* is present in God. He observes that free choice is said of someone who wills not out of necessity but of one's own accord *(sua sponte)*, and he refers back to his proof in c. 81 that God does not will other things of necessity to support his claim that God enjoys free choice. In ST I, q. 19, a. 10, he again attempts to prove that God possesses free choice. There he refers back to a. 3 in this same question, where he reasons in the same way as he had in *De veritate*, q. 23, a. 4, and in SCG I, c. 81. In brief, one who necessarily wills

48. In his Commentary on this text as found in the Leonine edition of Aquinas's SCG, Sylvester of Ferrara noticed this difficulty and proposed to resolve it by supplying the following after the troublesome proposition 4: "Ergo neque ipsa bonitas est realiter causa ipsius actus volendi: cum nihil sit sui ipsius causa" (Leon 13.238). Translation mine. A little farther on Sylvester adds: "Ideo, cum dixisset quod bonitas est causa volendi, subiunxit statim, *quae est etiam ipsum suum velle*, quasi diceret: Cum dico ipsam esse causam, non intelligo secundum realem causalitatem, cum sit idem cum ipso velle, sed tantum secundum nostrum modum intelligendi" (ibid.).

an end does not necessarily will things that are ordered to that end unless they are such that the end cannot be achieved without them. Because God's goodness is perfect and fully realized without the existence of other things, and because other things add nothing to the divine perfection, God is free to will or not to will anything other than himself.[49]

As for the Dionysian axiom that the good is diffusive of itself, Aquinas refrains from giving this a necessitarian application to God's creative activity, by insisting that it should be interpreted in terms of final causality rather than efficient causality. The divine goodness exercises its causality by serving as an end, a final cause, for other things. In other words, God produces things other than himself so that they may participate in and reflect that goodness; but since no created good is proportionate to the divine perfection and goodness, the production of other good things is not required for and does not add to the divine perfection and goodness. Thus God is perfectly free to produce or not produce things other than himself, and to produce this rather than any other creature or set of creatures. While this interpretation of the Dionysian principle may be both novel and counterintuitive, as Kretzmann charges, it is the reading Aquinas gives it, and it enables him to offer a benign interpretation of this supposedly Apostolic authority in the Christian world in accord with the medieval custom of offering "a reverential interpretation" of an accepted authority.[50]

---

49. See ST I, q. 19, a. 10 (Leon. 4.248) for the backward reference to article 3 (Leon. 4.235).

50. For Kretzmann see "A General Problem of Creation," 220. Fran O'Rourke, for instance, acknowledges that Dionysius likely interpreted this principle in terms of efficient causality. See his *Pseudo-Dionysius and the Metaphysics of Aquinas*, 242. Also see John D. Jones, "An Absolutely Simple God? Reading Pseudo-Dionysius Areopagite," 403–4, who cites two texts, including the one we have quoted above in the body of our text, as seeming "to argue against the view that for Dionysius God creates beings in the sense that he need not have willed them." The second text is taken from *De divinis nominibus* 1.5.593D. For other discussions of God's freedom to create or not in Aquinas see W. Norris Clarke, *Explorations in Metaphysics: Being, God, Person* (Notre Dame, IN: University of Notre Dame Press, 1994), 222–26; O'Rourke, c. 9; Bernhard Blankenhorn, "The Good as Self-Diffusive in Thomas Aquinas," *Angelicum* 79 (2002): 803–37. For an important earlier study on Aquinas's interpretation of the Dionysian axiom in terms of final causality see J. Peghaire, "L'Axiome 'Bonum est diffusivum sui' dans le néo-platonisme et le thomisme," *Revue de l'Université d'Ottawa* 2 (1932): 5*–30*.

IV

Finally, in light of the distinction Thomas makes between there being a reason *(ratio)* but not a cause for God's willing to produce other things, I will conclude by returning to our third main question: What would Aquinas say if we were to raise the ultimate why question about God himself and ask Thomas why does God exist? Aquinas is convinced on philosophical grounds that in all beings, with one possible exception, there is a distinction and composition of an essence principle, and an intrinsic *actus essendi,* an act of existing, which actualizes the essence, serves as the ultimate source of perfection in that being, and also accounts for the fact that it exists.[51] Indeed, in one of his best-known arguments for such distinction (*De ente,* c. 4), he maintains that it is impossible for there to be more than one being in which essence and *esse* are identical. And he often repeats this reasoning elsewhere.[52] Far from assuming that such a being exists, however, he concludes that in every other being, with this one possible exception, essence and act of existing differ. Then, on the strength of this, he concludes that any being in which essence and act of existing differ must receive its existence from something else; in other words, it must be efficiently caused. After considering but rejecting a regress to infinity of caused causes of existence as an adequate explanation of the existence of such a being, he concludes to the existence of an uncaused cause of existence, which is in fact identical with its act of existing, that is, which is subsisting *esse.*[53]

If one asks, therefore, why does this being exist, or why does God exist, Aquinas will, of course, deny that it is caused by anything, that is to say, it is not caused by itself, and it is not caused by anything else. God is not a *causa sui.* No efficient cause can be proposed to account for his existence. But he would also say that such a being exists because its essence

---

51. See, for instance, the oft-cited text from *De potentia,* q. 7, a. 2, ad 9: ". . . hoc quod dico *esse* est inter omnia perfectissimum: quod ex hoc patet quod actus est semper perfectio<r> potentia. Quaelibet autem forma signata non intelligitur in actu nisi per hoc quod esse ponitur. Nam humanitas vel igneitas potest considerari ut in potentia materiae existens, vel ut in virtute agentis, aut etiam ut in intellectu: sed hoc quod habet *esse,* efficitur actu existens. Unde patet quod hoc quod dico esse est actualitas omnium actuum et, propter hoc est perfectio omnium perfectionum" (*De potentia,* 192).

52. Leon. 43.376–77. See Wippel, *The Metaphysical Thought of Thomas Aquinas,* 137–57.

53. See Leon. 43.377.

is identical with its act of existing. Its very nature is to exist. Given this, it is not possible for God not to exist; he exists necessarily. While this is not to appeal to a cause to account for God's existence, it is, I would suggest, to offer an explanation or reason *(ratio)* for this. Here, in order to address the ultimate why question (Why does God exist?), I am adopting and adapting the distinction Thomas developed in SCG I, cc. 86–87 between a *ratio* and a cause. My suggested answer is that it is in accord with Aquinas's thought to respond that, while no causal explanation can be given for God's existing, a reason or explanation may be offered, namely, that God's essence is identical with his *actus essendi.*

Part Three

Contributions in Modern Philosophy

5 ⌀ *Causa sui* and Created Truth in Descartes

Why is there anything at all rather than absolutely nothing? This para-digmatically philosophical question is a request for an ultimate reason that renders existence fully intelligible. Some have insisted that this re-quest is reasonable—indeed, the very foundation of rationality—and have urged that, when pressed, it leads us to some ultimate cause of con-tingent objects that itself exists necessarily and so provides its own rea-son for its existence. This is of course the line of thought behind the so-called cosmological argument. Others have objected that the request is unreasonable, given the possibility that there is no ultimate cause of contingent objects, and thus no ultimate reason why there is something rather than nothing. In this view, the existence of such beings is a brute fact, incapable of further explanation.

But once the possibility of brute facts is rejected, it may not suffice to posit an ultimate cause of contingent objects. For there will remain the question of why this ultimate cause produced such objects in the first place. Once the question of why there is anything rather than nothing is accepted as legitimate, it seems that a complete answer requires the pos-tulation not only of an ultimate cause of the contingent universe, but also of an ultimate reason for the activity of that cause.

Descartes accepted as axiomatic that there is a "cause or reason" for the existence of everything. He appealed to this axiom in support of the conclusion that God is the cause of his own existence, and thus is a *causa sui*, a conclusion that I label the '*causa sui* doctrine'. In the first section, I consider this doctrine and its relation to the distinction between reasons and causes. We will see that, when confronted by the scholastic objection that nothing can be an efficient cause of itself, Descartes twisted himself in knots in order to explain how his causal axiom can apply to the only being that requires no efficient cause, namely, God. His ultimate conclusion is that this axiom applies to God only in a very special sense, since there is, in the case of his existence, a reason without an efficient cause.

However, this understanding of the *causa sui* doctrine seems to bring it into conflict with Descartes's notorious doctrine of the creation of the eternal truths. This doctrine, which I call for short the 'created truth doctrine', is the focus of the second section. According to the created truth doctrine, God not only is the efficient cause of eternal truths, but also is a wholly indifferent cause who is unconditioned by any antecedent reasons in creating them. An initial problem concerning the relation of this doctrine to the *causa sui* doctrine derives from the occasional suggestion in Descartes that the scope of the created truth doctrine is completely unrestricted, and thus includes even the truth that God exists. If the scope of the doctrine is unrestricted, however, it seems that, contrary to Descartes's understanding of the *causa sui* doctrine, there is in fact an efficient cause of the truth that God exists.

A second problem concerning the relation between Descartes's two doctrines arises from the requirement of the *causa sui* doctrine that there be an ultimate reason for God's existence. If the truth that God exists is subject to the created truth doctrine, then it seems that there can be no such ultimate reason. For God is supposed to be wholly indifferent with respect to all created truth, and so to lack any reasons that lead him to act in one way rather than in another.

The solution to both problems that I propose on Descartes's behalf depends on the restriction of the created truth doctrine to truths concerning creatures. Though Descartes himself did not consistently restrict the doctrine in this way, the most notable of those who later defended this doctrine did. In light of this later development, we can take the created truth doctrine to be compatible with the result of the *causa sui* doctrine that the truth that God exists has a reason without having an efficient cause. However, such a development also serves to reinforce the suggestion in Descartes that created truth has an efficient cause without having a reason. It turns out that in both cases the divergence of efficient causes from reasons is linked to the incomprehensibility of the divine essence that provides the ultimate causal ground for created truth and the ultimate rational ground for uncreated truth.

I. THE *CAUSA SUI* DOCTRINE

In a recent study, Vincent Carraud draws attention to the importance in the early modern period of the fact that Descartes took it to be axiomatic that there must be a "cause or reason" *(causa sive ratio)* that explains the existence of all actual beings, including God.[1] This axiom is part of the presentation in the Second Replies of the conclusions of the *Meditations more geometrico:* in geometrical order. The axiom itself states: "No thing exists of which it cannot be asked what is the cause why it exists [*Nulla res existit de qua non possit quæri quænam sit causa cur existat*]." Descartes anticipates the objection, which we will consider presently, that there can be no cause of existence in the case of God. Thus, he adds to his axiom the claim: "This can be asked even of God himself, not because he needs any cause in order to exist, but because the immensity of his nature itself is the cause or reason [*causa sive ratio*] why he needs no cause to exist" (AT 7:164–65).[2] Even though God has no external cause of his existence, the causal axiom requires that his nature provide a "cause or reason" that explains why he exists in the absence of any such cause.

In his *Ethics,* Spinoza offers the position that God is the cause of himself insofar as his essence includes existence. He also indicates in this text that the sort of causality involved here is *efficient* causality.[3] For Spinoza, then, there is no problem with taking God to be the efficient cause of himself. However, Descartes's suggestion in the Third Meditation that God derives his existence from himself was immediately rejected precisely on the grounds that it requires that some object be the efficient cause of itself. Thus, the Dutch critic Johan de Kater, or Caterus,

1. Vincent Carraud, *Causa sive ratio. La raison de la cause, de Suarez à Leibniz* (Paris: Presses Universitaires de France, 2002), esp. ch. 2.

2. AT = C. Adam and P. Tannery, eds., *Oeuvres de Descartes,* 11 vols. (Paris: J. Vrin, 1996). Translations of passages from original Latin and French texts are my own.

3. See the claim in *Ethics* Ip25s that "God must be called the cause of all things in the same sense in which he is the cause of himself," and the claim in Ip26d that in the case of any cause that has been determined to act in a particular way, "God, from the necessity of his nature, is the efficient cause both of its essence and of its existence" (in *Spinoza Opera,* ed. C. Gebhardt [Heidelberg: Carl Winter, 1925], 2:67–68).

responded to this suggestion in the first of the set of objections appended to the *Meditations* by protesting that God can derive his existence from himself only in a negative sense—that is, not from another—and not in a positive sense—that is, from a cause. He adds that this negative sense is the manner "in which everyone takes the phrase" in the case of God (AT 7:95). Indeed, the view that God has no cause was something of a scholastic commonplace. In his *Metaphysical Disputations,* for instance, Francisco Suárez insists that "not all beings comprehended under the object of this science [of metaphysics] have a true and proper cause, for God has no cause" (*MD* XII, 1:372).[4] This exception in the case of God explains his conclusion later in this text that although "what is said to be *ex se* or *a se* seems to be positive, it adds only a negation to being itself, for being cannot be *a se* by a positive origin or emanation" (*MD* XXVIII.1, §7, 2:2).[5]

In a letter to Mersenne, Descartes complains that "the common axiom of the Schools, 'Nothing can be the efficient cause of itself' [*Nihil potest esse causa efficiens sui ipsius*] is the cause of the fact that one does not understand the term *a se* in the sense in which it must be understood," adding that he nevertheless "did not want to appear to blame the schools openly" (March 18, 1641, AT 3:336). Moreover, he answers Caterus in the First Replies by claiming that it is legitimate to assume that everything requires an efficient cause of its existence, and so to inquire into its cause. Descartes goes on to say that even though the fact that God has "great and inexhaustible power" reveals that he does not require an external efficient cause for his existence, still since "it is he himself who conserves himself, it does not seem too improper for him to be called *sui causa*" (AT 7:109). Given that God can be called a *causa sui,* "we are permitted to think that in some manner [*quodammodo*] he stands in the same [relation] with respect to himself as an efficient cause stands with respect to its effect, and thus is positively from himself" (AT 7:111).

---

4. *MD* = Francisco Suárez, *Disputationes Metaphysicae,* 2 vols. (reprint, Hildesheim: G. Olms, 1965).

5. However, it is significant, in light of Descartes's causal axiom, that Suárez allows that there are certain reasons *(rationes)* for truths concerning God that "are conceived by us as if they are causes of the others" *(concipiuntur a nobis ac si essent causæ aliarum)* (1:372–73). In contrast to the *causa sive ratio* of Descartes's axiom, though, the claim here is not that reasons are a kind of cause, but rather that they are merely conceived "as if" causes. Borrowing from Carraud, we can express the alternative slogan for Suárez as: *ratio veluti causa* (*Causa sive ratio,* ch. 1).

Dissatisfied with this explanation, Arnauld notes in the Fourth Objections that we must reject the conclusion that God's existence has an efficient cause, since his existence is identical to his essence. Arnauld adds that since nothing can stand in the same relation to itself as an efficient cause does to its effect, God cannot stand in this relation to himself (AT 7:213–14).[6]

Though Descartes protests that Arnauld's complaint "seems to me to be the least of all his objections" (AT 7:235), he responds to it at some length. He begins by insisting that he had never said that God is an efficient cause of his own existence, but only that God *quodammodo* stands in the same relation to his existence as an efficient cause does to its effect. In order to explain more precisely the sense in which God can be said to be the cause of his existence, Descartes appeals to the claim in Aristotle that the essence of a thing can be considered as a "formal cause" of certain features of that thing (AT 7:242). He concedes to Arnauld that the fact that God's existence is identical with his essence reveals that he does not require an efficient cause, but he claims that God's essence provides a formal cause of his existence that "has a great analogy to the efficient [cause], and thus can be called an efficient cause as it were [*quasi causa efficiens*]" (AT 7:243).[7]

One has the sense that Descartes was not entirely on top of his game. For instance, it is understandable that Arnauld read the remarks in the First Replies as an attempt to apply the notion of efficient causality to the case of God's existence. After all, Descartes countered Caterus's suggestion that God can derive existence from himself only in a negative sense by claiming that he never denied that something can be the efficient cause of itself (AT 7:108). Moreover, we have seen that Descartes gave permission to Caterus to think that God stands to himself as an efficient cause to its effect.

Even so, it is perhaps clear enough that Descartes did not take God to be literally the efficient cause of his own existence and that, when

6. Arnauld's assumption is that an efficient cause must be distinct from its effect. Descartes himself explicitly denied that an efficient cause cannot act on itself; see Fifth Replies, AT 7:376; *To Hyperaspistes*, Aug. 1641, 3:428. What Arnauld is most concerned to deny, however, is that something can be the efficient cause of its own existence, and on this point Descartes would agree.

7. For more on Descartes's exchange with Arnauld on this point, see Carraud, *Causa sive ratio*, 266–88.

he spoke as if God's existence has such a cause, it was only, as he told Arnauld, "on account of the imperfection of the human intellect" (AT 7:235). Whereas in the case of all other beings the reason for existence is provided by an efficient cause, in the case of God the "cause or reason" for existence is merely the rational ground for the truth that his existence requires no efficient cause, which ground is provided by the immensity of his own power or essence. In the end, therefore, Descartes could not accept the suggestion in Spinoza that God is an efficient cause of his own existence.[8]

Descartes's causal axiom requires that there be a reason for the existence of everything, including God, even though in the case of God alone the reason is provided by his power or essence rather than by an efficient cause. However, his claim to Arnauld that we must conceive of the reason for God's existence as analogous to an efficient cause indicates the imperfection of our grasp of this reason. Descartes notes in the Fourth Replies that we are to understand this reason by extending our conception of an efficient cause to a case where the essence serves as a kind of "formal cause" of existence. He compares this sort of extension to the extension in geometry of the concept of a rectilinear polygon to the concept of a circle (AT 7:239–40). Even though the geometrical concepts are not commensurate, our grasp of the nature of polygons can lead us to recognize certain truths concerning circles. In a similar manner, Descartes suggests, the differences between efficient and formal causes do not prevent our understanding that the existence of finite beings must be grounded in efficient causes from yielding a recognition of the fact that a formal cause is required as the reason for God's existence.

But why do we need the comparison to efficient causes? Why can we not just see directly that God's nature provides a special kind of reason for his existence that does not involve true efficient causality? Descartes did not address this question directly, but it is significant that he appeals in the First and Fourth Replies alike to "great and inexhaustible power" *(tanta et inexhausta potentia)* as the "reason or cause" of God's existence (cf. AT 7:110 and 7:236). Even more telling is his claim in the First Re-

---

8. Thus, one must reject the view of Jean-Luc Marion that Descartes took God to be a *causa efficiens sui ipsius* (see *Questions cartésiennes II. Sur l'ego et sur Dieu* [Paris: Presses Universitaires de France, 1996], 143–82). For a critique of this view, see Carraud, *Causa sive ratio*, 266–76.

plies that this grounding power is "immense and incomprehensible" *(immensam et incomprehensibilem potentiam)* (AT 7:110). This reference to divine incomprehensibility is significant, given its prominence in Descartes's discussion of his created truth doctrine. Thus, in the 1630 correspondence with Mersenne that introduces the doctrine, Descartes claims that though "one can know that God is infinite and all-powerful," still it is the case that "our soul being finite he can be neither comprehended nor conceived; in the same way that we can touch a mountain with our hands, but one cannot embrace it as we could a tree or some other thing that is not too large for our arms" (May 27, 1630, AT 1:152).

Admittedly, this passage directly concerns not the dependence of God's existence on his essence, but rather the dependence of the eternal truths on his free will. Whereas Descartes was emphatic in his remarks to Arnauld that God is not the efficient cause of his existence, he was equally emphatic in this letter to Mersenne that "God disposed the eternal truths . . . as the efficient and total cause" (AT 1:151–52). Nevertheless, it seems that just as we cannot comprehend the power on which the eternal truths depend, so we cannot comprehend the power on which God's existence depends. It is for this reason that we cannot directly comprehend the unique case of the derivation of existence from the divine essence, and so must conceive of the derivation in terms of the production of an effect by its efficient cause.

God's incomprehensible power would seem to provide not only a reason for his own existence but also an efficient cause of everything else, including all eternal truths. As Descartes indicates to Mersenne, "I know that God is the author of all things [*de toutes choses*], and that these [eternal] truths are something, and consequently that he is their author" (AT 1:152). However, there would appear to be paradoxes lurking here. For one thing, the truth that God exists would seem to be something, and so to have God's will as its efficient cause. But as Descartes explains it, his *causa sui* doctrine requires that God's existence have only a reason that is not an efficient cause. The doctrine thus requires as well, contrary to the apparent implication of the created truth doctrine, that there be no efficient cause that makes it true that God exists. Moreover, the created truth doctrine appears to conflict with the requirement of the *causa sui* doctrine that there be an ultimate reason for God's existence. For Descartes insists in the Sixth Replies that it is repugnant that the will of God not be indifferent from eternity to all that has been made or will be made, since no good, or truth, or believing, or doing, or refraining from doing can be formed [*fingi potest*], the idea of which is in the divine intellect prior to his will determining or making it to be so. I am not speaking here of temporal priority; there is not any priority or order, or nature, or "reasoned reason" [*ratione rationcinata*], as it is called, such that this idea of good impels God to choose one thing rather than another (AT 7:431–32).

If the truth that God exists were among those the idea of which cannot be in the divine intellect prior to being determined to be true by the will, then there could be no conceptually prior reason why it is true rather than not. So what Descartes's *causa sui* doctrine seems to give—namely, a reason for God's existence, and thus an ultimate reason for why there is anything at all rather than absolutely nothing—his created truth doctrine seems to take away. In order to determine whether Descartes can in the end allow for an ultimate rational ground for the truth that something exists rather than nothing, we need to consider whether this doctrine precludes such a ground.

II. THE CREATED TRUTH DOCTRINE

The problems for the application of the created truth doctrine to the truth of God's existence derive from the assumption that this doctrine has unrestricted scope, and so includes even this truth. The attribution of such an assumption to Descartes would seem to be warranted by his remark in the Sixth Replies, just quoted, that *no* good or truth can be in the divine intellect by way of idea prior to God's will making it to be so. Moreover, in later correspondence with Arnauld he claims that "*every* basis [*ratio*] for truth and goodness depends on [God's] omnipotence" (July 29, 1648, AT 5:224; my emphasis).

On the basis of passages such as these, several commentators have taken Descartes's created truth doctrine to be unrestricted in scope. Such an understanding is reflected in the claim in Harry Frankfurt's ground-breaking discussion of this doctrine that the doctrine itself entails a "universal possibilism" on which all eternal truths, including truths concerning God, are "inherently as contingent as" or "no more necessary than" other contingent propositions concerning created existence.[9] In Frankfurt's view, Descartes took the apparent necessity of these truths "properly to be understood only as relative to the character of our minds."[10] God has created our minds such that we perceive the eternal truths to be undeniable, but he could just as easily have created us and the world and even himself differently. Indeed, Frankfurt insists that the created truth doctrine requires the "ultimate paradox" that truths concerning God "leave open the unintelligible possibility that God knows that he does not exist."[11]

Jonathan Bennett has proposed an alternative to Frankfurt's interpretation that avoids this ultimate paradox while still granting the unrestricted scope of the created truth doctrine. Bennett offers on Descartes's behalf a "conceptualist" account, in which the necessity of the eternal truths is to be analyzed in terms of our own mental capacities. To say that a truth is necessary is simply to say that we cannot distinctly conceive the opposite of such a truth.[12] Thus, the created truth doctrine amounts to the position that God has created our minds such that we cannot conceive the opposite of any eternal truth. As evidence for this reading of the doctrine, Bennett cites, for instance, Descartes's comment to Arnauld, from the letter just quoted, that "I do not think we should say of anything that it cannot be brought about by God," but "I merely say that he has given me such a mind that I cannot conceive" the opposite of the eternal truths, since "such things involve a contradiction in my conception" (AT 5:224).[13]

Bennett clearly rejects Frankfurt's view that Descartes accepted universal possibilism. According to Bennett, Descartes accepted rather the incompatible position that all eternal truths are necessary in a conceptualist sense. Thus, on his interpretation there is no need to allow that Descartes embraced the ultimate paradox that God could know that he does not exist. Nevertheless, in one crucial respect this interpretation is similar to Frankfurt's. For both Frankfurt and Bennett emphasize that the perceived necessity of the truths is tied to the constitution of our minds.

9. Harry Frankfurt, "Descartes on the Creation of the Eternal Truths," *Philosophical Review* 86 (1977): 42.

10. Ibid., 45.

11. Ibid., 53.

12. Jonathan Bennett, "Descartes's Theory of Modality," *Philosophical Review* 103 (1994): 647.

13. Ibid., 656–61. Bennett also mentions passages in which Descartes stressed that our "nature" compels us to accept clear and distinct perceptions when we perceive them. See, for example, AT 7:69, cited in Bennett, "Descartes's Theory," 666.

Admittedly, Frankfurt takes this sort of perceived necessity to be merely apparent, whereas Bennett takes it to constitute real necessity. But this difference does not matter with respect to the conflict between the created truth and *causa sui* doctrines. For whereas the fact that God is *causa sui* seems to require that the truth that he exists has a reason but no efficient cause, the versions of the created truth doctrine that Frankfurt and Bennett offer require that this truth has an efficient cause but no ultimate reason inasmuch as it depends on a feature of our minds that derives from God's indifferent will.

However, the consequence that the status of the truth of God's existence depends on a created feature of our mind is in fact difficult to square with certain claims in Descartes. Most notable is his insistence in the Fifth Meditation, with respect to the inseparability of essence and existence in God, that "it is not my thought that effects [*efficiat*] this, or imposes any necessity on anything, but on the contrary it is the necessity of the thing itself, namely, of the existence of God, that determines me to thinking this" (AT 7:67). Here it is something outside of my thought—namely, God's essence—that provides the reason for God's existence and thus grounds the determination of my thought to consider his existence as necessary. Though this line of reason is in considerable tension with a conceptualist understanding of the sort of necessity (or apparent necessity) that Descartes posited, it is to be expected, given the implication of his *causa sui* doctrine that God's existence has a reason that precludes the need for any sort of efficient cause.

Descartes elsewhere accorded eternal truths concerning God a special status that they cannot have on the interpretations Frankfurt and Bennett have offered. Thus, he insists in his 1630 correspondence with Mersenne that "the existence of God is the first and the most eternal of all possible truths and the one from which alone all others proceed" (AT 1:150). Moreover, Descartes closes out his initial discussion of the created truths doctrine in this correspondence by noting that the "essence of created things" is nothing other than eternal truths that are "no more necessarily attached to [God's] essence than are other created things" (AT 1:152–53). Given these remarks, the created truth doctrine would seem to be restricted to whatever is not necessarily attached to God's essence, and thus not to include those truths concerning this essence that surely are so attached. Even if the necessity of created eternal truths is bound up with the manner in which God creates our mind, the suggestion in these passages is that the necessity of truths concerning God's essence does not derive from his will, but rather serves as the uncreated ground for the necessity of created eternal truth.

The claim that at least in certain passages Descartes allowed for uncreated truths concerning God's own essence is not new.[14] What I think commentators have failed to appreciate, however, is that Descartes's *causa sui* doctrine itself requires that the truth that God exists have a reason but no efficient cause. This doctrine thus supports the suggestion that the created truth doctrine does not include within its scope truths concerning the essence—or, what is the same, according to the Fifth Meditation, the existence—of God.

I would not argue that Descartes consistently indicated that his created truth doctrine has a restricted scope. Indeed, it seems to me difficult to explain away all of the passages that Frankfurt and Bennett cite in support of the conclusion that this doctrine is unrestricted. But though Descartes may not always have insisted on the distinctive nature of truths concerning God, later partisans of his created truth doctrine did. Very few post-Descartes Cartesians explicitly defended this doctrine, but those who did so tended to emphasize its restricted scope. I offer as a case in point two Cartesians who to my mind offered the most philosophically sophisticated development of the doctrine, namely, Robert Desgabets and Pierre-Sylvain Regis.[15]

Desgabets was a French Benedictine who was active in promoting Cartesianism in the monastic schools where he taught. In a "Supplement" that he published to the *Meditations,* which dates from the 1670s, Desgabets cites Descartes's doctrine that "the will of God is the free cause of essences and of all that is immutable" as "being of the greatest importance

14. See, for instance, Norman Wells, "Descartes' Uncreated Eternal Truths," *New Scholasticism* 56 (1982): 185–99.

15. I draw on the discussion of the Cartesianism of Desgabets and Regis in my *Radical Cartesianism: The French Reception of Descartes* (New York: Cambridge University Press, 2002); see especially the consideration in ch. 2 of this text of their development of Descartes's created truth doctrine. Cf. Thomas Lennon, "The Cartesian Dialectic of Creation," in *The Cambridge History of Seventeenth-Century Philosophy,* ed. D. Garber and M. R. Ayers (Cambridge: Cambridge University Press, 1998), 1:331–62, esp. 350–56. Whereas I focus here on the insistence in Desgabets and Regis on the restricted scope of the created truth doctrine, though, Lennon makes the additional and more controversial claim that their acceptance of this doctrine led them to a kind of empiricism.

and having great and incomparable consequences."[16] Though this statement of the doctrine may seem to indicate that its scope is unrestricted, Desgabets makes clear that it is limited to truths concerning creatures. Thus, he notes that according to this doctrine, "before we conceive that [God] freely determined himself to produce or to establish things and truths, there is nothing real distinct from him" (RD 6:208–9). In another text, dating from as early as the 1650s, he also echoes Descartes's remarks to Mersenne in claiming both that "there is nothing subsisting or existing, nothing either true or intelligible, that has a necessary relation to [the] divine essence," and that God "has not been determined to make or to establish any thing or any truth by which this [thing or truth] is external to him" (RD 2:33).

In this earlier text, Desgabets acknowledges the traditional scholastic view that the divine act of creation is guided by God's knowledge of essences that reflect the manner in which his essence "can be participable in an infinity of ways by creatures" (RD 2:32). However, in claiming that creatures have no necessary relation to the divine essence, Desgabets intended to deny any pre-volitional conceptual connection between God and creatures. It is the lack of any such connection that reveals that divine perfections "are so elevated above our thoughts" and that both the essence and the existence of creatures have their source only in "this abyss of perfections" *(abîme de perfections)* in God (RD 2:33). Far from subjecting the divine essence to the created truth doctrine, then, Desgabets's version of this doctrine requires that divine perfections be absolutely distinct from what God creates, and so be fundamentally incomprehensible to us.

Our second Cartesian, Regis, was a popularizer of Cartesian physics whom the virulently anti-Cartesian Pierre-Daniel Huet called "the Prince of the Cartesians" (for Huet, not a compliment).[17] For his part, Regis called Desgabets (in what obviously was a compliment) "one of the great metaphysicians of our age." This comment is from Regis's 1704 *Use of Reason and Faith*,[18] which follows Desgabets in endorsing Descartes's

16. *Dom Robert Desgabets: Oeuvres philosophiques inédites* [RD], ed. J. Beaude (Amsterdam: Quadratures, 1983–85), 6:208.

17. For this and for more on the Huet-Regis connection, see my *Radical Cartesianism*, ch. 5.

18. *L'Usage de la raison et de la foy, ou l'accord de la foy et de la raison* (cited hereafter as *Use of Reason*), ed. J.-R. Armogathe (Paris: Fayard, 1996), 639.

created truth doctrine. Just as Desgabets had distinguished God's essence from the essences he has freely created, moreover, so Regis distinguishes in the *Use of Reason* between eternal truths concerning the divine nature, which are "immutable and necessary with an absolute necessity and immutability," and eternal truths concerning the nature of created things, which "are the consequences of the divine will" and thus have only "a hypothetical necessity and immutability" (*Use of Reason*, 276).

We have seen the view in Desgabets that the fact that created being bears no necessary relation to the divine essence reveals the fundamental incomprehensibility of the divine source of this being. If anything, such a view is even clearer in Regis. Thus, in the *Use of Reason* he responds to the traditional scholastic view that God sees creatures in his own perfections by claiming that "God does not see creatures in his perfections, because it has been proved that the perfections of God have nothing in common with creatures, and by consequence that they cannot represent them; we must say only that God sees creatures in his will, insofar as it is by his decree that he produces them and conserves them" (*Use of Reason*, 169).

It is important to notice, however, that the claim that God does not see creatures in his perfections serves to distinguish Regis not only from the scholastics but also from Descartes. Descartes was led by his axiom that the "reality or perfection" of the effect is contained in its cause "formally or eminently" to conclude that God "eminently" contains creatures in his infinite perfection.[19] However, Regis is led to reject this conclusion by his view that any cause that contains its effect must be similar to that effect in genus or species. For him, a "univocal cause," which is similar to its effect in both genus and species, formally contains the reality of its effect, as the father formally contains the reality of his offspring. In contrast, Regis holds that an "equivocal cause," which is similar to its effect only in genus, eminently contains the reality of its effect, as the sun

---

19. Descartes suggests that bodies are eminently contained in God, for instance, in his proof in the Sixth Meditation of the existence of the material world; see AT 7:79. In the Second Replies, Descartes defines formal containment as "whatever is in itself such as we perceive," and eminent containment as "whatever is not such [as we perceive], but greater, such that it can take the place [of what we perceive]" (AT 7:161). These definitions are less than clear, to say the least, but I try to make some sense of them in "Deflating Descartes's Causal Axiom," *Oxford Studies in Early Modern Philosophy* 3 (2006): 1–31, esp. 3–15.

eminently contains the reality of the plants it produces. Since divine simplicity precludes the applicability of the categories of genus and species to God, though, he can be similar to his effects in neither genus nor species. Regis's conclusion is that God is an "analogous cause" that contains its effects neither formally nor eminently (*Use of Reason*, 406–7).

There are good reasons, deriving from Descartes's created truth doctrine, for Regis's attempt to free God of the constraints on creation imposed by the perfections that Descartes took to be eminently contained in the divine nature. For in Descartes's own view, God's intellect is supposed to have no prior idea of created truth or goodness that determines his decision of what to create. In Desgabets's terms, there must be an "abyss" that separates divine perfection from truths concerning the created perfections that he freely creates. What Regis saw clearly is that such an abyss precludes the result in Descartes that God eminently contains created perfections.

To my knowledge, neither Desgabets nor Regis explicitly endorsed Descartes's argument that the axiom that the existence of everything must have a "cause or reason" requires that there be a reason even for the existence of God. By the same token, however, neither of these later Cartesians would have denied that there is a rational basis for the truth that God exists. For both offered as a reason for accepting the existence of God an "intentionality principle" that requires that all ideas of external objects must correspond to extra-mental reality. Given this principle, our idea of an infinitely perfect being must correspond to a being with infinite perfections.[20]

This "reason" may seem to be problematic insofar as the principle is subject to obvious counterexample. It seems possible, for instance, for us to conceive of a golden mountain that does not exist. Nevertheless, Desgabets and Regis alike indicated that their intentionality principle requires the presence only of some extra-mental essence that grounds our thought of an external object. They held that, in the case of created ob-

---

20. Cf. Desgabets's claim in his *Supplement* that "it is impossible to think of a thing that does not really and actually possess in itself external to the understanding all that we perceive of it, from which it follows clearly that God exists if one thinks of him or if one speaks of him" (RD 6:221), and Regis's claim in the *Use of Reason* that "the idea that we have of *the perfect Being* must have an exemplary cause, and this exemplary cause must formally contain all the perfections that the idea of the perfect Being represents (for such is the nature of an exemplary cause)" (*Use of Reason*, 129).

jects, these essences derive from God's indifferent will.[21] Yet their version of the created truth doctrine indicates that God's essence is special in serving as the necessary and uncreated ground of created essences.

The fact that God's essence serves as such a ground may seem to indicate that Desgabets and Regis allowed after all for an ultimate reason for the existence of something external to God. However, we need to take seriously their denial of any pre-volitional connection between creatures and God. In their view, not only is there no reason for divine creation that *we* can comprehend; there is no reason that *God* could comprehend either. Moreover, what is lacking here is not merely what Leibniz called a "sufficient reason" for action, namely, that which determines the existence of the best among a set of possibilities. Even if one holds, contra Leibniz, that there is no sufficient reason that determines God's choice of a certain world among an infinity of possible worlds, there still could be reasons drawn from his conception of possible worlds that inform this choice without determining it. But given the version of the created truth doctrine in Desgabets and Regis, it does not even make sense to claim that God has knowledge of possibilities that informs his act of creation. For what is possible with respect to creatures external to God is something that itself derives from this act. Thus, there cannot be any pre-existing possibilities that serve to explain why God chose to create as he did. Though Desgabets and Regis allow, and indeed insist, that God is the ultimate efficient cause of created essences and truths, they are committed to denying that there could be any reason for the fact that God created such essences and truths as opposed to creating other essences and truths, or no essences and truths at all.

We started with the demand in Descartes for a cause or reason for God's existence. We have seen that Descartes was forced under pressure to admit that the cause of divine existence is merely a reason (namely, the divine essence as formal cause) that reveals why it can have no efficient cause. The fact that we must conceive of this reason as analogous to an efficient cause turns out to be merely an indication of the incomprehensibility to us of the divine essence. But whereas divine incomprehensibility is linked in the case of Descartes's *causa sui* doctrine to the fact

21. For a further defense of this interpretation of Desgabets and Regis, see my *Radical Cartesianism*, ch. 3.

that there can be a reason that is not an efficient cause, it is linked in the case of his created truth doctrine to the fact that there can be an efficient cause without a reason. I have proposed that we can reconcile Descartes's claim that divine existence has an ultimate reason without having an efficient cause with his conclusion that God is the ultimate efficient cause of created truths that have no reason by following Desgabets and Regis in restricting his created truth doctrine to truths concerning creatures. By so restricting this doctrine, we end up with a view in Descartes that offers not only an ultimate reason lacking efficient causality that explains why God exists rather than absolutely nothing, but also an ultimate efficient cause lacking a reason that explains why anything is even true of objects external to God.

Daniel O. Dahlstrom

6 ∽ Being and Being Grounded

I. THE AGE OF LEIBNIZ

The world today stands under the spell of Leibniz's thought. Or, perhaps more carefully, we might say that the world today stands under the spell of what Leibniz thought only too well. With uncanny perceptiveness, he managed to articulate a basic principle of thinking and being in the early modern world that is arguably as vital today as it was at the outset of the eighteenth century. Looking for reasons, causes, and grounds of things was, to be sure, hardly novel then; indeed, it was second nature for human beings long before Leibniz's day. Yet Leibniz possessed the philosopher's gift of articulating and thereby giving wings to the principle under which humanity, particularly in the modern age, labors with an ever-mounting sense of urgency. The mantra of his genius has, indeed, become the mantra of an age fully committed to the promise of science and technology. I am referring, of course, to what has been called, since Leibniz's time, the principle of sufficient reason.

Many of the foregoing sentiments were voiced by Heidegger in lectures and an address held some fifty years ago and published in 1957 as *Der Satz vom Grund,* the German abbreviation for Leibniz's principle of reason.[1] According to Heidegger, only by looking back at what Leibniz was thinking when he elaborated the principle of sufficient reason can we understand our present age. "The thinking of Leibniz," he contends, not only prefigures mathematical logic and the subjectivity of German

---

1. M. Heidegger, *Der Satz vom Grund* (Pfullingen: Neske, 1957), 51 (hereafter "SvG 51"). All translations into English are my own.

idealism; it also "bears and stamps the chief tendency of what we can name the metaphysics of the modern age, thought broadly enough" (SvG 65). Thus, Heidegger insists that the name "Leibniz" by no means stands for some by-gone system of philosophy. In today's seemingly unrestricted "technological-scientific construction of the world," he contends, the principle of sufficient reason first comes fully into its own. In terminology perhaps more familiar a half-century ago, Heidegger emphasizes how the self-proclaimed "atomic age" adapts human thinking to modern technology and underwrites computational thinking to give "scientific thinking an axiomatic form." Modernity in this sense is only beginning, Heidegger submits, and modernity is the age of Leibniz, the age in which the principle of sufficient reason is the supreme principle (SvG 40f, 65f).

Heidegger gives mixed signals about this development. Sometimes he tells his students that this modern development is both necessary and promising, as is retracing the path through it (SvG 41f, 66). More often he makes it clear that he regards the unrestricted pursuit of reasons and grounds *(Grund)* as a threat, a threat to another sort of ground *(Boden)*, the soil that is allegedly vital to human flourishing. The fact that Heidegger continues to employ the term *Boden* in a way that reverberates with its checkered past use (by him and others) in National Socialist rhetoric is hardly accidental. It remains to be seen whether it can have a redeeming significance that is not parasitic on a parasite.

Nevertheless, if we can manage to bracket these important political ramifications of his rhetoric for the moment, we can readily appreciate the experience motivating his lament about modernity, captivated by the principle of sufficient reason. As he puts it, the more doggedly we pursue the grounds and reasons for things, the more uprooted we seem to be; the more we penetrate the causes of things in the sciences, the more that vital ground *(Boden)* recedes from view (SvG 60; SvG 137f). Heidegger also bemoans the fact that though modern science—and thereby modern technology and the modern university as well—are beholden to this principle, consideration of it is not to be found in the sciences themselves or, for that matter, in the university (SvG 48f, 56f). In fact, Heidegger submits, given the way the sciences correspond to the demand contained in the principle of sufficient reason, they are unable to reflect on it (SvG 59). But it is not only "the usual scientific-technical way of presenting things" that fails here; the philosophical doctrine that the principle of sufficient reason is an immediately illuminating principle "evades the decisive questions of thinking" (SvG 66). Not surprisingly, when Heidegger infamously remarks that science does not think, he is quick to add that neither does philosophy.

Accordingly, Heidegger's own strategy for dealing with the principle of sufficient reason is not to discard it. Instead he pleads for distinguishing two basic ways of reading the principle. On the standard, Leibnizian reading, the principle of sufficient reason is a statement about beings or whatever is; on the reading proposed by Heidegger, it is a way of saying what it means to be. Heidegger makes the case for this reading by contending that certain aspects of being are allegedly irreducible to and, indeed, occluded by Leibniz's account of the principle of sufficient reason, not least the utter self-sameness and individuality, the historicity and non-dependence of being. Thus, Heidegger's central contention is that we become oblivious to being to the extent that, taking our bearings from the principle as Leibniz conceives it, we engage in a wholesale pursuit of rational explanation, giving full sway to the standpoint of reason (SvG 181). Paradoxically, thanks to pursuit of the sufficient reason of beings, we are said to lose sight of being as—in some sense—the ground of or reason for beings.

I think that there is something right about this contention. However, as I hope to show by means of the following considerations, the issue is far more complicated than Heidegger lets on. In particular, his way of painting Leibniz's principle with the same colors that he applies to the so-called "atomic age" is, I argue, misleading to a fault. But the main thrust of my following remarks is to establish what is wrong with Heidegger's interpretation of Leibniz's principle of sufficient reason as a means of clarifying what I take to be right about it.

My comments are divided into three parts. In the first part I discuss Leibniz's complex account of the principle of sufficient reason with an eye to its bearing on his conception of the contingency of finite existence. In the second part I turn to Heidegger's account of Leibniz's principle of sufficient reason and his "argument" for a different, nonconventional reading of the principle.[2] In the third part I address the trenchancy of the argument.

2. In order to keep the discussion from becoming unwieldy, I omit two important, related themes of Heidegger's account, namely, his treatment of language and his treatment of transla-

II. LEIBNIZ ON THE NATURE AND SCOPE OF THE PRINCIPLE OF SUFFICIENT REASON

One of Leibniz's early (if not earliest) formulations of the principle is the abbreviated version: "nothing is without reason" *(nihil est sine ratione)* from around 1671.[3] Writing to a student of Spinoza in 1677, Leibniz adds the crucial qualification that the reason be sufficient: "nothing exists for which a sufficient reason of its existence cannot be given."[4] 'Sufficient' in this context does not mean what it typically means today in talk of sufficient conditions, as when, for example, a condition is said to be sufficient to identify membership in a class. When Leibniz speaks of a sufficient reason, he has in mind the complete satisfaction of all the conditions requisite for something to be. As he himself puts it: "For existence it is necessary that the aggregate of all that is requisite also exist [*adesse*]. Something is requisite if a thing cannot exist without it; the aggregate of all that is requisite is the full cause of the thing. Nothing is without a reason. For nothing is without the aggregate of all that is requisite."[5] A decade or more later (in the 1680s) in an essay entitled "A specimen of discoveries," Leibniz adds yet another qualification, by stipulating that the reason must be given, that is, *principium reddendae rationis*. In this same connection, he writes that for every truth, the *ratio* can be given *(quod omnis veritatis reddi ratio potest)* or, as is commonly if less precisely said, "nothing comes to pass without a cause" *(vel ut vulgo ajunt, quod nihil fit sine causa)*. This principle and the principle of contradiction are, he asserts, the principles of all rational operations *(ratiocinationum)*.[6] Finally, in the *Monadology* (§32) he combines the two already-mentioned qualifi-

---

tion, particularly, as it bears upon the differences among the terms *logos, ratio, Vernunft,* and *Grund* that historically underlie precursors and variations on the principle.

3. *Opuscules et fragments inédits de Leibniz,* ed. Louis Couturat (Paris: Alcan, 1903), p. 515; *Die philosophischen Schriften von Gottfried Wilhelm Leibniz,* ed. G. I. Gerhardt (Hildesheim: Olms, 1965), Band IV, 232.

4. *Die philosophischen Schriften* IV, 138.

5. Leibniz, *Textes inédits d'après les manuscrits de la biblothèque provinciale de Hanovre,* ed. G. Grua, 2 vols. (Paris: Presses universitaires de France, 1948), 267: "Ad existentiam necesse est aggregatum omnium adesse requisitorum. Requisitum est id sine quo res esse non potest, aggregatum omnium requisitorum est causa plena rei. Nihil est sine ratione. Quia nihil est sine aggregato omnium requisitorum." See, too, *Die philosophischen Schriften* VII, 310. Heidegger gives a clear interpretation of the sufficient reason along these lines; see SvG 64.

6. *Die philosophischen Schriften* VII, 309.

cations into the formulation *principium reddendae rationis sufficientis* or "the principle of the sufficient reason that is to be given."[7]

Leibniz puts the principle of sufficient reason to many uses. It underlies his arguments for the relativity of time, the identity of indiscernibles, and the existence of God. Thus, there would not be a sufficient reason to create the world at one time or another if time were absolute;[8] nor would there be a sufficient reason for the different placement of two things if they differed only in number;[9] God exists since otherwise there would not be a sufficient reason why this world rather than another exists.[10] The principle of sufficient reason also plays a fundamental role in establishing the nonexistence of relations and the nature of monads as well as their pre-established harmony and immortality. As these examples indicate, for Leibniz the existence of something stands or falls in some important sense with the presence or absence of a sufficient reason for it. There is a pattern to these arguments, a pattern of disarming simplicity and enormous consequence: either something exists or it does not; if it exists, then there is a sufficient reason for it; if there is no sufficient reason for it, then it does not exist. Why is there something rather than nothing? For Leibniz, there is something rather than nothing because nothing can exist without a sufficient reason for doing so, although nothing in nature contains within itself the sufficient reason for its being. In this sense the principle of sufficient reason is an ontological principle, articulating what it means for something to be at all. It is not enough to be a bounded variable; to be is to have an adequate reason for being. In the first step in a proof of God's existence, Leibniz asserts that "*reason [ratio]* is why in nature something exists rather than nothing." He immediately

---

7. The story does not by any means end here; there are competitors to the principle of sufficient reason in later writings, namely, the principle of perfection (*Textes inédits*, 287) and experience; on this matter and on the role of "experimenta" as principles of knowledge countenanced by Leibniz after 1679, see R. C. Sleigh, Jr., "Leibniz on the Two Great Principles of All Our Reasonings," in *Essays on Early Modern Philosophers*, ed. Vere Chappell, Volume 12: Gottfried Wilhelm Leibniz (New York–London: Garland, 1992), Part II, 305f.; see, too, Leibniz, *Sämtliche Schriften und Briefe*, ed. German Academy of Sciences (Darmstadt: Reichl, 1930), sechste Reihe, Band 6, S. 4.

8. *Die philosophischen Schriften* II, 515.

9. *Opuscules et fragments*, 519.

10. *Die philosophischen Schriften* VI, 603; VII, 289ff., 356; for additional examples, see Benson Mates, *The Philosophy of Leibniz: Metaphysics and Language* (Oxford: Oxford University Press, 1986), 155f.

adds that this claim follows from the principle that nothing comes to be without reason.[11]

While Leibniz seems to think that the principle of sufficient reason, together with the principle of contradiction, holds for all true propositions, he distinguishes the scope of what depends upon it from the scope of what depends upon the principle of contradiction. Thus, in *The Principles of Nature and Grace* as well as in the correspondence with Clarke two decades later, he regards the principle of sufficient reason as the foundation of metaphysics, natural theology, and physics. Mathematics rests, by contrast, upon the principle of contradiction.[12] So, too, in *Cum animadvertem* (1679) as well as much later in the *Théodicée,* the principle of sufficient reason is said to encompass all contingent propositions, in contrast to necessary propositions, which fall under the principle of contradiction.

However, there is an important qualification made, even a shift, some scholars (notably, Robert Sleigh) would argue, in Leibniz's thinking about the nature of the principle of sufficient reason that occurs during the 1680s, as he distinguishes necessary truths from contingent truths, explaining the difference between them as a difference between the finite and infinite analysis required to demonstrate them. He instructively likens the difference to one between commensurable and incommensurable numbers. As a result, Leibniz's considered view of the matter seems to be that if something is contingently the case, then there is a sufficient reason for it, but in the form not of an a priori proof but of a progressive convergence. Thus, in the *Generales Inquisitiones* he writes:

There can be relations which, however far an analysis is continued, will never reveal themselves sufficiently for certainty, and are seen perfectly only by Him whose intellect is infinite. It is true that as with asymptotes and incommensurables, so with contingent things we can see many things with certainty, from

11. *Die philosophischen Schriften* VII, 289: "(1) *Ratio* est in Natura, cur aliquid potius existat quam nihil. Id consequens est magni illius principii, quod nihil fiat sine ratione, quemadmodum etiam cur hoc potius existat quam aliud rationem esse oportet. (2) Ea ratio debet esse in aliquo Ente Reali seu causa. Nihil aliud enim *causa* est, quam realis ratio, neque veritates possibilitatum et *necessitatum* (seu negatarum in opposito possibilitatum) aliquid efficerent nisi possibilitates fundarentur in re actu existente. (3) Hoc autem Ens oportet necessarium esse, alioqui causa rursus extra ipsum quaerenda esset cur ipsum existat potius quam non existat, contra Hypothesin. Est scilicet Ens illud ultima ratio Rerum, et uno vocabulo solet appellari DEUS."

12. *Die philosophischen Schriften* VI, 603; VII, 355f.

the very principle that every truth must be capable of proof. . . . But we can no more give the full reason for contingent things than we can constantly follow asymptotes and run through infinite progressions of numbers.[13]

Similarly, in remarks entitled (by Grua) "On contingency" he introduces experience as a means of knowing not only contingent things but the principle of sufficient reason itself:

Since we cannot know the true formal reason for existence in any particular case because it involves a progression to infinity, it is therefore sufficient for us to know the truth of contingent things a posteriori, that is, through experience, and yet, at the same time, to hold, universally or in general, that principle divinely implanted in our mind, confirmed both by reason and experience itself (to the extent that we can penetrate things), that nothing happens without a reason, as well as the principle of opposites, that that which has the more reason always happens.[14]

This passage is striking, since it expresses clearly the fact that Leibniz continues to accord the principle of sufficient reason an unrestricted provenance (at least for finite minds), despite his acknowledgment of the infinite analysis (or synthesis, as the case may be) required *per impossibile* in the case of contingencies.[15] This differentiation of the sorts of sufficient reason that can be given coincides with a more precise conception of logical or a priori necessity. Logical necessity requires demonstrability, that is, complete analysis of the concepts contained in a proposition (and not merely consideration of the relations holding between those concepts).[16]

This dual understanding of the principle of sufficient reason, applying diversely to the necessary and to the contingent, has a bearing on Leibniz's compatibilism. By his lights, the universal sweep of the principle is not inconsistent with divine freedom and the contingency of the world.[17] He is able to hold this position because the sufficient reason for

13. *Opuscules et fragments* 388–89; see, too, Leibniz, *Nouvelles Lettres et Opuscules inédits de Leibniz*, ed. Foucher de Careil (Paris: Durand, 1857), 182; Sleigh has listed the texts in which the thesis of infinite analysis is advanced; see Robert Sleigh, "Truth and Sufficient Reason in the Philosophy of Leibniz," in Chappell, *Essays on Early Modern Philosophers*, vol. 12/part II, 271, 279 n. 2, and 283, n. 38.
14. *Textes inédits*, 304f.; see, too, ibid., 343, and *Opuscules et fragments*, 19.
15. Ian Hacking, "Infinite Analysis," *Studia Leibnitiana* 4 (1974): 127f.
16. Robert Merrihew Adams, "Leibniz's Theories of Contingency," in Chappell, *Essays on Early Modern Philosophers*, vol. 12/part I, 18.
17. *Essai de Théodicée*, Sections 288–302 (*Die philosophischen Schriften* VI, 288–96); in a

contingent existence—in contrast to mere possibility and necessary existence—can reside only in something other than that existence itself. Whereas the status of mere possibility and necessary existence can be explained solely by appeal to the principle of noncontradiction, the principle of sufficient reason is the key to explaining possibilities that exist but not in virtue of themselves. Thus, Leibniz characterizes the actual, contingent world as something necessary on the supposition of something else *(necessarius ex alterius hypothesi)* and distinguishes it both from what enjoys the status of simply being possible (by reason of being noncontradictory) and from what is necessary of itself or, as he puts it in the manuscript entitled *The Philosopher's Confession,* "what has within itself the reason for its existence and truth."[18] What alone suffices to explain contingent existence is God. However, importantly and more precisely, it is not God's existence as something necessary through itself but God's own free choice to actualize this world that is the sufficient reason for contingent, individual existence. In other words, there is a contingency to the existence not only of the actual world but of the act of its creation. A contingency compatible with the principle of sufficient reason runs deeply through actual beings in Leibniz's conception of them.

Not everyone accepts this aspect of Leibniz's argument that he has a place for contingency. Since God cannot choose anything but the best possible world, a defense of contingency resting on the idea of such a choice might seem to give way to a system as necessitarian as Spinoza's. But this inference, whatever its merits otherwise, must discount Leibniz's contention that God's choice is morally, but not metaphysically necessary. Whereas metaphysical necessity "leaves no place for any choice, presenting only one possible object," the moral necessity obliging the wisest to choose the best is necessary only in an analogous sense, since it does not eliminate other, contrary possibilities.[19]

By itself, this solution is not very satisfying, since it leaves open the

---

1671 letter Leibniz seems to require only voluntariness and intelligence for freedom; for a discussion, see Adams, "Leibniz's Theories of Contingency," 3f.

18. Leibniz, *Confessio Philosophi,* ed. Otto Saame (Frankfurt am Main: Klostermann, 1967), 66; see, too, *Textes inédits,* 273; on noncontradictoriness as equivalent to possibility, even if its coexistence with God implies a contradiction "in some way or other [*aliquo modo*]," see *Textes inédits,* 289f.; *Essai de Théodicée,* Section 173 (*Die philosophischen Schriften* VI, 217).

19. *Essai de Théodicée,* Sections 236 and 367 (*Die philosophischen Schriften* VI, 258 and 333).

question of the relation between moral and metaphysical necessities. Moreover, there is strong evidence that, as Robert Adams has argued, Leibniz himself vacillated considerably on the issue of whether God's choice of the best is necessary or contingent. Thus, while passages from the *Théodicée* and elsewhere stress the contingency of the choice, there are other passages, most notably from 1706, where Leibniz emphasizes the logical necessity of God's choice.[20]

Yet even if it is necessary in some sense—logical as well as moral— that God choose the most worthy of possible worlds, Leibniz insists in his later writings that it is not a matter of necessity that this world enjoys that status. This point deserves particular emphasis since it further underscores the contingency of this world in relation to divine causation. Leibniz says quite plainly that, while it is true that the world of God's making is the most worthy, its being the most worthy "is not a necessary truth; it is indemonstrable, contingent, a truth of fact."[21]

So the contingency of this world lies for Leibniz in (a) the fact that it is not necessary of itself, (b) the fact that its existence is the result of a choice (tabling the issue of whether the choice is only morally necessitated), and (c) the fact that the superiority of this world over others is indemonstrable and, indeed, indemonstrable because of the infinite aspects of the world. At the same time, this contingency is, like that of the world's existence at all, fully compatible with the universal if qualified reach of the principle of sufficient reason with respect to nature. Reconstructing what all this means is notoriously difficult, to be sure, but it should be clear that it does not mean that one world is superior to all the others because God thinks or knows as much. What qualifies this world to be the actual world is a contingent truth that God immediately recognizes.

20. Adams, "Leibniz's Theories of Contingency," 24: "There seems to have been more vacillation and uncertainty in Leibniz's mind about whether it is necessary or contingent that God chooses what is best than about any other main issue in the problem of contingency. I shall argue, however, that the view that it is necessary is required by other features of Leibniz's philosophy." Adams has in mind here the question of logical or metaphysical necessity. He observes, however, that if the *Essai de Théodicée* and, suitably interpreted, section 13 of the *Discourse on Metaphysics* were our only sources, we would have to conclude that Leibniz considers God's choice of what is best to be contingent, but in other texts Leibniz seems to hold the opposite; see Adams, 25f.

21. *Textes inédits,* 493, probably dating from 1706; as Robert Adams notes, the thesis of the contingency of the property of being best has met with resistance among scholars; see Adams, "Leibniz's Theories of Contingency," 15.

There remain problems with this account, not least Leibniz's contention that God is the source of what is real in the possible worlds. Yet, however such problems are to be resolved, the dependency of possible worlds on God by no means rules out their contingency in more than one sense of the term, and that contingency is something that Leibniz seems clearly to have underscored. For the purposes of this paper, what is important is that Heidegger overlooks this contingency and its compatibility with the universal existential scope of the principle of sufficient reason. It is important because, by underscoring this contingency, Leibnizian rationality presents a particular challenge to Heidegger's contention that we can think what it means to be only by taking leave of that sort of rationality.

III. HEIDEGGER ON READING THE PRINCIPLE OF SUFFICIENT REASON

There is much more to be said about Leibniz's principle of sufficient reason and, especially, there are notable complications to be addressed. Yet the foregoing perhaps suffices to explain why Couturat in his *La logique de Leibniz* (1903) was able to convince Russell that the entire *Monadology* and, indeed, Leibniz's entire metaphysics derives from the principle of sufficient reason.[22] The priority accorded the logic in Leibniz's thinking has been a matter of contention, to be sure. Ernst Cassirer and A. H. Johnson have emphasized the influence that Leibniz's studies of nature and the mind (among other things) exercised on his metaphysics.[23] A case can also be made that Leibniz in the 1680s argues for the principle on the basis of certain metaphysical assumptions. But, whatever the motivations for the principle, there is general agreement that for Leibniz, to be is to have a reason or ground for being.

Heidegger seems to have had his own take on these issues. A former

---

22. Louis Couturat, *La logique de Leibniz d' après des documents inédits* (Paris: Alcan, 1901); Bertrand Russell, *A Critical Exposition of the Philosophy of Leibniz,* second edition (London: George Allen & Unwin, 1937), preface to the second edition, v–vi.

23. Ernst Cassirer, *Leibniz' System in seinen wissenschaftlichen Grundlagen* (1. Auflage, Marburg an der Lahn: Elwert, 1902; reprint: Hildesheim: Olms, 1962), 532–48; A. H. Johnson, "Leibniz's Method and the Basis of his Metaphysics," in *Gottfried Wilhelm Leibniz: Critical Assessments,* ed. R. S. Woodhouse, Volume 1: *Metaphysics and Its Foundations. 1: Sufficient Reason, Truth, and Necessity* (London/New York: Routledge, 1994), 24ff.

student of Husserl, Heinrich Ropohl, had completed a dissertation on Leibniz under Heidegger's direction, defending it in June 1932. In Heidegger's positive evaluation of the defense, he writes that Ropohl's dissertation shows in a new way "that the Leibnizian metaphysics is not built up on 'the logic' but instead the *reverse.*" However, Heidegger completes the sentence by adding, "supposing that it makes any sense at all to divide up the original whole of the Leibnizian philosophy in these terms."[24] The implication is that Leibniz's views on the principle of sufficient reason are best understood as expressing an equivalence or parallel between metaphysics and logic.

Heidegger's approach here also explains his indulgent attitude toward what is often regarded as Leibniz's reduction of causes to the principle of sufficient reason. Though Heidegger notes the standard criticism that Leibniz mistakenly equates reasons and causes, he interprets Leibniz generously on this score, suggesting that the principle of causation is one form of the principle of sufficient reason, as Leibniz himself sometimes suggests.[25] The significance of the principle of sufficient reason, at least in Heidegger's interpretation of Leibniz, reaches across any divide between reasons and causes as it does between logic and metaphysics.

Nonetheless, across that logical/metaphysical divide, Heidegger does take exception to one interpretation of the principle of sufficient reason that he traces back to Leibniz. In keeping with the phenomenological tradition's dogged refusal to accept supposedly self-evident views without scrutiny, Heidegger does not regard the principle of sufficient reason as something beyond question. He accordingly endeavors to explain the hold of the principle of sufficient reason on us or, in other words, why it seems so self-evident.

24. Renato Cristin and Kiyoshi Sakai, eds., *Phänomenologie und Leibniz* (Freiburg/Munich: Alber, 2000), 294; Heinrich Ropohl, *Das Eine und die Welt. Versuch zur Interpretation der Leibnizischen Metaphysik* (Leipzig: Hirzel, 1936).

25. Heidegger notes the usual criticism that Leibniz mistakenly equates reasons and causes (see SvG 43ff., 52; Mates, *The Philosophy of Leibniz,* 158–62) but, cautioning against the presumption, he suggests that the principle of causation is one form of the principle of sufficient reason. For a set of texts that corroborate Heidegger's more generous reading, see Mates n. 34 on pp. 158f.

1. Empowerment: Explaining the Hold of the Principle of
   Sufficient reason on Modernity

On the standard reading of the principle of sufficient reason, it is a principle governing every being. It stipulates, moreover, not only that every being insofar as it exists has a ground or reason, but also that the
ground or reason needs to be given and, indeed, literally "given back."
Thus, it is the *principium reddendae rationis*: for every being insofar as
it exists, the reason must be adduced, retrieved, or, again, literally "given
back."[26] But why given back and to whom? This stipulation, Heidegger
contends, implicates the standard reading of the principle in modernity's project of absolutizing subjectivity, since it is precisely the knowing
subject to whom the ground or reason is supposed to be given.[27] "The
ground or reason is such as must be supplied to the person who enter-
tains and thinks [things]" and, indeed, does so with a view to knowing
them (SvG 47). Heidegger maintains that the sort of knowing in question here for Leibniz is scientific and the ground or reason to be given is
that of a true sentence or assertion in the context of proof or justification.
Glossing this character of the principle of sufficient reason, Heidegger
observes: "The enormous power of the principle consists in the fact that
it pervades, guides, and carries all knowing that expresses itself in sentences" (SvG 46).

This last remark may seem to imply that the principle of sufficient
reason is essentially epistemological. Heidegger is particularly adamant,
however, that such a restricted understanding of the principle of sufficient reason is misguided. For modern thinking in general, he claims,
being is equated with being an object, that is, objecthood, being presented or represented to a subject. The principle of sufficient reason simply
asserts that this presenting and what is presented to it must be some-

26. *Die philosophischen Schriften* VII, 309; not *a* reason, as Mates suggests; Mates, *The Philosophy of Leibniz*, 155.
27. Noting the variations on *facere*, namely, *efficere, sufficere, perficere*, informing Leibniz's
views, something that, Heidegger observes, is "certainly no accident," he links the principle of
sufficient reason to the production of things (SvG 64). This linking deserves more attention,
given Heidegger's critique of the role that production plays in the Western metaphysical tradition; see his 1927 lecture course published as *Die Grundprobleme der Phänomenologie*, Gesamtausgabe Band 24, ed. Friedrich-Wilhelm von Herrmann (Frankfurt am Main: Klostermann,
1975), 140–65.

thing sufficiently grounded or justified *(begründet)*. In this way the principle of sufficient reason holds of every object (what "is" in that sense). In other words, to be is identical to being an object and being an object is identical to being grounded. We can say with certainty that something exists only if it presents itself to us as grounded or, equivalently, if the ground is "delivered" or "conveyed" *(zugestellt)* as the ground.[28] As Heidegger puts it, "Something 'is', that is to say, it is pointed out as an entity, only if it is asserted in a sentence that satisfies the basic principle of the ground [sufficient reason] as the basic principle of justification" (SvG 47).

To the question of what grounds the principle of sufficient reason or, equivalently, why it is modernity's supreme principle, Heidegger thus gives at least part of an answer. The principle of sufficient reason enjoys this status precisely because of what is packed into that gerund *"reddendae,"* which he translates as *zustellen,* meaning "to deliver" as in delivering the mail, a warning, a bill, etc. Though the gerundive expression *"reddendae"* is open, to be sure, to different interpretations (which are signaled, for example, by the variants on "should" or "must"), it does suppose, as Heidegger rightly sees, someone to whom the sufficient reason is given back. But it is also clear that this emphasis on the subjectivity tacitly presupposed by the principle of sufficient reason can only be a finite subjectivity. This finite subjectivity is not to be confused with a contingent, individual subject; instead it is the sort of subjectivity, elaborated in modernity, that suffices for there to be objects (SvG 137). At the same time, in the context of Leibniz's specific system, while a sufficient reason must be given to us why God creates this world, the sufficient reason was never absent from God such that it must or should be given back to Him—a point that Heidegger ignores.[29]

In any case Heidegger casts this answer, it bears stressing, completely in historical terms. In addition to being based upon Leibniz's own historical wording of the principle, Heidegger elaborates its decisive impact

28. SvG 54ff. Or, to paraphrase yet another way that Heidegger puts it, only what exhibits itself to us as we entertain or represent it, only what we encounter in such a way that it is grounded, obtains as something that stands secure. "Only what stands in this way is the sort of thing of which we can say with certainty: it *is*" (SvG 54). Lost in the translation of this paraphrase is a wordplay on *sicher Stehendes* and *Gegenstand.*

29. One might ask whether it is meaningful to say that God has a sufficient reason since there is no sufficient reason why this world is better than the others (assuming that a sufficient reason entails an inference); or is this just a matter of semantics?

on subsequent philosophers and on contemporary thinking, as we noted at the outset. "The *reddendum*, the claim on the delivery of the ground or reason, has now interposed itself between the human being who thinks and his world, in order to take control [*sich bemächtigen*] of human consciousness [*Vorstellen*] in a new way" (SvG 48). What is typically complex in Heidegger's account is this attempt to think what characterizes being-in-the-world in a way that does not fall back on a subject or a world. Accordingly, the powerfulness of the principle of sufficient reason—what exerts power *(machtet)* in it—cannot be reduced to what human subjects do or what the world does.[30] Nevertheless, its power is precisely its demand to deliver to the human subject the grounds or reasons of whatever is. "What exerts power in the principle of sufficient reason is the demand for the delivery of the ground or reason" (SvG 54).

Heidegger's aim here, it bears recalling, is to try to explain why the principle of sufficient reason has the hold on our thinking that it does and, indeed, such that we find ourselves unable to question it. The key to Heidegger's explanation is the *"reddendae"* stipulation, that is, the necessity of giving the reason back to a subject,[31] a stipulation that supposedly explains why the principle of sufficient reason is the defining principle of modernity and, indeed, is the defining principle as something explicitly demanded by modern subjectivity. It is in this connection that Heidegger makes the critical, tendentious observations, cited earlier, that contemporary sciences and philosophies generally do not question or even find any need to question the principle of sufficient reason even while supposing it. The explanation for this obliviousness, Heidegger submits, is the fact that the principle of sufficient reason is at once a principle of empowerment and a principle of being, historically conceived as the *vis viva* and the *Wille zur Macht*.[32] In the *reddendum* stipulation, he notes in

30. Crucial here is the relation obtaining between Seyn and Da-sein; a relation that Heidegger designates a "grounding" *(Gründung)*, the event *(Ereignis)* of Da-sein's appropriation by Seyn; see *Beiträge zur Philosophie (Vom Ereignis)*, Gesamtausgabe Band 65, ed. Friedrich-Wilhelm von Herrmann (Frankfurt am Main: Klostermann, 1989), 260f.

31. SvG 63: "In der ratio reddenda zeigt sich der Grund im Charakter des Anspruches auf Zustellung." See, too, SvG 45, 54.

32. Heidegger traces Nietzsche's thought back to its Leibnizian roots (via Schelling): "Das erste und zwar metaphysische Gespräch mit Leibniz hat Schelling eingeleitet, es erstreckt sich bis in Nietzsches Lehre vom Willen zur Macht" (SvG 43). Later in the lectures he identifies the conception of the being as the objecthood of things with the conception of being as will, though his discussion is abbreviated to a fault; see SvG 115.

the final hour of his lectures, "lies the aspect of the unconditioned and thoroughgoing claim to supplying the mathematically-technically computable grounds, the total 'rationalization'" (SvG 173).

Heidegger's rhetorical guile here is noteworthy. By asking why the principle of sufficient reason has the hold on us that it does, Heidegger has already moved beyond a consideration of the principle of sufficient reason as a principle of the relationship between beings to a consideration of it in terms of an historical manner and dispensation of being. He shifts the center of focus to the way that the principle of sufficient reason prevails or holds sway as a grounding condition of modern subjects and their world, irreducible to either. Thus, before formally and explicitly introducing his audience to the nonstandard reading of the principle of sufficient reason, Heidegger is already employing that reading.

2. What the Principle of Sufficient Reason Presupposes:
Being as a Groundless Ground

In elaborating what the principle of sufficient reason says about being, Heidegger recounts two familiar themes: a sense in which being—and not being-here (Da-sein), not human beings, not subjectivity—is groundlessly grounding and a sense in which it grounds precisely by holding back.[33] Being is what dispenses itself to us precisely by concealing itself and, indeed, in more than one sense of the term. The fact that we do not observe the being of beings in any way analogous to the way we observe other properties of them is one sense in which being conceals itself. Yet it would be a mistake to suppose that, by identifying the presence of beings in contrast to their colors or sizes, we then have gotten hold of their being. It would be a mistake because an absence, for example, what is merely imminent or forever lost, can be no less integral than a presence to what it means for something to be. Being, as Heidegger is fond of saying in Der Satz vom Grund as elsewhere, speaks to us, exhorting and consoling, like a kind of clearing for which it and nothing else is respon-

---

33. SvG 109: "Wenn wir das Wort 'Geschick' vom Sein sagen, dann meinen wir, daß Sein . . . sich lichtet. . . ."; SvG 110: "Sein schickt sich uns zu, indem es zugleich sein Wesen entzieht, dieses im Entzug verbirgt"; SvG 118f.: "In solchem Falle beginnen wir mit dem Versuch: Sein als Sein zu denken. Dies sagt: Sein nicht mehr durch etwas Seiendes erklären." See, too, SvG 143: "Sein währt als sich entziehendes Zuschicken des Zeit-Spiel-Raumes für das Erscheinen dessen, was, dem Geschick und seinem Geheiß entsprechend, jeweils das Seiende heißt." For other texts on the "Zeit-Spiel-Raum," see SvG 129f., 146.

sible, a clearing that makes way for the play of time-space, an interplay of presences and absences in which beings are able to appear.[34] As Heidegger is quick to add in an attempt to forestall misconstruals of what he is saying, presence and absence, bestowal and withdrawal, are not properties of being as something that otherwise obtains, for example, like the changing color of someone's hair. "The self-concealing, the withdrawal, is a manner in which being as being endures, dispenses itself, that is to say, affords [*gewährt*] itself" (SvG 122). Heidegger here is maintaining the constancy of being in a way that supposedly does not collapse into the metaphysics of presence, since it is precisely the absence or withdrawal that characterizes the way being persists; so, too, he speaks of being as "wielding power" *(Machtende)*—the same terms he used to explain the principle of sufficient reason's hold on modernity—but precisely as the way being dispenses itself "in the manner of the withdrawal" (SvG 123).

Heidegger attempts to demonstrate what he means by this fate or dispensation of being in the form of a withdrawal by turning to ancient and modern approaches that supposedly signal this aspect of being. In this connection, he mentions Aristotle's strictures about proceeding from what is more apparent to us to what is more apparent by nature, that is, in its being (*Physics* 184a16ff.) and Heraclitus' observation that being loves to hide. Aristotle's methodology and Heraclitus' cryptic remark each evidence a Greek appreciation of how being's withdrawal or concealment of itself is essential to the way it dispenses and displays itself.[35]

In regard to modern philosophy, Heidegger emphasizes how a commitment to the principle of sufficient reason, rigorously construed, underlies Kant's critical philosophy. The *Kritik der reinen Vernunft* is the attempt, against the backdrop of an equation of subjectivity and rationality, to identify the sufficient reason for objects, "that is to say, for ob-

---

34. SvG 109; 129f. Moreover, while 'being' says something different in the various epochs of its dispensation, the way in which it epochally dispenses itself to us by withholding its essence, concealing this in the withdrawal, is "something the same" (SvG 110).

35. Heidegger contends that being's character of withdrawing is entailed by Aristotle's methodological considerations at the outset of the *Physics*: "Das Sein des von-sich-her-Aufgehenden und -Anwesenden heißt *physis*. . . . Der Weg dahin empfängt seinen eigenen Charakter aus der Weise, wie das Sein des Seienden für den erkennbaren Menschen offenbar ist. Nun zeigt sich überall leicht, daß uns das jeweilig Seiende . . . jederzeit offenkundig gegenüberliegt. Dagegen liegt das, wohindurch all dieses von-sich-her Anwesende auf seine Weise anwest und aufgeht, uns niemals gegenüber wie das hier und dort jeweils Anwesende" (SvG 111; see, too, SvG 120ff., 154).

jects of the representing, self-conscious subject" (SvG 132). The sufficient reason in this case comprises those a priori conditions of the possibility of experiencing the object, conditions projected by the transcendental subject and expressed in the form of eight transcendental principles. The import of this critical appropriation of Leibnizian rationality is not simply that an entity respectively exists only as an object and thus for a subject, but that the subject is equated with reason, a reason that assembles the conditions of the possibility of nature and freedom precisely in the sense of determining the sphere of what counts as a sufficient reason (SvG 127, 134, 137).

In this way Kant's appropriation of Leibnizian rationality provides a modern version of the Parmenidean identification of being and thinking. Being and rational thinking are the same, but in the sense that only that for which a sufficient reason can be given can be said to be or, what is the same, can be said to be thought. But this identification—including, not least, its historical character—illustrates how being withdraws or withholds itself precisely in this way of presenting or dispensing itself. The objectness *(Gegenständigkeit)* of objects is, as Heidegger puts it, the being of beings for Kant, insofar as they can be experienced. As Heidegger puts it: "The new manner in which being dispenses itself consists not only in the fact that being now appears as objectness but that this appearing displays a decisiveness as a result of which being determines itself in the realm of the subjectivity of reason and only here" (SvG 137, 149). The question of being and its essential origin does not even surface, testifying to yet another way in which being withdraws here, and that question does not surface "because in the completely measured realm of *ratio* as reason and subjectivity, the complete justification of beings as such is decided and closed at the same time" (SvG 150). As we emphasized earlier, Heidegger is insistent that this philosophical conception persists in the present. Thus, he contends that the virulence of the atomic age rests upon the historical fact that being affords itself "as objectness for the subjectivity of reason" or, in other words, on "the unconditioned claim of the principle of sufficient reason in the form of complete rationality." There is a claim to power, a *Machtanspruch,* in this claim of reason, determined by the *principium rationis,* one that, as Heidegger puts it, "unleashes the universal and total miscalculation of everything [as] . . . something computible" (SvG 138). Revealing what he understands positively by being, he also observes how, in the atomic age's wholesale pursuit of computible sufficient reasons, "the particularity, individuation, and validity of the individual disappear in favor of total uniformity."[36] However, as the Greek experience amply attests (SvG 139f., 148, 154), what it means to be need not be identified with being an object.

Heidegger accordingly suggests that, if we consider this development properly and, that means, in a genuinely historical way, we may appreciate its limitations and lack of inevitability. The first condition for thinking this way is recognizing that we ourselves belong to this history and are called upon to respond to it. That is to say, we are called upon to respond to the epochal interplay of time-space in which being affords itself to us.[37] Thinking historically and responding to the fateful way being affords itself are thus one and the same and, indeed, one and the same in a way that steers clear of both nostalgia and prophecy. Such thinking is a reverential appropriation of that fateful interplay and Heidegger stresses how this thinking is possible only as a leap, a leap that enables us to grasp what has been *(das Gewesene)* by thinking ahead to what is yet unthought in it. "Thinking is reverentially thinking-ahead" (SvG 159). This leap in thinking, a leap that constitutes thinking being genuinely, that is, historically, is, Heidegger also remarks, "no repetition and no recurrence." This telling remark underscores the radically epochal, individual, and contingent character of being, something that eludes all thought of history in terms of tokens and types (including any "eternal recurrence of the like"), in terms of a realization of supra-temporal ideas and values or a distinction between the absolute and the relative (SvG 159f). Not

---

36. SvG 138; to this telling passage (telling because it identifies in terms of individuality what the "modern" conception of being supposedly neglects) one might add Heidegger's remark about the difference between being and beings: "Denn das Seiende ist ein jeweiliges und so ein vielfältiges; dagegen ist das Sein einzig, der absolute Singular in der unbedingten Singularität" (SvG 143).

37. SvG 146: "Aber wir stehen in dieser Lichtung keineswegs unangesprochen herum, sondern stehen in ihr als die vom Sein des Seienden in dessen Anspruch Genommenen. Wir sind als die in der Lichtung des Seins Stehenden die Beschickten, die in den Zeit-Spiel-Raum Eingeräumten. Dies sagt: Wir sind die in diesem Spielraum und für ihn Gebrauchten, gebraucht, an der Lichtung des Seins zu bauen und zu bilden, im weiten vielfältgen Sinne: sie zu verwahren." SvG 147: "Nur insofern der Mensch seinem Wesen nach in einer Lichtung des Seins steht, ist er ein denkendes Wesen." In this connection (in the eleventh lecture) Heidegger introduces a fourth sense of "Satz" in the *Satz vom Grund,* coupling it with the third sense of it as a leap (first: *Satz* as *Aussage,* second: *Satz* as *Sagen*). That fourth sense is that of the musical "set" that carries the musician into the oncoming, requisite movement.

surprisingly, Heidegger regards the ever-increasing flight from history as symptomatic of the atomic age and the dawning of the time of the unconditioned claim of the principle of sufficient reason in the form of a consummate (complete and perfect) rationality (SvG 138).

IV. EXPLANATION, JUSTIFICATION, AND THE CONTINGENCY OF BEING

Hopefully, the preceding remarks have at least made clear, not only Heidegger's reasons for examining Leibniz's metaphysics, but also reasons why that examination deserves critical scrutiny itself. Heidegger contends that modernity's commitment to the universal sweep of the principle of sufficient reason, a commitment typified and cemented by Leibnizian rationality, blinds it to the irreducible contingency, individuality, and inexhaustibility of being.

However, Leibniz is a modern who recognizes that God's being is not grounded in something else, and he recognizes, too, that there are contingent truths about possible worlds, necessarily known by God, but no less contingent for being so. Moreover, this ungroundedness runs throughout his entire metaphysical system inasmuch as every entity not only expresses the self-groundedness of the primary being from a particular point of view but also instantiates contingent truths by virtue of membership in a possible world. In other words, contrary to Heidegger's claims, Leibniz clearly countenances aspects of being that are ungrounded in various senses of the word and, perhaps more importantly, suggests how that contingency and necessity can be thought together, irreducibly, in a metaphysical conception of being. Moreover, even if it is true in some sense for Leibniz that no absence is completely hidden, he nonetheless countenances a contingent aspect of finite being that explanation and justification presuppose but for which there is no explanation or justification. On all these counts, Leibniz can hardly be said to be oblivious to being, precisely if, following Heidegger, we take being to be in some respects utterly contingent, individual, and inexhaustible, with hidden and absent or at least inexplicable characteristics that are no less telling than features that are transparent or explicable.

This reading of Leibniz's metaphysics, to the extent that it can be sustained, presents a hefty challenge to Heidegger's interpretation of it.

Contrary to what Heidegger maintains, Leibnizian rationality, given the complexity of Leibniz's account of the principle of sufficient reason, does not without further ado cancel what Heidegger understands as the historicity of being. In order to make good on his criticism, Heidegger needs to demonstrate that Leibnizian rationality, with its appeal to creation, necessarily reduces being to being created, to being made. Heidegger does not provide the necessary demonstration and there are good reasons, some suggested by Leibniz and recounted above, to think that such a demonstration cannot be given.[38] The absence of such a demonstration calls into question the trenchancy of Heidegger's claim that that it is necessary to take leave of Leibnizian rationality and bracket causation completely in order, as he puts it, to "correspond to being" (SvG 95). What is questionable is not merely the rigid bifurcation of being and causation (or, equivalently, justification and explanation), but also the supposition that we can clearly draw the line of demarcation between being and causation.

Nevertheless, what Heidegger clearly gets right in his reading of the principle of sufficient reason is the notion that being in some sense grounds the beings that are cause and effect, ground and grounded. In this grounding, being is hidden and sustaining, present as the presence of beings yet in such a way that that very presencing is absent in some respects from any finite point of view. In other words, if Heidegger is wrong to think that explanation is, of necessity, ontologically reductive, he is right to think that being is in some sense irreducible to explanation. At the risk of redundancy, let me stress the fact that, on this score, Leibniz is in far more agreement with Heidegger than Heidegger appreciates. After all, creating does not exhaust what it means to be in the case of the creator and, as Leibniz seems to have seen quite clearly, what it means to be in the case of the created is not reducible to being created.

That said, the domain of disagreement between the two thinkers remains profound, inasmuch as Heidegger suspends any pretensions to a conception of the historically transcendent. His insistence on thinking

38. One reason would be the fundamental difference in the supposition about what it means to be (e.g., Heidegger might argue that his interpretation of the principle of sufficient reason requires a leap from the conventional, Leibnizian reading, a leap that suspends that reading). Another reason is the fact that the opposite holds (i.e., that contingency and the universal sweep of the principle of sufficient reason are compatible) and that Leibniz's philosophy provides a template for demonstrating as much.

being historically presents a considerable challenge to thinking being metaphysically. It does so not only because being is said to be inherently tied to our being-here *(Da-sein)* and thus historical, and not only because thinking being metaphysically is said to miss, that is, to forget this eventfulness *(Ereignis)* as such, but also because it proposes an explanation, indeed, an historical explanation of this obliviousness. In other words, his position can only be trenchantly dismissed if it can be demonstrated that we have access to metaphysical truths rather than, as Heidegger submits, only historical access to being. If we are, indeed, barred as finite beings from the sort of knowledge that only an infinite mind could have, then there is reason to be suspicious of presumptions—again, on the part of the age of Leibniz, if not Leibniz himself—that being in some sense or another, despite its infinity, is fully determinate. For if the future of being is, indeed, pre-determined, so is ours.

Holger Zaborowski

7 ∽ Why Is There Anything at All Rather than Absolutely Nothing?

F. W. J. Schelling's Answer to the Ultimate Why Question

I. IMMANUEL KANT, GERMAN IDEALISM, AND THE SYSTEM OF PHILOSOPHY

The last decades of the eighteenth century and the first decades of the nineteenth belong to the most interesting and important periods of German philosophy, if not even of modern Western philosophy *tout court*. Frederick C. Beiser rightly calls this time of Kant's critical philosophy and of German Idealism "one of the most revolutionary and fertile" periods "in the history of modern philosophy."[1] F. W. J. Schelling argued in 1830 that since Kant, philosophy had not come to rest yet. "The effect of Kant," he stated a few years later, "was indeed exceptional."[2] What happened in

---

1. Frederick C. Beiser, *The Fate of Reason: German Philosophy from Kant to Fichte* (Cambridge, Mass.: Harvard University Press, 1987), vii. For the pre-history of German Idealism see particularly Dieter Henrich's masterful *Grundlegung aus dem Ich. Untersuchungen zur Vorgeschichte des Idealismus. Tübingen—Jena (1790–1794)* (2 vols., Darmstadt: Wissenschaftliche Buchgesellschaft, 2004). For the development from Kant's critical philosophy to Hegel's idealism see also his *Between Kant and Hegel: Lectures on German Idealism*, ed. David S. Pacini (Cambridge, Mass.–London: Harvard University Press, 2003). For important primary sources in English translation see *Between Kant and Hegel: Texts in the Development of Post-Kantian Idealism*, trans. George di Giovanni and H. S. Harris (Albany: State University of New York Press, 1985). For a general introduction to German Idealism see *The Age of German Idealism*, ed. Robert C. Solomon and Kathleen M. Higgins (London–New York: Routledge, 1993); *The Cambridge Companion to German Idealism*, ed. Karl Ameriks (Cambridge: Cambridge University Press, 2000).

2. F. W. J. Schelling, *Einleitung in die Philosophie* (= Schellingiana 1), ed. Walter E. Ehrhardt

this period to make it, even from a merely philosophical perspective, so "revolutionary," "fertile," agitated, and even turbulent that scholars such as Dieter Henrich argue that "this philosophical period was, from a historical standpoint, possibly more influential than any other"?[3]

A brief look at the 1780s and early 1790s may explain the philosophical significance of this period. Immanuel Kant published the *Critique of Pure Reason* in 1781 (2nd edition 1787), the *Critique of Practical Reason* in the beginning of 1788, and the *Critique of Judgment* in 1790. Shortly before and after the publication of his *Religion within the Boundaries of Mere Reason Alone* in 1793 (2nd edition 1794), and, starting with the publication of Fichte's *Attempt at a Critique of all Revelation* in 1791 (2nd edition 1793) and the first edition of his *Science of Knowledge* in 1794, the philosophical world could witness the rise of a new movement that continued to be both revolutionary and fertile—and is so still, after more than two hundred years since its inception, thought-provoking.

This new movement, German Idealism, was led by a younger generation of philosophers, all of them born in the second half of the eighteenth century, who claimed to bring the Kantian project to its fulfillment, radicalizing some of his ideas and at the same time leaving many of his ideas far behind. With Kant's works, as Schelling states, "the way to idealism was . . . opened."[4] In developing their new philosophy, the idealists took very seriously, not the letter of Kant's philosophy, but its spirit.[5] Kant provided them with the results, but failed to manifest the principles, as they maintained.[6] He furthermore has, as the author of the anonymous "Oldest Systematic Program of German Idealism" argues, "given only an example and exhausted nothing."[7] In the idealist view, Kant did not

(Stuttgart–Bad Cannstatt: Frommann-Holzboog, 1989), 29. F. W. J. Schelling, *On the History of Modern Philosophy*, translation, introduction, and notes by Andrew Bowie (Cambridge: Cambridge University Press, 1994), 94. All translations are, if not otherwise indicated, my own.

3. Dieter Henrich, *Between Kant and Hegel*, 3.

4. F. W. J. Schelling, *On the History of Modern Philosophy*, 106.

5. See also in this context Fichte's three lectures "Concerning the Difference between the Spirit and the Letter within Philosophy," in Johann Gottlieb Fichte, *Early Philosophical Writings*, trans. and ed. Daniel Breazeale (Ithaca-London: Cornell University Press, 1988), 185–215.

6. See also F. W. J. Schelling, *Vom Ich als Prinzip der Philosophie oder über das Unbedingte im menschlichen Wissen*, in *Sämmtliche Werke*, ed. Karl Friedrich August Schelling (Stuttgart-Augsburg: Cotta, 1856–64), Abt. I, vol. 1 (= SW I/1), 152; idem, *Einleitung in die Philosophie*, 37; idem, *Urfassung der Philosophie der Offenbarung*, vol. 1, ed. Walter E. Ehrhardt (Hamburg: Felix Meiner Verlag, 1992), 3ff.

7. "The Oldest Systematic Program of German Idealism," trans. Diana I. Behler, in *The*

succeed in providing a unified account of his philosophy. He thus failed to develop an all-comprehensive system that showed how his three *Critiques* belonged together and how reality as well as knowledge of reality could be explained with respect to merely one main principle.[8]

This main principle, the idealists argued, the "first idea," is naturally "the conception of my self as an absolutely free being."[9] In order to understand fully this formulation of the main principle of German Idealism, it is important to remember that not only Kant's "Copernican turn" of philosophy, but also other, less philosophical factors need to be taken into account in order to understand German post-Kantian philosophy with its emphasis on the absolutely free Ego. These include the lasting impact of Christian theology and of the Reformation as a yet-to-be-finished project, which focused on the individual and his freedom,[10] and the French Revolution with its radical program of freedom and its emphasis upon a new political and social order.[11] It is this complex histori-

---

Philosophy of German Idealism, ed. Ernst Behler (New York: Continuum, 1987), 161–63, p. 161. The author of this program is—presumably—either Hegel or Schelling. For a discussion of this program see particularly *Mythologie der Vernunft. Hegels 'ältestes Systemprogramm des deutschen Idealismus'*, ed. Christoph Jamme (Frankfurt am Main: Suhrkamp, 1984).

8. For this view see F. W. J. Schelling, *Über die Möglichkeit einer Form der Philosophie überhaupt* (1794), SW I/1, 87ff.; idem, *System der Weltalter. Münchener Vorlesung 1827/28 in einer Nachschrift von Ernst von Lausaulx*, ed. Siegbert Peetz (Frankfurt am Main: Vittorio Klostermann, 2nd ed., 1998), 41ff.

9. "The Oldest Systematic Program of German Idealism," 161.

10. For Schelling's view of the Reformation and of theology see the ninth lecture of his *Vorlesungen über die Methode (Lehrart) des akademischen Studiums* (1803; SW I/5, 207–352). For his later view of the Reformation and of Protestantism see the eighty-second lecture of his *Philosophy of Revelation* (F. W. J. Schelling, *Urfassung der Philosophie der Offenbarung*, vol. 2, ed. Walter E. Ehrhardt [Hamburg: Felix Meiner Verlag, 1992], 691–700). For the religious and theological background of German Idealism see also Wilhelm G. Jacobs, *Zwischen Revolution und Orthodoxie? Schelling und seine Freunde im Stift und an der Universität Tübingen. Texte und Untersuchungen* (= Spekulation und Erfahrung II/12) (Stuttgart–Bad Cannstatt: Frommann-Holzboog, 1989); Holger Zaborowski, "'Reason and Freedom Remain Our Shibboleth and the Invisible Church Our Point of Unity': The German Idealist View of the Church and Its Political Implications," in *Church ag Politeia: The Political Self-Understanding of Christianity. Proceedings of a Becket Institute Conference at the University of Oxford, 28 September–1 October 2000. With forewords by Bishop Hans Christian Knuth and Cardinal Walter Kasper* (= Arbeiten zur Kirchengeschichte 86), ed. Christoph Stumpf and Holger Zaborowski (Berlin: Walter de Gruyter, 2004), 191–218.

11. For this historical context see also Terry Pinkard, *German Philosophy 1760–1860: The Legacy of Idealism* (Cambridge: Cambridge University Press, 2002), 82ff. and passim; Dieter Sturma, "Politics and the New Mythology," in *The Cambridge Companion to German Idealism*, 219–38.

cal context in which Fichte, Schelling, and Hegel, the most important
philosophers of German Idealism, developed all-comprehensive systems
of philosophy, or at least outlines of such systems, which "will contain
nothing other than a complete system of all ideas."[12]

While Hegel has much been studied for two centuries, Fichte and
Schelling were long somewhat neglected. It was too tempting simply to
follow the Hegelian account of the history of modern philosophy, which
considered Fichte's "subjective" idealism and Schelling's "objective" idealism to be mere steps toward the mature and ultimate position of Hegel's
"absolute" idealism.[13] In the second half of the twentieth century, inspired
particularly by the historical-critical editions of Fichte's, Hegel's, and
Schelling's works, scholars have frequently questioned this widespread
reading of the rise and genesis of German idealist philosophy. They have
increasingly explored the sources of German idealist philosophy, its history, immediate context, and main ideas (and have also edited many new
sources for the first time) so that they could develop a more comprehensive and much more nuanced account of German idealist philosophy and
its development. Not only Fichte, but also Schelling, the *enfant terrible*,
as it were, of eighteenth- and early-nineteenth-century German philosophy, have been of interest to many scholars, who have spent a considerable
amount of scholarly energy in interpreting his early and later philosophy
and its development. Thereby they have contributed to a deeper understanding of Schelling's complex thinking as well as of nineteenth- and
twentieth-century post–Schellingian philosophy.[14]

12. "The Oldest Systematic Program of German Idealism," 161.

13. For Hegel's view of the history of philosophy and its development see Holger Za-
borowski, "Reason, Truth, and History: The Early Hegel's Philosophy of History," in *Hegel's
Phenomenology of Spirit: New Critical Essays*, ed. Alfred Denker and Michael Vater (New York:
Humanity Books, 2003), 21–58.

14. For the best account of Schelling's thought and life see Xavier Tilliette, *Schelling. Une
philosophie en devenir. I. Le Système vivant. 1794–1821* and *II. Le Dernière Philosophie. 1821–
1854* (Paris: Vrin, 2nd ed. 1992); Xavier Tilliette, *Schelling. Biographie*, trans. Susanne Schaper
(Stuttgart: Klett-Cotta, 2004). Important contributions to Schelling research are published
in *Schellingiana* (ed. by Walter E. Ehrhardt [Stuttgart–Bad Cannstatt: Frommann-Holzboog,
1989–]). See Dale E. Snow's *Schelling and the End of Idealism* (Albany: State University of New
York Press, 1996) for a good English discussion of Schelling's philosophy. For an overview of
the first period of the rejuvenated interest in Schelling see Hermann Zeltner, *Schelling-Forschung seit 1954* (Darmstadt: Wissenschaftliche Buchgesellschaft, 1975); Harald Holz, "Nach-
wort: Einige Überlegungen zur Wirkungsgeschichte Schellings heute," in *Die Idee der Philosophie bei Schelling. Metaphysische Motive in seiner Frühphilosophie* (Freiburg-Munich: Verlag
Karl Alber, 1977), 127–37.

150   *Holger Zaborowski*

II. "FREEDOM IS OUR AND THE GODHEAD'S HIGHEST": SCHELLING'S SYSTEM OF FREEDOM

Some early interpreters (and critics) of Schelling's philosophy such as Heinrich Heine distinguished very sharply between the early and the later Schelling. This distinction very often would allow the critic to accuse the later Schelling of abandoning the principles of his own early thinking, of falling subject to a philosophically unjustifiable irrationalism and esotericism, or of returning to a closed dogmatic system.[15] Recent scholars, however, by and large agree that there is "only one Schelling"[16] and that his later philosophy did not at all betray his beginnings. His later philosophy is, as he himself argued, rather a "plus," a "consequence" of his earlier thinking that "is related to it like the fruit to a blossom."[17]

Schelling, it is now uncontroversial to argue, follows one particular trajectory of thought which finds its center in the question of freedom. Schelling claims always to have thought freely for himself.[18] Philosophy as such, he would maintain until his death in 1854, requires one to think for oneself; it is in its highest form freely produced out of oneself.[19] So freedom is, as he argues in one of his earliest writings, the beginning and the end of philosophy.[20] It is, he would later maintain, "our and the Godhead's highest."[21]

15. See, for example, Heinrich Heine, "Zur Geschichte der Religion und Philosophie in Deutschland," in *Über Deutschland 1833–1863. Aufsätze über Kunst und Philosophie* (= Säkularausgabe 8), ed. Renate Francke (Berlin and Paris: Akademie-Verlag, 1972), 224.
16. For this see particularly Walter E. Ehrhardt, "Nur ein Schelling," in *Studi Urbinati di Storia, Filosofia e Letteratura*, Anno LI, Nuova Serie B, N. 1–2 (1977), 111–22; see also Walter Kasper, *Das Absolute in der Geschichte. Philosophie und Theologie der Geschichte in der Spätphilosophie Schellings* (Mainz: Matthias Grünewald, 1965), 10.
17. Schelling, *Einleitung in die Philosophie*, 39.
18. F. W. J. Schelling, *Vom Ich als Prinzip der Philosophie* (1795), SW I/1, 152.
19. Schelling, *Einleitung in die Philosophy*, 1; see also 34.
20. F. W. J. Schelling, *Vom Ich als Princip der Philosophie* (1795), SW I/1, 101. For a good introduction to the early Schelling's view of freedom see Alfred Denker, "Freiheit ist das höchste Gut des Menschen. Schellings erste Auseinandersetzung mit der Jenaer Wissenschaftslehre Fichtes," in *Sein—Reflexion—Freiheit. Aspekte der Philosophie Johann Gottlieb Fichtes* (= Bochumer Studien zur Philosophie 25) ed. Christoph Asmuth (Amsterdam-Philadelphia: B. R. Grüner, 1997), 35–68.
21. Schelling, *Urfassung der Philosophie der Offenbarung*, vol. 1, p. 79. For Schelling's understanding of freedom see also Walter E. Ehrhardt, "'Freiheit ist unser und der Gottheit Höchstes'—ein Rückweg zur *Freiheitsschrift?*" in *Schellings Weg zur Freiheitsschrift. Legende und Wirklichkeit* (= Schellingiana 5), ed. Hans Michael Baumgartner and Wilhelm G. Jacobs (Stuttgart–Bad Cannstatt: Frommann-Holzboog, 1996), 240–51.

Schelling, however, was not only a philosopher of freedom; he was also a modern systematic philosopher whose goal was the all-comprehensive philosophical system and who understood philosophy as the primordial science.[22] But unlike many seventeenth- and eighteenth-century philosophers who maintained that a system could be developed only at the cost of freedom, that is to say that any system must necessarily be deterministic,[23] Schelling held that a system of freedom is not only possible but the very challenge that philosophy—particularly at his time—had to face. His intention, so he states in one of his later lectures concerning the philosophy of revelation, is to develop a "system that would be strong enough to pass the test of life sometime,"[24] that is, that is not systematic at the cost of neglecting, or even of dismissing, the realities of life and freedom.

It is in this context that he raises the ultimate why question, the question why there is anything at all rather than absolutely nothing. A system of philosophy would have to deal with this question and *think* about why there is anything rather than nothing.[25] Philosophy, he argues throughout his career, is the "science that starts plainly from scratch."[26] This is

22. For his (as well as Fichte's and Hegel's) systematic claim see Adolf Schurr, *Philosophie als System bei Fichte, Schelling und Hegel* (Stuttgart–Bad Cannstatt: Frommann-Holzboog, 1974). For the early Schelling's understanding of philosophy as a systematic science see also F. W. J. Schelling, *Über die Möglichkeit einer Form der Philosophie überhaupt* (1794), 5ff. For his understanding of philosophy see also Karl Jaspers, *Schelling. Größe und Verhängnis* (Munich-Zurich: Piper, 1986), 64–121.

23. Schelling expresses this view himself in *Vom Wesen der menschlichen Freiheit*, SW I/7, 336f. For an interpretation of Schelling's philosophical claim see Jochem Hennigfeld, *Friedrich Wilhelm Joseph Schellings, Philosophische Untersuchungen über das Wesen der menschlichen Freiheit und die damit zusammenhängenden Gegenstände* (Darmstadt: Wissenschaftliche Buchgesellschaft, 2001), 37; for the philosophical claim of Schelling's *Vom Wesen der menschlichen Freiheit* see also Martin Heidegger, *Schelling: Vom Wesen der menschlichen Freiheit* (1809), ed. Ingrid Schüßler (Gesamtausgabe 42) (Frankfurt am Main: Vittorio Klostermann, 1988).

24. Schelling, *Urfassung der Philosophie der Offenbarung*, vol. 1, p. 3.

25. For Schelling's answer to this question see also Jaspers, *Schelling. Größe und Verhängnis*, 124–30. Jaspers also mentions important passages in which Schelling raises the ultimate why question or at least implicitly refers to it: F. W. J. Schelling, *System der gesammten Philosophie und der Naturphilosophie insbesondere* (1804), SW I/6, 155; *Aphorismen zur Einleitung in die Naturphilosophie*, SW I/7, 174; *Einleitung in die Philosophie der Offenbarung oder Begründung der positiven Philosophie*, SW II/3, 7, 163ff.; 242; 270.

26. Schelling, *Urfassung der Philosophie der Offenbarung*, vol. 1, p. 19: "Man kann die Philosophie erklären als die schlechthin von vorne anfangende Wissenschaft." With his understanding of philosophy, Schelling stands, of course, particularly in the Aristotelian tradition (see for example *Metaphysics* 1003a26f.). For the later Schelling's interest in Aristotle, see

why, on his account, philosophy is the discipline that "ought to explain the fact of the world."[27] All philosophical systems, however different they may be, Schelling further argues, converge in their attempt "to demonstrate *(nachweisen)* the ultimate ground of being and of knowledge."[28]

Given his philosophical self-understanding, Schelling could not have allowed that the ultimate why question is philosophically meaningless or utterly unanswerable; nor could he have accepted a doctrinal answer to the ultimate why question that, for instance, would merely have made reference to the theological doctrine of creation. For such a doctrinal answer may simply state *that* God exists and created the world and *that,* therefore, there is something at all, but does not necessarily contribute to a deeper and, according to Schelling, philosophically satisfying understanding as to *why* God created the world and *why,* therefore, there is anything rather than absolutely nothing. Even if God (as a possible theological answer may run) created the world out of love, it is, according to Schelling, both possible and necessary to know this much better by means of philosophical reasoning.[29] Schelling argues that "he who knows God as cause, does not yet know the kind of cause" that God is.[30] So in addition to knowing *that* God created the world, we also need to know what kind of cause God is and why he created the world, as much as this can be *known* at all.

Schelling holds that all previous metaphysics admitted that it could not say anything about "the way in which God is the creator of the world."[31] For God as the ultimate cause of reality and knowledge could be a necessarily existing Being—the God, according to Schelling, of Descartes or of Spinoza, who, necessarily or not, creates the world—or, alternatively, could be a freely existing God who freely created the world.[32]

Alfred Denker, "Schelling und Aristoteles," in *Das antike Denken in der Philosophie Schellings* (= Schellingiana 11) ed. Rainer Adolphi and Jörg Jantzen (Stuttgart–Bad Cannstatt: Frommann-Holzboog, 2004), 305–20.

27. Schelling, *Einleitung in die Philosophie,* 37.

28. Ibid., 6.

29. See for Schelling's philosophical claim in this context also F. W. J. Schelling, *Ideas on a Philosophy of Nature as an Introduction to the Study of this Science,* trans. Priscilla Hayden-Roy, in *The Philosophy of German Idealism,* ed. Ernst Behler, 167–202, at 202.

30. Schelling, *Einleitung in die Philosophie,* 31.

31. Schelling, *Urfassung der Philosophie der Offenbarung,* 67.

32. For Schelling's critique of Descartes' and Spinoza's concepts of God see his *On the History of Modern Philosophy,* 42–75. For Descartes' view of God as necessarily existing see his proofs of the existence of God in his *Meditations* III and V; for Spinoza's concept of God see

The question as to which kind of cause God is—that is, who God is—stands particularly in Schelling's later thought in the center of his philosophical attention.[33] It is his continuous attempt to answer the ultimate why question (implicitly or explicitly) that shows to what extent he remained faithful to his own origins. For in his later philosophy also, freedom is the beginning and the end of philosophy. When, in his later lectures on the philosophy of revelation, he states that "*freedom* is our and the Godhead's highest," he continues to argue that "we want freedom as the ultimate reason of all things."[34] So he never abandons the fundamental insight into the significance of freedom that he developed in his early thinking, even though he would substantially develop his own philosophy. As his philosophy, however consistent, did undergo major changes, it is appropriate to explore the ultimate why question both with respect to the early Schelling and with respect to his later philosophy. It is important, however, not to forget that in his early philosophy he does not explicitly ask the ultimate why question. This does not at all mean that he is not interested in this question in his early philosophy; it means that he raises and answers this question differently.

III. SCHELLING'S (IMPLICIT) ANSWER TO THE ULTIMATE
WHY QUESTION IN HIS EARLY PHILOSOPHY

In order to understand Schelling's early development and his early philosophy, it is necessary to consider more closely four major influences on his thinking: the philosophies of Spinoza, Kant, Fichte, and Plato. Schelling's early philosophy is characterized by the attempt to overcome

---

particularly the "pars prima" ("De Deo") of his *Ethica Ordine Geometrico Demonstrata*. For a discussion of Schelling's critique of Descartes' ontological proof of the existence of God see Jeffrey Kinlaw, "Schellings ursprüngliche Einsicht. Das ontologische Argument und die Aufgabe der Philosophie," in *System—Freiheit—Geschichte. Schellings Einleitung in die Philosophie (1830) im Kontext seines Werkes* (= Schellingiana 16), ed. Holger Zaborowski and Alfred Denker (Stuttgart: Frommann-Holzboog, 2004), 123–60.

33. For an account of the later Schelling's understanding of God see Walter Kasper, *Das Absolute in der Geschichte. Philosophie und Theologie der Geschichte in der Spätphilosophie Schellings*; Klaus Hemmerle, *Gott und das Denken nach Schellings Spätphilosophie* (Freiburg i. Br.: Verlag Herder, 1968); Josef Kreiml, *Die Wirklichkeit Gottes. Eine Untersuchung über die Metaphysik und die Religionsphilosophie des späten Schelling* (Regensburg: S. Roderer Verlag, 1989); Walter E. Ehrhardt, "Schelling's Gottesbegriff," in *Religion und Gott im Denken der Neuzeit*, ed. Albert Franz and Wilhelm G. Jacobs (Paderborn: Ferdinand Schöningh, 2000), 126–35.

34. Schelling, *Urfassung der Philosophie der Offenbarung*, vol. 1, 79.

Spinoza's philosophical system "in its fundament."[35] He acknowledges Spinoza's important and radical contribution for the search of an "ultimate point of all knowledge" and remains deeply indebted to his enterprise, but also does not overlook its limits. According to Schelling, Spinoza bases his philosophy on the concept of God as necessarily existing substance as first principle, but he fails to do justice to the fact of freedom.[36] God, he argues, is in Spinoza's philosophy no longer a "free cause."[37] "Spinozism, then," as he would later argue, "shows itself . . . as a system which is not wholly and completely developed."[38] The further development of the history of philosophy, he holds, would have to lead toward a system of freedom that does take the fact of freedom as seriously as it should be taken. For a "system of freedom—but with just as great contours, with the same simplicity, as a perfect counter-image *(Gegenbild)* of the Spinozist system—this would really be the highest system."[39]

Immanuel Kant's philosophy was of great significance for Schelling as he came to understand freedom better and developed his own philosophy of freedom. He read the history of modern philosophy from Descartes to his own time as a progressive discovery of freedom that would finally lead to the complete system of freedom—his own later system.[40] Kant's critical philosophy, then, is a major (though, as we have already seen, insufficient) step toward the completion of philosophy insofar as he focuses mainly on the subject and on freedom and not, as did Spinoza, on the concept of God as an infinite substance.[41] So for Schelling, Kant's critical philosophy was essentially a philosophy of the subject and of freedom.[42] Kant, he argued, "*directed philosophy towards the subjective,* a direction which it had completely lost since Spinoza."[43] This is the

35. F. W. J. Schelling, *Vom Ich als Prinzip der Philosophie* (1795), SW I/1, 151ff.
36. See F. W. J. Schelling, *Über die Möglichkeit der Form einer Philosophie überhaupt* (1794), AA I/I, 102.
37. F. W. J. Schelling, *Einleitung in die Philosophie*, 28; see also 29.
38. F. W. J. Schelling, *On the History of Modern Philosophy*, 72. For Schelling's relation to Spinoza see also F. W. J. Schelling, *Vom Ich als Prinzip der Philosophie* (1795), SW I/1, 151f.
39. Schelling, *On the History of Modern Philosophy*, 66.
40. See particularly the account of modern philosophy that Schelling provides in his *On the History of Modern Philosophy*.
41. For Schelling's later critique of Kant's concept of God see Schelling's *On the History of Modern Philosophy*, 105ff.
42. For this dimension of Kant's philosophy see also Henrich, *Between Kant and Hegel*, 46–61.
43. Schelling, *On the History of Modern Philosophy*, 106.

direction that subsequent German idealist philosophy, beginning with Fichte, would further follow.[44]

There are, however, according to Schelling also serious shortcomings in Kant's philosophy. Kant only developed what Schelling in his later philosophy calls a "regressive philosophy."[45] A "regressive philosophy," as contrasted with a "progressive philosophy," is an a priori philosophy that takes its beginning in the produced *(das Hervorgebrachte)* or *posterius* to go back to the producer *(der Hervorbringende)* or *absolute prius*.[46] Kant's philosophy is thus, Schelling further argues, a "merely logical" and subjective philosophy and cannot but fail to discover as its starting-point what is an *absolute prius,* that is, the freedom of God. The freedom and, based on this, the existence of God, however, need to be experienced a posteriori through the world, as Schelling argues, but cannot be deduced from the standpoint of an a priori transcendental philosophy.[47]

This is, of course, the later Schelling's criticism of Kant's philosophy. In his earlier works, Schelling's criticism of Kant was somewhat different. It is particularly Schelling's early insight into the shortcomings of the Kantian project that made it necessary for him to go beyond Kant— with Kant, however, always still on his side. Schelling, as Wilhelm G. Jacobs nicely summarizes the difference between the early Schelling and Kant, "does not like Kant ask for the conditions of possibility, but conversely how the conditioned is to be thought in its condition."[48] This marks indeed a considerable difference between Kant and Schelling. In thinking about the conditionedness of the conditioned (in other words, in raising a particular form of the ultimate why question) from within the general framework of Kant's philosophy, Schelling goes beyond Kant's radical critique of metaphysics and moves toward the foundations of a new, post-Kantian, rational metaphysics.[49] The answer to this ques-

---

44. For a very helpful account of Fichte's transcendental philosophy see Frederick Neuhouser, *Fichte's Theory of Subjectivity* (Cambridge: Cambridge University Press, 1996).

45. Schelling, *Einleitung in die Philosophie,* 33.

46. Ibid., 24.

47. Ibid., 24ff.

48. Wilhelm G. Jacobs, *Schelling lesen* (Stuttgart–Bad Cannstatt: Frommann-Holzboog, 2005), 77.

49. For a helpful interpretation of Schelling's re-turn toward metaphysics, see Harald Holz, *Die Idee der Philosophie bei Schelling;* see also Manfred Schröter, "Der Ausgangspunkt der Metaphysik Schellings, entwickelt aus seiner ersten philosophischen Abhandlung 'Über

tion leads him to a philosophy of the unconditional that conditions all that is conditioned.

Philosophy as such, he argues in one of his earliest publications, is "a whole, that stands under the form of unity."[50] This unity, he further states, is possible only on the basis of an unconditional basic principle *(Grundsatz)*. This is why philosophy must be conditioned and justified by an "absolute basic principle."[51] In close proximity to Fichte's *Science of Knowledge*,[52] Schelling finds this unconditional principle in the transcendental Ego that is originally posited through itself (so it is not conditioned by anything or by anyone else).[53] The Ego, he argues, is posited through itself and, with it, a non-Ego is also posited out of freedom *(aus Freiheit)*.[54] Initially, so Schelling states, "there is nothing but the Ego, namely, given as highest condition."[55]

Thus in his earliest writings Schelling answers the ultimate why question (as the question why there are conditioned things rather than nothing at all) with respect to the absolute Ego as the absolutely unconditional basic principle. The absolutely unconditional can only be the transcendental Ego, freedom itself. This is what it means to say that freedom is the beginning of philosophy: the ultimate why question finds its answer in what is ultimately unconditioned and the condition of all that is conditioned—freedom itself.

In developing his philosophy of freedom, which is deeply indebted to Spinoza's, Kant's, and Fichte's philosophies, Schelling increasingly attempted to overcome the gap between nature and freedom that he considered one of the most important shortcomings of Kant's critical philosophy (as well as of Fichte's subjective idealism). In so doing, he benefited from a close reading of Kant's third critique, *The Critique of Judgment*, but also from his interest in the Platonic tradition of philosophy.

At age nineteen, Schelling wrote a commentary on Plato's *Timaeus*

---

die Möglichkeit einer Form der Philosophie überhaupt' (1795)," in Manfred Schröter, *Kritische Studien. Über Schelling und zur Kulturphilosophie* (Munich: R. Oldenbourg, 1971), 11–51.

50. Schelling, *Über die Möglichkeit* (1794), SW I/1, 90.
51. Ibid., SW I/1, 92.
52. See Johann Gottlieb Fichte, *Science of Knowledge (Wissenschaftslehre) with the First and Second Introductions*, ed. and trans. Peter Heath and John Lachs (New York: Appleton-Century-Crofts, 1970), §1.
53. Schelling, *Über die Möglichkeit*, SW I/1, 96.
54. Ibid., SW I/1, 99.
55. Ibid., SW I/1, 100.

which particularly focuses on those passages that refer to the genesis of the world.[56] In his commentary Schelling uses Kant's terminology to interpret Plato while at the same time attempting to read Kant from a Platonic position. What is important about this early and, given the historical circumstances, rather unusual work (which has been much discussed since its first publication in 1994)[57] is the extent to which it anticipates many of the ideas that Schelling would develop later in his life.

Among other questions, he discusses Plato's famous answer to the question why the creator of the world created the world. Plato's answer, that the creator is good and that he thus never experiences jealousy,[58] is, according to Schelling, "the purest, most magnificent idea of God's intention in creating the world."[59] So also in the context of his *Timaeus* interpretation, Schelling implicitly raises the ultimate why question, and answers it, from the perspective of his particular reading of Plato, with reference to God's intentions. This approach implicitly presupposes freedom on the side of God, for God did not create out of some kind of necessity.

In this early commentary, he also anticipated his objective idealism of the late 1790s that would find the workings of freedom in the objective realm of nature and would provide an account of nature as productively developing toward full freedom and self-consciousness. Plato, Schelling argues for example, has "always transferred the subjective to the objec-

56. F. W. J. Schelling, *"Timaeus"* (*1794*) (= Schellingiana 4), ed. Hartmut Buchner (Stuttgart–Bad Cannstatt: Frommann-Holzboog, 1994).

57. For a good and very helpful interpretation of Schelling's reading of the *Timaeus* see Hermann Krings, "Genesis und Materie—Zur Bedeutung der 'Timaeus'-Handschrift für Schelling's Naturphilosophie," in Schelling, *"Timaeus"* (1794), 115–55; Denker, "Freiheit ist das höchste Gut des Menschen," 40ff.; Tanja Gloyna, *Kosmos und System. Schellings Weg in die Philosophie* (= Schellingiana 15) (Stuttgart–Bad Cannstatt: Frommann-Holzboog, 2002), 172–98; Federica Viganó, "Schelling liest Platons 'Timaeus'. Die Erneuerung zwischen Platon und Kant," in *Das antike Denken in der Philosophie Schellings* (= Schellingiana 11), ed. Rainer Adolphi and Jörg Jantzen (Stuttgart–Bad Cannstatt: Frommann-Holzboog, 2004), 227–35; Leonardo V. Distaso, *The Paradox of Existence: Philosophy and Aesthetics in the Young Schelling* (= Topoi Library 5) (Dordrecht, Boston, London: Kluwer Academic Publishers, 2004), 37–47.

58. For Plato's view, see Plato, *Timaeus*, 29D and following.

59. Schelling, *"Timaeus."* (*1794*), 27. Schelling's reading of Plato is, of course, not unproblematic from a philological and historical perspective, insofar as he identifies the Demiurge with God and speaks of the "world's creation." I would like to thank Msgr. John Wippel for drawing my attention to this problematic feature of Schelling's interpretation of Plato's *Timaeus*. For Schelling's own "interest" in his early approach to Plato, see also Hermann Krings, "Genesis und Materie," in Schelling, *"Timaeus"* (1794), 115–55, at 126ff.

tive."[60] Transferring the subjective to the objective and thus overcoming the modern Cartesian and Kantian gap between the subject and the object is also one of the main interests of Schelling's own philosophy. The Platonic dimension of Schelling's philosophy (or at least his reading of Plato), then, made it possible even for the young Schelling to raise a question that Kant could not have raised in this particular form, the question how a sensible world could have come into existence.[61] This, of course, is for Schelling to ask a deeply metaphysical question that according to Kant cannot meaningfully be either asked or answered, as it concerns the supersensible realm and thus transcends the limits of reason. In his move toward a more metaphysical philosophy, Schelling, however, does not adopt a pre-Kantian metaphysical position but explores the possibility of asking a metaphysical question *after* Kant's critical turn of philosophy.[62]

Particularly in the years after the publication of *Vom Ich,* Schelling develops his position and tries to overcome the subjectivism of his own and Fichte's early idealism. He argues that subjective idealism did not allow for an adequate understanding of (the objectivity *and* subjectivity of) nature. A new *transcendental* philosophy of nature, based upon the most recent physical research (with which Schelling familiarized himself while studying at Leipzig), but in "a region higher than mere natural science,"[63] was necessary if philosophy did not want to abandon its systematic, all-comprehensive claim. This is why Schelling worked inten-

60. Schelling, *"Timaeus"* (1794), 31. For this concept see also Tanja Gloyna, *Kosmos und System,* 172–76.

61. For the Platonic dimension of Schelling's philosophy, see also Harald Holz, "Das Platonische Syndrom beim jungen Schelling. Hintergundtheoreme in der Ausbildung seines Naturbegriffs," in his *Die Idee der Philosophie bei Schelling,* 19–63. For a short comparison of the difference between Kant's philosophy of nature in his *Metaphysical Foundations of Natural Science* and Schelling's philosophy of nature, see Myriam Gerhard, *Von der Materie der Wissenschaft zur Wissenschaft der Materie. Schellings Naturphilosophie im Ausgang der Transzendentalphilosophie Kants und Fichtes und ihre Kritik einer systematischen Bestimmung des Verhältnisses von Natur und Vernunft* (Berlin: Duncker & Humblot, 2002), 149–75.

62. For a brief discussion of this, see also Jacobs, *Schelling lesen,* 78f. For Schelling's relation to Kant see also Wilhelm G. Jacobs, *Gottesbegriff und Geschichtsphilosophie in der Sicht Schellings* (= Spekulation und Erfahrung II/29) (Stuttgart–Bad Cannstatt: Frommann-Holzboog, 1993), 122–51. For Schelling's later critique of Kant see his *On the History of Modern Philosophy,* 94–106.

63. F. W. J. Schelling, *Ideas for a Philosophy of Nature as an Introduction to the Study of this Science,* trans. Errol E. Harris and Peter Heath (Cambridge: Cambrige University Press, 1988), 177.

sively on the philosophy of nature in the second half of the 1790s and in the early nineteenth century and tried to show—in close agreement with Spinoza—how nature is both product (object/*natura naturata*) and productive (subjective/*natura naturans*) at the same time.[64] "Nature shall be visible spirit, and spirit invisible nature," as Schelling pointed out in his *Ideas on a Philosophy of Nature as an Introduction to the Study of this Science.*[65]

He also continued his work in the field of transcendental idealism. One of the most important documents from this period of Schelling's thinking is his *System of Transcendental Idealism,* published in 1800. Still following Kant and Fichte,[66] Schelling takes knowledge as the starting-point of his reflection. He argues that "all knowledge is founded upon the coincidence of an objective with a subjective."[67] The task of philosophy, then, is to explain this coincidence, the "concurrence" of the subjective and the objective in each knowing. There are two possible ways to do this, he says (and not only one, as Fichte and Schelling himself a few years earlier would have argued). The first way makes the objective "primary" and asks the questions "how a subjective is annexed thereto, which coincides with it." This is the way of the natural sciences, and it will, Schelling holds, eventually lead to a philosophy of nature, as "nat-

64. For his philosophy of nature see F. W. J. Schelling, *Ideas for a Philosophy of Nature as an Introduction to the Study of This Science*; idem, *First Outline of a System of the Philosophy of Nature,* trans. Keith R. Peterson (Albany: State University of New York Press, 2004). For Schelling's later interpretation of his own early philosophy of nature, see his *On the History of Modern Philosophy,* 114–33. For interpretations of Schelling's philosophy of nature, see Ludwig Hasler, in *Schelling. Seine Bedeutung für eine Philosophie der Natur und der Geschichte. Referate und Kolloquien der Internationalen Schelling-Tagung 1979,* ed. Ludwig Hasler (Stuttgart–Bad Cannstatt: Frommann-Holzboog, 1981), 73–172; Snow, *Schelling and the End of Idealism,* 67–92; Michael Rudolphi, *Produktion und Konstruktion. Zur Genese der Naturphilosophie in Schellings Frühphilosophie* (= Schellingiana 7) (Stuttgart–Bad Cannstatt: Frommann-Holzboog, 2001), particularly 87–126, for the transcendental character of Schelling's philosophy of nature; Pinkard, *German Philosophy 1760–1860,* 178–83.

65. Schelling, *Ideas on a Philosophy of Nature as an Introduction to the Study of This Science,* 202.

66. Dieter Jähnig rightly points out that in his lecture on the history of modern philosophy, Schelling discusses his *System of Transcendental Idealism* in the same lecture in which he discusses Kant's and Fichte's philosophies (Dieter Jähnig, *Schelling. Die Kunst in der Philosophie. Erster Band: Schellings Begründung von Natur und Geschichte* [Pfullingen: Neske, 1966], 133).

67. Schelling, *System of Transcendental Idealism* (1800), trans. Peter Heath (Charlottesville: University Press of Virginia, 2001), 5. All quotations in the remainder of this paragraph are taken from the same work, pp. 5–6.

ural science has a necessary tendency to render nature intelligent." So natural science shows that nature's highest goal is to become an object to herself in human reason "whereby nature first completely returns into herself." The second way is the way of transcendental philosophy, which makes the subjective "primary" and raises the question "how an objective supervenes, which coincides with it."

In the *System of Transcendental Idealism,* Schelling focuses on this latter question; philosophy of nature, or nature-philosophy, raises the former question. So the *System of Transcendental Idealism* is only one part of Schelling's philosophical system. This means that in his thought around 1800, his (still implicit) dealing with the ultimate why question is somehow divided: As he starts from knowledge as a unity of the subjective and the objective and as there are two ways of understanding this very unity, there are necessarily two basic sciences of philosophy. The important question, now, is whether there is an overarching unity of nature philosophy and transcendental philosophy. Schelling, to be sure, did not develop such a unity of these two basic sciences at the time (and from the philosophical position) in which he wrote the *System of Transcendental Idealism.* He even explicitly argues in the *System of Transcendental Idealism* that, so far as the depiction of the "parallelism of nature with intelligence" is concerned, "neither transcendental philosophy nor the philosophy of nature is adequate by itself; *both sciences* together are alone able to do it, though on that very account the two must forever be opposed to one another, and can never merge into one."[68] The key problem of this attempt at developing a system of philosophy lies exactly in this relation of the two sciences to each other. If the two sciences must "forever be opposed to one another," the system is essentially a dualistic system and thus does not fulfill the requirements for any all-comprehensive system, that is, that there is a unity of the system and only one main principle. So in the time in which Schelling wrote the *System of Transcendental Idealism* and in which he positioned transcendental philosophy and nature philosophy on the same level (and did not subject one to the other as, incidentally, he did in previous years when his nature philosophy was dependent upon his transcendental philosophy), the ultimate why question finds two different answers simply because there are two pri-

68. Ibid., 2.

maries, two unconditionals: the Ego, the subjective subject-object, and nature, the objective subject-object. This means that the question why there is anything at all and not rather nothing, is, strictly speaking, not answered, at least not as the *ultimate* why question.[69]

The answer would lie in a philosophy that unifies transcendental idealism and nature philosophy in a way that transcends the distinction of the subjective and the objective altogether and would thus be able to find a point of ultimate unity. Schelling, however, moved on and attempted to create such a philosophy in his philosophy of identity, which he would develop after the publication of the *System of Transcendental Idealism*. His starting-point, or basic principle, is now the absolute that lies beyond the division of subject and object and that leads Schelling to a philosophy of absolute identity of freedom and necessity, the subjective and the objective. Within the limits of this essay, we cannot examine Schelling's philosophy of identity and its intrinsic problems any further but must simply offer a few remarks that explain the subsequent development of Schelling's thought.

Even the philosophy of identity does not help Schelling in answering the ultimate why question. It even becomes increasingly difficult for Schelling to explain why there is anything rather than nothing. At this point of his thinking, the difficulty lies, not so much in finding the one basic principle, but in explaining how the relation between the absolute and the manifoldness of what is not absolute can be adequately understood. This problem led to a crisis in Schelling's thinking, so that he revised the foundations of it and finally supplemented what he would call his "negative" transcendental philosophy with a "positive" historical philosophy.[70] At this point, therefore, it is appropriate and possible to move on to discuss his later positive philosophy. In so doing, we will find a somewhat different answer to the ultimate why question, in which Schelling nonetheless does not abandon the claims of his early philosophy, namely that freedom is the beginning and end of philosophy.

---

69. For the limits of his own position around 1800 and the hidden new system "under the exterior of Fichtean thinking" in the *System of Transcendental Idealism,* see his *On the History of Modern Philosophy,* 111.

70. For his view of negative philosophy, see his *Einleitung in die Philosophie,* 30 and passim, and his *System der Weltalter,* 128ff. and passim.

IV. GOD AS "LORD OF BEING": SCHELLING'S LATER POSITIVE PHILOSOPHY

Schelling became increasingly aware of the limits of explaining reality and knowledge from within the transcendental-philosophical framework that he had developed in his early thought. To some interpreters it seems that he lost himself in his bold speculations about a distinction-free absolute that are characteristic of his philosophy of identity. After publishing *Of Human Freedom* in 1809,[71] Schelling did not publish a large amount any more. He seemed to struggle in his attempt to develop the system of philosophy, the *System of the Ages of the World*[72] and his later positive philosophy as outlined in his lectures on mythology and revelation, which some take to be the completion, others the self-limitation or even the overcoming and end, of German Idealism.[73]

Schelling's main critique of his early philosophy concerns its merely logical and unhistorical character. It is a philosophy of merely logical reasoning about *what* something is, but not a philosophy of that "of which one can merely say that it is."[74] It is also a philosophy, as Schelling argues, that has not yet taken God as its starting-point and center, as does his later "progressive" philosophy. He realized, however, that without taking God as a starting-point one could not possibly answer the ultimate why question. As he noted already in 1806, only God or "the All" could provide the answer to the question "why is there not nothing? Why is there anything at all?"[75] This answer to the ultimate why question, in

71. For a new English translation of this important work see F. W. J. Schelling, *Philosophical Investigations into the Essence of Human Freedom*, trans. and introduction Jeff Love and Johannes Schmidt (Albany: State University of New York Press, 2006).

72. For an English translation see F. W. J. Schelling, *The Ages of the World (Fragment)*, trans. Jason M. Wirth (Albany: State University of New York Press, 2000).

73. For this discussion see (with different positions on the question) Walter Schulz, *Die Vollendung des Deutschen Idealismus in der Spätphilosophie Schellings*, 2d ed. (Pfullingen: Neske, 1975); Thomas Buchheim, *Eins von Allem. Die Selbstbescheidung des Idealismus in Schellings Spätphilosophie* (Hamburg: Felix Meiner 1992); Snow, *Schelling and the End of Idealism*.

74. For this view, see Schelling, *System der Weltalter*, 18.

75. Schelling, *Aphorismen zur Einleitung in die Naturphilosophie*, SW I/7, 174: "Auf die Frage, die der am Abgrund der Unendlichkeit schwindelnde Verstand aufwirft: Warum ist nicht nichts, warum ist überhaupt etwas? Ist nicht das Etwas, sondern nur das All oder Gott die vollgültige Antwort. Das All ist dasjenige, dem es schlechthin unmöglich ist nicht zu sein, wie das Nichts, dem es schlechthin unmöglich ist zu seyn." See also his *System der gesammten Philosophie und der Naturphilosophie insbesondere* (1804), SW I/6, 155: "Die absolute Position der Idee Gottes ist in der That nichts anderes als die absolute Negation des Nichts, und so gewiß die

its reference to "the All or God," still betrays Schelling's somewhat Spinozistic philosophy of identity (be it pantheistic or rather panentheistic). But in its explicit emphasis upon God, it also shows, at least initially, the direction that Schelling would subsequently take. This is the way of a philosophy of God that acknowledges the freedom of God.[76] Given that he does not abandon his claim to develop a philosophy of freedom and even radicalizes his philosophy of freedom,[77] the answer to the ultimate why question that Schelling develops in his later philosophy still focuses on freedom. Freedom, however, is no longer the unconditional transcendental freedom of the Ego. It is God's freedom.

It is not simply that God now plays a much more prominent role than in his early philosophy; Schelling also understands God much more against the background of the biblical understanding of him as a historical and living God. He defines God as "Lord of Being" *(Herr des Seins),* thus claiming to do justice to the biblical understanding of God. What particularly comes into play here is Schelling's reading of Exodus 3:14. He knew that the translation of this key passage of the Judaeo-Christian understanding of God as "I am who I am" is problematic. Of course, it allowed Christian theologians to synthesize classical Greek metaphysics of Being with the biblical understanding of God. But in this translation, Schelling maintains, an important dimension of this divine self-predication was lost. For Schelling, however, rediscovering this dimension does not imply divorcing the biblical understanding of God from a philosophical understanding of God. It allows him to rethink philosophically his concept of God on the basis of, or at least with respect to, God's self-predication as "I am he who I will be," as Schelling translates Exodus 3:14.[78] This is for Schelling the true name of God. He consequent-

---

Vernunft ewig das Nichts negirt, und das Nichts nichts ist, so gewiß affirmirt sie das All, und so ewig ist Gott. Es gibt also auch keine Erkenntnis, als inwiefern die Idee von Gott ist; es gibt keine andere Erkenntnis, die zu dieser leitete, sondern erst nachdem diese absolute affirmirt ist, ist auch jede Erkenntnis affirmirt. Denn erst dann erkenn wir, dass nicht nichts ist, sondern dass notwendig und ewig das All ist."

76. Schelling's philosophy ultimately moves toward a philosophical religion. For this, see particularly Albert Franz, *Philosophische Religion. Eine Auseinandersetzung mit den Grundlegungsproblemen der Spätphilosophie F. W. J. Schellings* (Amsterdam: Rodopi, 1992).

77. For this and a further explanation of Schelling's philosophical claim, see his *Urfassung der Philosophie der Offenbarung,* 25–30.

78. See, for instance, his *System der Weltalter,* 136, and his *Urfassung der Philosophie der Offenbarung,* 88.

ly argues that only one "who can say: I will be who I will be, that is who I want to be—nothing is predetermined about my own being—nobody can determine what I will be—it depends only on my will" deserves the name "God."[79] God is free to be a creator or not, and if there is anything at all (as there is), this is the case because of God's free will to be a creator and thus to create.

Examining this divine self-predication further, Schelling is not only interested in why there is anything at all rather than nothing; he is interested in understanding philosophically also why there *is* God. He is looking for an ultimate "source of Being."[80] This is why Schelling developed a very radical philosophy of divine freedom. He is not simply arguing that God freely called things into existence out of nothing. He argues that God willfully called himself, his own Being *(Sein),* into existence because he is the one "who will be." What does this mean? Schelling calls the idea that "there is in Being—in the world—wisdom" the "first presupposition of philosophy": So "philosophy," as he argues, "presupposes a Being which already in the beginning develops with foresight, with freedom."[81] From the perspective of his historical philosophy, he cannot simply take Being, not even God's Being, as his starting-point. He requires a wisely and "intentionally posited Being"[82] and thus needs to explore the wisdom and intentionality behind or before Being.[83] God, according to Schelling, is free; freedom (and not Being) is the Godhead's highest. This means that God was free to be or not to be,[84] free to start a theogonic process or not to do so. For freedom requires that "the choice of Being is totally undetermined."[85]

This is how he understands the idea that God—"who will be"—is the Lord of Being[86] and that "something positive, will, freedom, action"

79. Schelling, *Urfassung der Philosophie der Offenbarung,* 89.
80. Ibid., 25.
81. Ibid., 23: "Die Philosophie setzt ein Sein voraus, welches gleich anfangs mit Voraussicht, mit Freiheit, entsteht."
82. Ibid.; see also 69.
83. See ibid., 23: "Die Philosophie will hinter das Sein kommen; ihr Gegenstand ist also nicht das Sein selbst, sondern das, was vor dem Sein ist, um eben das Sein zu begreifen."
84. For this idea see also ibid., 50–56.
85. Ibid., 89.
86. Schelling, *System der Weltalter,* 85: "Eine Philosophie ohne Positives die also nichts sezt und behauptet, kann nur definierend sein und empfiehlt sich bei allen die nichts Positives wollen."

needs to be presupposed in explaining the world.[87] There are, therefore, three main characteristics of his later positive philosophy. First, the existence of the world is not merely accidental and also cannot be understood through a mere necessity of thinking. Second, the existence of the world can be explained through a free *actus*, and this is why, third, the cause of the world organism is a free creator who stands in a free relation to Being.[88] This is, *in nuce*, the later Schelling's answer to the ultimate why question, which he now often explicitly raises and explores.[89]

Schelling's reference to Exodus 3:14 has already shown that in his later work he does claim to provide a deeper understanding of the very essence of Christianity. Schelling is very well aware of the difference between philosophy and theology. There are, however, close links between philosophy, as understood by Schelling at this time, and theology. According to the 1827/28 *System of the Ages of the World*, Christianity in its literal and historical sense must be the object of philosophy.[90] In this lecture series, Schelling does not argue, however, that Christianity equals reason; he is very keen on distinguishing his own thinking from Hegel's logical rationalism, which, as he has it, fails to take history in its reality seriously.[91] In contrast to Hegel, Schelling in the 1827/28 lectures considers himself a historical thinker and his philosophy a truly "Christian philosophy."[92] He takes as a basis of Christianity a system that continues from the beginning to the very end.[93] And it is the very task of his thinking, of the *System of the Ages,* to provide a *philosophical* account of this system that can only be a system of *freedom.*

So in developing his positive philosophy, Schelling claims to leave behind any kind of deterministic rationalism, as well as any kind of irra-

87. Schelling, *Einleitung in die Philosophie,* 13; see also his *System der Weltalter,* 17.

88. Schelling, *Einleitung in die Philosophie,* 21.

89. The limit on the length of this essay do not permit us to provide a sufficient account and critique of his later philosophy, so we limit ourselves to the heart, as it were, of his later answer to the ultimate why question. For the ultimate why question in Schelling's later philosophy, see particularly his *Einleitung in die Philosophie der Offenbarung oder Begründung der positiven Philosophie,* SW II/3, 7; 163ff.; 242; 270.

90. Schelling, *System der Weltalter,* 9: "Das Christentum in seiner Buchstäblichkeit und Geschichtlichkeit muß Gegenstand der Philosophie sein."

91. Ibid., 52f.

92. Ibid., 9: "Der eigentlich entscheidende Name für meine Philosophie, ist *christliche Philosophie* und dies Entscheidende habe ich mit Ernst ergriffen" (Schelling's emphasis).

93. Ibid.: "Meine Philosophie legt dem Christenthum ein System zu Grunde, das vom Anfang bis zum Ende dauern wird."

tionalism or dogmatism that does not strive for an understanding where understanding is very well possible. That there is anything at all rather than nothing is not a mere necessity, nor is what is caused by an unintentional emanation or efflux from God. It is a consequence of the free Divine decision, as it were, to be and to be as a creator. He thus claims to go beyond Hegel, his own early philosophy, and, even more, the whole history of modern philosophy. All previous philosophy is negative philosophy, a philosophy, therefore, that does not acknowledge the unpreconceivable *(unvordenklich)* act of freedom that cannot be (pre-)conceived prior to the event of it actually happening. From the position of negative philosophy, God is the necessarily existing being. God, then, is subject to a necessity, the necessity of his own existence. God, Schelling, realizes, is not only more than a moral world order (as Kant and the early Fichte would have argued).[94] He is also more than a necessarily existing being; he is the ultimate source and "Lord of Being."[95]

V. THE CHALLENGES OF SCHELLING'S PHILOSOPHY

Schelling's questioning of and answer to the ultimate why question stands within a long tradition. Of particular importance for Schelling may have been Leibniz, who raised this question in his *Principes de la nature and de la grace fondés en raison* (1714). In this short treatise, Leibniz argues that it is an important metaphysical principle *(grand principe)* that nothing happens without sufficient reason. On the basis of this principle, he further argues, we could ask the question why there is anything rather than nothing *(pourquoi il y a plus tôt quelque chose que rien)*.[96] Leibniz now concludes that the sufficient reason for there being anything at all rather than nothing does not need another reason, but must lie outside of the chain of contingent things. It can be found, he argues, in a

94. For Schelling's critique of a "moralized" notion of God, see his *Vom Wesen der menschlichen Freiheit*, SW I/7, 356.

95. This is a view, of course, that betrays not only the Christian, but also the continuous (Neo)Platonic dimension of Schelling's later thought.

96. G. W. Leibniz, *Principes de la nature and de la grace fondés en raison*, ed. André Robinet (Paris: PUF, 1954), § 7. See also G. W. Leibniz, *Monadologie*, ed. André Robinet (Paris: PUF, 1954), §§ 36ff. For Leibniz on the ultimate why question, see also Jaspers, *Schelling. Größe und Verhängnis*, 124; Martin Heidegger, "Einleitung zu, 'Was ist Metaphysik?'" (1949), in Martin Heidegger, *Wegmarken* (= Gesamtausgabe 9), ed. Friedrich-Wilhelm von Herrmann (Frankfurt am Main: Verlag Vittorio Klostermann, 1976), 365–83, at 381ff.

substance which is the reason, or cause, for the chain of things and in itself a necessary being *(un Être necessaire)* "that carries the reason for its existence in itself." This ultimate reason, he concludes his argument, is called God.[97] So Leibniz finds an answer to the ultimate why question that is, at first look, very similar to the later Schelling's answer. There are, however, important differences. For Schelling, God is not simply a necessary being. This, he thinks, would mean to subject God to the necessity of his own existence. God, Schelling thinks, must be thought to be free to be or not to be, for he, as free *causa sui,* is the Lord, the subject, as it were, of Being, not the object of the necessity of Being. In providing this answer to the ultimate why question, Schelling goes beyond Leibniz and opens up a new philosophical way of thinking about God and the question why there is anything at all rather than nothing.

Another important source and inspiration for Schelling's dealing with the ultimate why question was certainly also Immanuel Kant's thought. Schelling himself quotes a passage of Kant's *Critique of Pure Reason* in which Kant refers to the ultimate why question:[98] "The unconditioned necessity," Kant writes, "which we need so indispensably as the ultimate sustainer of all things, is for human reason the true abyss. Even eternity . . . does not make such a dizzying impression on the mind; for eternity only measures the duration of things, but it does not sustain that duration. One cannot resist the thought of it, but one also cannot bear it that a being that we represent to ourselves as the highest among all possible beings might, as it were, say to itself: 'I am from eternity to eternity, outside me is nothing except what is something merely through my will; but whence am I?' Here everything gives way beneath us, and the greatest perfection as well as the smallest, hovers without support before speculative reason, for which it could cost nothing to let the one as much as the other disappear without the least obstacle."[99] Schelling, too, experi-

---

97. G. W. Leibniz, *Principes de la nature and de la grace fondés en raison,* §8.

98. F. W. J. Schelling, *Einleitung in die Philosophie der Offenbarung oder Begründung der positiven Philosophie,* SW II/3, 163.

99. Immanuel Kant, *Critique of Pure Reason,* trans. and ed. Paul Guyer and Allen W. Wood (Cambridge: Cambridge University Press, 1998), 574 (A 641). For an implicit reference to the ultimate why question, see also Immanuel Kant, "The Only Possible Argument in Support of a Demonstration of the Existence of God," in Immanuel Kant, *Theoretical Philosophy 1755–1770,* trans. and ed. David Walford with Ralf Meerbote (Cambridge: Cambridge University Press, 1992), 124: "That, by means of which all possibility whatever is cancelled, is absolutely impossible, for the two expressions are synonymous. Now, to start with, the formal element

enced the force of this question and attempted to answer it in a way that Kant, one might imagine, might not have entirely approved, even though Kant emphasizes, as does Schelling, the divine will as ultimate source of all things. In his speculative philosophy of God, Schelling radicalizes the concept of God's will, or freedom, and claims to provide an answer to a question that even Kant could only raise but not answer.

The ultimate why question has struck philosophers ever since Leibniz, Kant, and Schelling raised it in explicit terms. It is Max Scheler who explores the existential experience of the "*possibility* of 'absolute nothingness'" which, he argues, then leads to the question "'why there is a world at all, why and for what reason am I at all?'"[100] Martin Heidegger also explicitly deals with this question in his later philosophy.[101] Following Heidegger, philosophers such as Bernhard Welte raised this question and gave it central significance in their thought about being and nothingness.[102]

The ultimate why question is a question that continues to puzzle, to fascinate, and to inspire thinkers up to our time. Schelling's attempt at an answer belongs perhaps among the most interesting and challenging answers. In dealing with the ultimate why question, it is impossible simply to go back to Schelling without being aware of the historical distance that separates us from his time and his thinking. It is not possible simply to revitalize his early negative philosophy or his later positive phi-

---

of all possibility, namely, agreement with the law of contradiction, is cancelled by that which contradicts itself. Hence, that which is self-contradictory in itself is absolutely impossible. This, however, is not the case where we have to consider the complete elimination of all existence. For, as we have proved, the complete cancellation of all existence whatever involves no internal contradiction. However, the means by which the material element, the data, of all that is possible is cancelled, is also the means by which all possibility itself is negated. Now, this is effected by the cancellation of all existence. Thus, when all existence is denied, then all possibility is cancelled as well. As a consequence, it is absolutely impossible that nothing at all should exist."

100. Max Scheler, *Die Stellung des Menschen im Kosmos*, ed. Manfred S. Frings, 15th ed. (Bonn: Bouvier Verlag, 2002), 88. Similarly Schelling, *Einleitung in die Philosophie der Offenbarung oder Begründung der positiven Philosophie*, SW II/3, p. 7: "Gerade er, der Mensch, treibt mich zur letzten verzweiflungsvollen Frage: warum ist überhaupt etwas? warum ist nicht nichts?"

101. See Martin Heidegger, *Einführung in die Metaphysik* (= Gesamtausgabe 40), ed. Petra Jaeger (Frankfurt am Main: Verlag Vittorio Klostermann, 1983); idem, "Was ist Metaphysik?" in Martin Heidegger, *Wegmarken* (= Gesamtausgabe 9), 103–22; idem, "Einleitung zu 'Was ist Metaphysik?'" (1949).

102. See Bernhard Welte, *Religionsphilosophie*, ed. Bernhard Casper and Klaus Kienzler, 5th ed. (Frankfurt am Main: Verlag Josef Knecht, 1997), 89ff.

losophy. But it is equally impossible to dismiss Schelling's contribution to an answer to the ultimate why question altogether. He still makes us think about the ultimate why question, and there are at least two insights that one should take very seriously. One concerns his emphasis on the significance of freedom; the other concerns his concept of God and his attempt to develop a concept of God that does justice to the Godly character of God, as it were, as a Being "than which nothing greater can be conceived." If there is a God, God can indeed not merely be a necessarily existing being, the God of many philosophers, but certainly not the God of Schelling.

Edward C. Halper

8 ∽ The Ultimate Why Question:
The Hegelian Option

The question posed in the title of this volume, "The Ultimate Why Question," is a venerable one that is usually understood to ask why there is something rather than nothing and answered by positing a highest cause, a transcendent God. The aim of this chapter is to introduce and explore an alternative interpretation of the question along with an answer that I ascribe to Hegel. Among other advantages, this alternative throws light on the more traditional approach to the problem. By the same token, the traditional account points up a difficulty in the Hegelian account. My strategy here is to set the one account against the other. To put the contrast briefly, whereas the traditional account moves to a higher level, the Hegelian account stresses interlinked comprehensiveness. The former account aims to discover the source of everything, the latter to explain everything.

I

Hegel often presents his philosophy as the culmination of a historical development. It is, therefore, appropriate to use the traditional account to justify Hegel's. The traditional account can be found in Plotinus, Aquinas, and Leibniz, among others, and it is motivated by a perceived deficiency in ancient philosophy. Ancient philosophers do not ask the ultimate why question. They are content to account for the way things are. Consider the following argument that appears at least twice in Aristotle:[1] A house or a human being has multiple material constituents that somehow form a unity. It is only when these constituents are unified that the house or person exists. Boards or bricks in a heap, for example, are not a house. There must be something that holds these material elements together, something that could hold any other collection of material elements into a single thing. If this unifier is itself another material element, it will be necessary to find something else that unifies it and the other material elements. If this new unifier is, again, a material element, we will need still another thing to unify it with the other material elements, and so on. Now there cannot be an infinite number of unifiers or we would never have unities. Since the only way to block the regress is to recognize that the unifier is something quite different from matter, something whose unity with matter does not need to be explained by anything else, there must be some non-material principle of unity. This principle is the form, and it unifies whenever it is present in matter.

Now it is clear that the composite of form and matter must come to be, but neither the form nor the matter could come to be *with* the composite, for if they were generated, each would need to come to be from something else, some matter, which matter must, again, come from something else, and so forth. In other words, if either matter or form is created in the creation of the composite, we again risk infinite regress.[2] Before it comes to be in some matter, the form must exist somehow in another composite. And that other composite acquires its form from still another composite. There is a claim that an infinite transfer of form is not possible without some eternal causal power to sustain it.[3] Aristotle calls this eternal agent the unmoved mover. In sum, what emerges from this account is that there must be an eternal first principle that sustains the temporal, finite beings.

What does *not* emerge is a way to account for the constituent principles of the composite that the first principle sustains. That is to say, plants and animals pass along their forms to their offspring, and the unmoved

1. *Metaphysics* VII, 17, 1041b11–33 (cf. 1041a26–32); *De anima* I, 5, 411b11–14.

2. *Metaphysics* VII, 8, 1033a24–b19.

3. Aristotle claims that the transfer of a torch in a relay race is a consecutive motion, not a continuous motion (*Physics* V, 4, 228a26–29). He argues later that, because motion is eternal, a series of things, the one moving the next, could not be sustained without some unmoved cause (VIII, 5). Motion is eternal because at least one thing is eternally moving, and it, in turn, is moved by something that is itself unmoved.

mover sustains reproduction. But the unmoved mover is not an explanation of what forms are passed along. The first principle sustains and orders. It does not explain why what is is what it is, rather than something else. Nor does it explain why there is what is rather than nothing at all. Aristotle's first principle is not an *ultimate* why principle.

Plato is in much the same position. The forms are the principles of everything, and everything not a form is whatever it is by imitating a form. So the world of non-forms is a world of things imitating forms in various degrees, some more than others. The Demiurge makes the cosmos by taking matter moving in a disorderly way and fashioning it so that it imitates the forms.[4] A good bit of the *Timaeus* aims to account for physical structures by showing how they imitate the forms.[5] While it is quite clever, what it shows is the rationality of the world; it crucially does not derive the world from the forms, for that would mean showing that *only* such a world could emerge from the forms. Anyway, because matter and form both exist before the world, neither the Demiurge nor the Good could be an ultimate cause.

Perhaps a better place to look for a Platonic ultimate cause would be the so-called unwritten doctrine, according to which everything derives from the one and the indefinite dyad.[6] Unfortunately, we do not have any texts from Plato or the Academy on the derivation, and it is unclear how they understood the derivation. The one passage from the *Parmenides* that is sometimes taken to present such a derivation suggests that Plato is concerned to show merely that the one is prior to and organizes what follows from it.[7] The unit is prior to any number and the latter is some con-

---

4. *Timaeus* 30A1–7.

5. This is the aim of the so-called "Works of Reason" section; see esp. *Timaeus* 29D7–40D5.

6. Aristotle ascribes to Plato the notion that the forms (or numbers) derive from the one and the indefinite dyad, and everything else from these forms and (again) the dyad (*Metaphysics* I, 6, 987b14–29). Since this view is not asserted in the extant dialogues, it is generally considered a reference to Plato's "unwritten doctrine." Anglo-American scholars have been skeptical that the doctrine is genuinely Plato's and, if it is, that it is significant. A group of German scholars, known as the "Tübingen School" arrive at the opposite conclusions. For a detailed discussion of their position see Hans Joachim Krämer, *Plato and the Foundations of Metaphysics: A Work on the Theory of the Principles and Unwritten Doctrines of Plato with a Collection of the Fundamental Documents,* trans. and ed. John R. Catan (Albany: State University of New York Press, 1990). For a brief, accessible, and excellent presentation from another member of this school see: Thomas A. Szlezák, *Reading Plato,* trans. Graham Zanker (London: Routledge, 1999).

7. *Parmenides* 142D. See R. E. Allen, *Plato's Parmenides: Translation and Analysis* (Minneapolis: University of Minnesota Press, 1983), 220, who asks whether the unlimited multitude that is

junction of units, but being prior and structuring hierarchies characterize organizing causes. Since the unit does not have agency, it cannot be an *ultimate* cause. The ancient Greeks recognize no *creatio ex nihilo*.

Once we see what Aristotle and other ancient philosophers did not explain, we can see the possibility of and need for an ultimate cause. Plotinus makes the One an ultimate cause by not only placing it at the top of a hierarchy but giving it agency. He tries to show how the succeeding levels emerge out of the One. In itself the One is not thinkable; it is beyond our knowledge. However, the One's first act as an agent is to think itself. In the process of thinking itself, One is both object thought and subject thinking. This duality is not simply One, but an entirely different level, the intellect. The intellect, in turn, becomes soul when it moves itself.[8] Whether these deductions are successful is, of course, a matter of debate. But the point is that for Plotinus the higher unity not only sustains and preserves the lower reality, but *generates* its substance. Let us look at it from the other direction. Start from any particular thing. To ask "why?"—that is, to seek its cause—is to seek a principle on a higher ontic level that is responsible for its existence. This higher ontic level owes its existence to something on a still higher level that is more of a unity, until ultimately there is the One itself that is the ultimate cause of everything else and is itself uncaused.

There are two important variations on this picture that I want to mention. The first is Thomas Aquinas, who discovered how to ask the ultimate why question in an Aristotelian context. What he needed was a principle that would be generative. His key move was to make Being *(esse)* be a higher level of actuality than form so that form could become a potential for reality; since this potential can be actualized only by something already fully actual, and since only the first principle is fully actual, the existence of everything depends on the first principle. Since it is responsible for being or existence, it is a creative principle.[9] Again, con-

---

generated from the one is a process or a product, that is, whether, the infinite is potential or actual infinite. He argues that it is actual (p. 224). That would exclude the passage's being a generation of parts.

8. This brief summary cannot possibly do justice to the richness of Plotinus' account. His discussions of emanation from the one occur in many places. One very brief account appears in *Ennead* V, 1, 1.

9. See St. Thomas Aquinas, *Summa Contra Gentiles*, trans. Anton C. Pegis (Notre Dame: University of Notre Dame Press, 1975), Book I, c. 16, par. 3, 5, 7.

sidered from the other direction, any composite will be held together by
its form, but that form cannot by itself explain the composite's existence.
For that, we need something on any entirely different level, a fully actual
causal agent. This latter is not the One, but a pure Being responsible for
the being of everything else.[10]

Still another variation is that of Leibniz. He begins with the perfection of the first cause. If it were not perfect, it would need another cause,
and thereby not be the first cause. Since, on the other hand, it is perfect,
whatever it produces is also the best possible of its type.[11] This is a very
simple move, but it has profound consequences. Plotinus and Thomas
Aquinas can account for the existence of anything by referring to a higher level and, ultimately, to the highest level. So if we ask them why there
is something rather than nothing, their answer is going to be that it derives from the first principle. Leibniz has this answer, but he also has a
more specific answer. Because the first principle is perfect, that of which
it is the principle must also be perfect, in its kind, to the extent possible. Hence, Leibniz answers the ultimate why question by referring to
the first principle, God, but also by referring to the perfection, within its
kind, of what is caused. That makes the ultimate cause of any X not only
God but God's perfection. Voltaire makes fun of Leibniz' assertion that
this is the best of all possible worlds because he thinks the world far from
perfect.[12] However, Leibniz does not rely on observation to measure perfection; rather, he infers perfection by a priori argument.

What is common to all three versions of the traditional approach to
the ultimate why question is the idea of explaining things by finding some
higher principle. The basic mode of reasoning starts from the existence
of some X and asks why X exists. We might be tempted to ascribe X's existence to some other thing; say, X's parents or the craftsman who made
X. But these answers could explain only why there is X instead of something else, Y: why there is this table instead of wood, nails and glue in a
heap. They do not explain why there is X rather than nothing at all. For

10. For a brief and clear statement of this point, see Thomas Aquinas, *On Being and Essence,*
2d ed., trans. Armand Maurer (Toronto: Pontifical Institute of Mediaeval Studies, 1968), 55–57.

11. G. W. Leibniz, "Discourse on Method," §§1–2 in Gottfried Wilhelm Leibniz, *Discourse
on Method and Other Essays,* ed. and trans. Daniel Garber and Roger Ariew (Indianapolis:
Hackett Pub. Co., 1991), 1–2.

12. Voltaire, *Candide and Other Writings* (New York: Modern Library, 1956), see esp. cc. 1,
3, and 6.

that, we need to move to a higher level, a level that can somehow generate X from nothing. That is to say, in order to give an *ultimate* cause for some thing, we need to justify not just its state or its form—that is what Aristotle was doing—but to explain why there is this rather than nothing, and that cannot be done by anything like the thing, because the existence of the cause would be equally problematic. The only apparent solution is to posit a higher level that makes the thing possible and is responsible for its existence. Clearly, this higher level cannot be subject to the same concerns about its existence—otherwise it too will require a cause, and we will not have given an ultimate answer to the ultimate question. And just as clearly, this higher level must be richer in being; it must be, to summarize the tradition, the highest one, the most real, and completely perfect.

II

My aim in developing this line of thought is to set the stage for Hegel. We can understand Hegel by reflecting on the traditional answer. The question we need to ask is, what is the connection between the thing explained and the higher level? I think this question catches us in a dilemma: On the one hand, we need to say that the higher, causal level *exists,* is *one,* and is *perfect.* Were it lacking any of these, the cause would require a still higher cause and, thus, not be an ultimate cause. Moreover, the cause must have these features in respect of itself. It follows that we do know something about the ultimate cause. On the other hand, it is clear that we cannot know the ultimate cause. The reason is that, first, everything we know is finite and delimited, but everything delimited has a cause. Hence, the ultimate cause, itself uncaused, would necessarily lack delimitation and thereby be beyond knowledge. Second, since the ultimate cause is itself uncaused, it cannot be like anything else in our world; since we know things by comparing them with what we experience, we cannot know the ultimate cause. Thus, we find ourselves in the uncomfortable position of denying that we know the first cause while insisting that that cause must, through its own nature, exist, be one, and be perfect.

This is not a new problem. It is confronted explicitly by Maimonides, Averroes, and Thomas Aquinas.[13] Their responses to it are well known; I

---

13. Moses Maimonides, *The Guide of the Perplexed,* trans. Shlomo Pines (Chicago: University of Chicago Press, 1963), Bk. I, c. 56, pp. 130–31. Maimonides is struck by the impossibil-

pass over the details here. Let me note only that all three think we need to recognize that the first cause is so different from what it causes that even the terms we apply to it cannot apply in the usual way.

This "solution," however, creates a new difficulty: the more grand and mysterious the first cause is, the less successful it is in accounting for what it causes. Ironically, it is just the cause's power of explaining everything that seems to render this cause less than enlightening. Because the first cause is responsible for *everything*'s being what it is, it explains nothing in particular. I think that Leibniz tacitly recognizes this difficulty; that is why he puts so much stress on God's perfection. He uses this perfection to infer that each substance contains within its concept everything that it will ever do and that will ever happen to it, and he derives the laws of mechanics from Divine perfection.[14] This is clever, and the completeness of individual substances nicely imitates the perfection of their ultimate cause. But even Leibniz does not try to deduce the states of an individual substance from the first cause. These states should follow, in principle, at least; but we cannot see how they could be derived. I want to suggest that it is the cause's elevated status, its complete separation from what it is supposed to explain, that renders it unable to account for the world in a sufficiently determinate way. The problem is not, as Voltaire thinks, that the world could not be the best of all possible worlds, but that knowing this about it tells us very little about why storms occur when and where they do or about very many other details in the world.

The issue can be posed as a dilemma: In order to be an ultimate cause, the first cause needs to be unlike what it causes; but if this cause is truly unlike the world, then we cannot know it. If we cannot know it, we are

---

ity of ascribing positive attributes to God and the necessity to ascribe such attributes to him in respect of his creation of the world. He holds that these apparently positive attributes should be understood as negative attributes, and that we should seek to know God through his actions; see c. 58, pp. 134–37.

Averroes, *Faith and Reason in Islam: Averroes' Exposition of Religious Arguments,* trans. Ibrahim Najjar, Great Islamic Writings (Oxford: Oneworld, 2001), 54–56, 75–77. Averroes' solution seems to be, much as Maimonides', to focus on God's actions in the world instead of divine attributes.

Like Maimonides, Thomas Aquinas, in his *Summa Contra Gentiles,* Bk. I, c. 14, par. 2–3, endorses knowing God by what he calls the method of "remotion" on the ground that this would allow us some knowledge of what is beyond our grasp. However, he also claims that it is possible to know divine attributes analogically through the effects God causes, Bk. I, c. 29, par. 2; c. 30, par. 2–3; c. 31.

14. Leibniz, *Discourse on Method and Other Essays.* See esp. §§13, 17.

unable to use it to explain the details of the world. In short, its very nature as ultimate cause renders it unable to be the ultimate cause. Another way to formulate the issue derives from asking whether the first cause is or is not knowable. If we can know it, it must be like us and therefore not ultimate; if we cannot know it, we cannot explain how it is responsible for the world as it is. Again, either we cannot explain how the cause acts as a cause, in which case we are in the dark about it, or we can explain how it acts, and it is among the finite knowables and not a transcendent first cause. In short, there is something fundamentally problematic about appealing to a transcendent cause. It either explains nothing or explains everything. Either we cannot know it, or we know it in the way we know everything else.

III

This difficulty is hardly unrecognized, but I will not discuss responses to it further. Instead, I want to talk, finally, about Hegel's move. There are two issues here. One is the knowability of the cause, and the other is the working of the causal relation. It is a contradiction to say that there is a cause that accounts for something but that we do not know this cause; for if we know that the cause is at work as a cause, then we *do* know the cause. Hegel does not avoid this contradiction; he embraces it—or so we can surmise even if he does not present his position in this way. The sticking point is the existence of a transcendent cause, but once we recognize that the cause cannot be determinately thought, we *are*, in some sense, grasping it: we understand this cause to be *indeterminate*. Hence, the problem for Hegel becomes: how does determinacy emerge from indeterminacy? This is his version of the question about the efficacy of a transcendent ultimate cause. But it is now posed differently because the starting point is indeterminate. The problem is how any causal relation could come from an indeterminate cause. Hegel's answer lies in his dialectic. Simply put, the indeterminacy's being indeterminate is the first vestige of determination.[15] Hegel does not himself present his starting point in quite this way, but he does make it clear that the first category

15. Georg Wilhelm Friedrich Hegel, *Wissenschaft der Logik. Erster Teil. Die Objektive Logik. Erster Band. Die Lehre vom Sein (1832)*, vol. 21 of *Gesammelte Werke*, ed. Friedrich Hogemann and Walter Jaeschke (Hamburg: Meiner, 1985), 68–69. [Hereafter: *WL* I, 68–69.] Georg

of his *Science of Logic,* Being, is tantamount to God.[16] I do not think it is accidental that he gives God the same name that Thomas Aquinas did. Hegel's Being, like Aquinas's, is simple and unlike everything else; it is "only like itself."[17] This connection is obscured because Aquinas presents Being as a cause, whereas indeterminate Being seems unable to cause anything. Indeed, at the start of the *Logic,* there is no proper causality. There is only Being, and it has no determination. But, again, its lack of determination is its determination; hence, its determination is Nothing. Insofar as Being is Nothing and the two are identical, the category of Becoming has emerged.[18]

What is important for now is not the detail of the dialectic but the fact that it represents an intelligible path from what serves as a cause to thing caused, a path in which the content of the thing caused emerges from the character of the cause. Again, Hegel solves the problem of the nature of the cause by insisting that the first cause be indeterminate but also knowable as such. This empty, indeterminate Being is properly counterposed to the full, perfect, and transcendent Being of Thomas Aquinas and the tradition. Because Hegel's Being is indeterminate, it admits of determination in a way that Aquinas's Being does not. Hence, Hegel can solve the problem of making a first principle's causality intelligible by having it determine itself. It is the self-determination of the cause that produces what is caused.

This solution comes with a heavy price: the cause, Being, cannot be an *ultimate* cause because it is not transcendent. In determining itself, it transforms itself, and any cause that is transformed in the act of causation cannot be ultimate. In transforming itself, Being generates a new category, which, in its turn, transforms itself into still another category. The entire *Science of Logic* is a kind of odyssey that reaches completion when the category's transformation is not a new category but exists fully within the transformed category. That is, the final category of the *Logic,* Absolute Idea, contains within itself the entire series of transformations through which it comes to be.[19] The categorial unfolding begun with in-

Friedrich Hegel, *Hegel's Science of Logic,* trans. A. V. Miller, Muirhead Library of Philosophy (London: Allen & Unwin, 1969), 82. [Hereafter: *SL* 82.]

16. *WL* I, 65; *SL* 78. The title of this section is "With What Must the Science Begin?"

17. *WL* I, 68–69; *SL* 82.

18. *WL* I, 68–69; *SL* 82–83.

19. See "The Absolute Idea," in Georg Wilhelm Friedrich Hegel, *Wissenschaft der Logik.*

determinate Being is completed in a category that is also Being but now fully determined with all the logical categories and the process of their entire unfolding.[20] But this completion is short-lived; for in attaining it, the Absolute Idea acquires a different sort of Being, one external to itself, and begins to unfold a second time, through Nature and Spirit, eventually to reach completion a second time.[21] The final category, Philosophy, includes within itself the entirety of the system. It is, Hegel holds, what Aristotle must have meant when he spoke of "God thinking himself"; more obviously it is God that makes himself material (incarnate), in order to return to himself.[22]

Hegel's first cause, Being, is not the ultimate cause, but that does not leave him unable to answer the ultimate why question. The answer comes not at the beginning of the unfolding, but at its end. The ultimate cause is the category that contains within itself the unfolding that constitutes the entirety of the system. This ultimate cause is not a transcendent creator, but the *comprehensive* creation. The final paragraph of Hegel's system, as he expounds it in the *Encyclopedia,* speaks of the idea of Philosophy that serves as a kind of middle term that unifies Nature and Mind, because the movement or development that constitutes Nature is also the action of cognition: "The eternal Idea, in full fruition of its essence, eternally sets itself to work, engenders and enjoys itself as absolute Mind."[23] Hegel concludes with a lengthy quotation from Aristotle's *Metaphysics* XII (1072b18–30) to the effect that God is eternally thinking of him-

Zweiter Band. Die subjektive Logik (1816), vol. 12 of *Gesammelte Werke,* ed. Friedrich Hogemann and Walter Jaeschke (Hamburg: Meiner, 1985), esp. 251 [hereafter: *WL* II, 251]; *SL* 841.

20. *WL* II, 252–53; *SL* 842–43.

21. That *Realphilosophie* is a second unfolding is explained in the closing paragraphs of the *Science of Logic.* Discussions of this passage and the second unfolding appear in Edward C. Halper, "The Logic of Hegel's *Philosophy of Nature:* Nature, Space and Time," in *Hegel and the Philosophy of Nature,* ed. Stephen Houlgate, SUNY Series in Hegelian Studies (Albany: State University of New York Press, 1998), 31–35, and Edward C. Halper, "The Idealism of Hegel's System," *The Owl of Minerva* 34 (2002): 19–58.

22. Georg Wilhelm Friedrich Hegel, *Enzyklopädie der philosophischen Wissenschaften im Grundrisse (1830),* vol. 20 of *Gesammelte Werke,* ed. Wolfgang Bonsiepen and Hans-Christiane Lucas (Hamburg: Felix Meiner, 1992), 569–72; Georg Wilhelm Friedrich Hegel, *Hegel's Philosophy of Mind: Being Part Three of the "Encyclopaedia of the Philosophical Sciences" (1830),* trans. A. V. Miller (Oxford: Clarendon Press, 1971), 213–15. See also Georg Wilhelm Friedrich Hegel, *Lectures on the History of Philosophy,* trans. E. S. Haldane (Lincoln: University of Nebraska Press, 1995), III, 546. I explain these remarks in the next paragraph of my text.

23. Hegel, *Enzyklopädie (1830),* 571; Hegel, *Hegel's Philosophy of Mind,* 314–15.

self and is thereby a living actuality. Again, Hegel means to say that the dialectical unfolding that constitutes the development of his system is, somehow, God manifesting Himself. Since God's nature is to manifest himself, this entire development is God thinking himself: "Philosophy in its development [is] the revelation of God, as He knows himself to be."[24] The final category of the system includes the entire system and, indeed, everything else.

The contrast between Hegel and the traditional answer to the ultimate why question could hardly be starker: (1) Hegel takes a cause to be ultimate because it is comprehensive; the traditional answer is that the ultimate cause is transcendent. (2) Hegel's ultimate cause comes at the end, the traditional one at the beginning. (3) Hegel's ultimate cause is the whole, and he aims to account for everything through the cause's interconnection with everything else; the traditional ultimate cause depends on finding a higher plane of reality that will account for the existence of everything on our level. (4) Hegel's comprehensive cause is transparently knowable; the traditional cause is unknowable by us except as far as it is a cause.[25]

Perhaps the simplest way to grasp the difference between the traditional perspective and Hegel's is to think of the disagreement between advocates of intelligent design and certain proponents of evolution. The former insist that the organization of the universe could only have come from an intelligent creator on a higher level; the latter that *all* organized structures can be explained by the operations of scientific laws on randomly distributed matter. This is a disagreement that cannot be resolved; for the comprehensiveness of the latter account seems to render intelligent design unnecessary, whereas proponents of intelligent design see comprehensiveness as itself an *organization* that needs a transcendent cause.

24. Hegel, *Lectures on the History of Philosophy,* III, 547.

25. Kant seems to have these contrasts in mind when he notes that the concept of "highest" is ambiguous, meaning either "supreme" or "perfect": Immanuel Kant, *Critique of Practical Reason,* trans. Lewis White Beck (New York: Macmillan, 1993), 116. The former is a transcendental condition (such as virtue), the latter a complete whole (like happiness). Kant combines virtue and happiness by an a priori postulate: the virtuous must be happy. But because there is no empirical connection between virtue and happiness, the postulate requires the further assumptions of God and of immortality. Kant sees no way to combine the two notions of "highest" other than by positing an ideal world. But because this completion is merely ideal, it remains distinct from the physical world we know empirically, a world governed by quite different laws.

My example is, however, a bit misleading because Hegel does not advance the comprehensive ultimate cause as a way to disable the hypothesis of God. On the contrary, he thinks the development just *is* God, as I said. Strangely, however, his notion of ultimate causality has become part of contemporary scientific thought, where it often serves an end he would never have endorsed. My concern here is with comprehensive causality as a general approach to ultimate why questions—not with the particular way this approach has been developed or the particular conclusions it has been used to support.

IV

There are, of course, many questions we could raise about the comprehensive account that Hegel advances, but it is more pertinent to our concerns here to consider comprehensive accounts generally. The beginning is always going to be an issue. The usual strategy is simply to posit some starting points and proceed to show that they can account for everything. This is how Lucretius develops his atomism: there are atoms and void, and everything else can be explained through them.[26] Evolutionary biologists take the same tack. Starting assumptions are taken to be justified retrospectively through their success. The real justification lies at the end: it is the power to account for everything that the comprehensive account usually relies upon.

In scientific contexts, the hypothesis that is most powerful is accepted, provided there are no contrary considerations. But, then, the aim of science is not to find an ultimate cause. Just how comprehensive could its account be if it does not deduce its own starting points? Or, to put it differently, any account that begins from an arbitrary assumption is not comprehensive unless it also accounts for its initial assumptions. If this is right, then any comprehensive account must be circular in some way. Once we see this, our appreciation of Hegel's beginning must increase; for he avoids merely positing assumptions as Lucretius and modern science do. Hegel begins with Being, but a Being that is without any determination. Such a Being is Nothing, and it is as if the starting point is

---

26. Lucretius, *On the Nature of the Universe*, trans. R. E. Latham (Middlesex, England: Penguin, 1970), 39.

Nothing. Suppose, on the other hand, that Being had been determinate, full instead of empty. We could still ask about this determinate Being, why does it exist rather than nothing? It must derive its determination either from a higher Being or from itself. In the former case, Being is not ultimate and, to avoid regress, we need a transcendent cause. In the latter, Being's determination is responsible for itself, and we again face the problem of explaining why it generates other things and how it could account for the specific determinations in the world. The nice feature of Hegel's indeterminate beginning is that there is obviously no need to account for its determinations: no need to explain why it exists in the way that it does, for it does not exist in any particular way. It is just Being. Lacking determination, it is Nothing. That Being is Nothing also seems to obviate the need to seek a higher cause. Nor need Hegel account for Being's existence, for surely Being must be. Moreover, the completion of the system constitutes a kind of recovery of this Being. Initially, Being is reflexive insofar as it is "only like itself," but by the end Being is the reflexivity of thought thinking itself. If there is a higher cause of Being, it would seem to be Being itself as fully unfolded.[27]

One question we should raise is whether this fully unfolded categorial system is truly comprehensive. As I have suggested here, there are really two unfoldings. The first encompasses all the logical categories, the second, what Hegel terms *"Realphilosophie,"* produces Nature and Spirit in succession before returning to itself. Nature includes Space, Time, the laws of Newtonian mechanics, and much else; Spirit includes all living things. This is a remarkable achievement, but Hegel does *not* derive particulars. He speaks of the "impotence of Nature" that allows its concept to deduce only abstractions and leaves "detailed specification to external determination."[28] This may suggest that particulars will always escape philosophical knowledge. However, this discussion makes clear that Hegel also thinks that the distinction between particulars and kinds be-

27. At the end of the *Science of Logic*, Hegel declares that the Absolute Idea itself is a "pure concept that relates itself only to itself; it is therefore the *simple self-relation* that is *Being*. But it is now also *fulfilled Being*, the *concept that comprehends* itself": WL II, 252; SL 842 (translation revised slightly). The very last sentence of the *Logic* claims that this self-comprehending concept completes itself when it finds in the science of spirit the supreme concept of itself. This supreme self-relation seems to be yet another recovery of Being.

28. See Hegel's "Remark" to §250, Hegel, *Enzyklopädie (1830)*, 240–41; Georg Wilhelm Friedrich Hegel, *Hegel's Philosophy of Nature: Being Part Two of the "Encyclopaedia of the Philosophical Sciences" (1830)*, trans. A. V. Miller (Oxford: Clarendon Press, 1970), 23–24.

longs somehow to the concept of Nature. It follows that Nature knows that it does not know particulars. In this respect, particulars would seem parallel to a transcendent cause, according to the notion of the latter I have ascribed to Hegel; and if he thinks that even such a cause can somehow be grasped, then there is hope of eventually deriving particulars. Indeed, famously challenged to deduce Herr Krug's pen, Hegel indicates that Philosophy of Nature has more important things to do—not that it would be impossible.[29] Hegel gives a quite interesting derivation of body and matter from his logical categories, as I argue elsewhere.[30] So, that Hegel does not derive everything is not in itself problematic

A more serious problem for Hegel arises from his dialectic. He consistently uses some form of self-relation as the motor principle of his dialectic: he derives one category from another by showing that the category stands in some relation with itself or with another category.[31] The relation adds content to the category, transforming it into another category. This type of process can work only if the category belongs to *thought*. One thought determination is transformed into another by further thinking that expands its content, and only a thought can be transformed merely by thinking.

Hegel is, after all, an idealist. On the one hand, the scope and power of his idealism is truly impressive. On the other, the recognition that his entire philosophy is a determination of *thought* raises exactly the sort of question that the traditional ultimate cause is supposed to resolve: why is there any thought at all? The comprehensive structure of the Hegelian categories, that is, their self-contained development that fulfills and attains itself—in short, all that makes the Hegelian system so attractive—makes the question of its ultimate origin all the more pressing. And that origin cannot be in thought—because thought completes itself in the system. That is to say, the very virtue of the comprehensive cause as the ultimate cause of everything—a virtue that is most readily seen in a system like Hegel's where the development is internal and the connections between stages so strong—makes the comprehensive cause bear the organization that requires a transcendent cause.

29. Hegel, *Philosophy of Nature*, 23 n.
30. Edward C. Halper, "A Tale of Two Metaphysics: Alison Stone's Environmental Hegel," *Bulletin of the Hegel Society of Great Britain*, no. 51/52 (2005): 1–12.
31. Halper, "The Idealism of Hegel's System," esp. 26–28, 50.

Hegel's version of comprehensive causes is designed to skirt to this conclusion. The system is supposed to be self-generating and self-sustaining, the cause of its own existence. The link between beginning and end is supposed to tie the system together so as to avoid the need for an external cause. It is Being's self-determination that begins the process that culminates at the end of the system with a richly differentiated Being that is its own unfolding. Hegel's version of self-caused Being avoids the central objection to a transcendent self-caused Being, the problem that we cannot understand how this cause either sustains itself or generates the world. Hegel's system sustains itself through thought thinking; he speaks of the world as God, that is, thought engaged in this thinking. When we work through the processes of categorial unfolding that constitute his system, we also participate in sustaining the world. However, it is precisely the system's being self-sustaining that also calls the system into question. The problem here is not that we can find a thought or a cause that falls outside of the system, but that we recognize that *thought* itself needs to be accounted for as much as anything else. The tight interconnectedness of thought does not allay our concerns: it exacerbates them. If Hegel counts even what is other than thought as thought, then he can allow nothing but thought. Why, then, does *thought* exist? It does not suffice to answer that the categories are all modes of Being and that Being must surely be (= exist); for, insofar as they are categories, they belong to thought. In short, Hegel's system ties thought so tightly together that it forces us to ask for its cause.

To recap, I have been describing two notions of ultimate causes here along with their attendant difficulties. According to the first notion, the ultimate cause is a transcendent reality that is supposed to account for why there is something rather than nothing, inasmuch as existence somehow flows from its higher level of reality to the lower levels on which everything else resides. The first difficulty we saw with this approach is that, in order to account for the reality of everything, the cause needs to exist *beyond* the faculty of thought because the things whose existence it causes can be thought and because it needs to account for thought; but the cause cannot exist beyond thought, for it must itself be thought in order to be recognized as the cause, and we do, indeed, recognize it as the cause. The second attendant difficulty with this approach is that insofar as the higher level accounts for every other being's *existence*, it does not also account for its *nature*. According to the second notion of ultimate cause, a cause is ultimate if it is completely comprehensive. This is Hegel's approach, and he argues that the whole of reality unfolds, through categorial self-determination, from indeterminate Being into a category of Being that somehow includes this entire unfolding within itself. We saw that the difficulty with this approach is that, insofar as all things are connected with each other, they have an order and structure that unifies them into a whole, but to account for each thing in the whole through other things in the whole is not to account for the *existence* of the whole. Even though the whole is the category of self-related *Being*, we cannot take its existence (being) for granted because it is also a comprehensive whole of thought.

To put the dichotomy between the two types of causes more forcefully, we could say that whereas the transcendent cause fails to be comprehensive and to account for everything or to account for any particular nature, the comprehensive cause, in accounting for all things through each other, fails to explain why the well-structured whole should exist. The more the latter cause succeeds at weaving all things into a tightly knit whole, the more compelling the question, why does this whole exist rather than nothing?

V

The obvious solution to the dilemma is to look for an account that is both transcendent and comprehensive. Why not simply say that there are two primitive ultimate causes? The objection is that, on the one hand, the transcendent account cannot in principle explain the details of the created universe; so that the transcendent cause never produces a comprehensive effect. A comprehensive account, on the other hand, must always omit the transcendent cause and can therefore never be truly comprehensive.

Still, I want to mention very briefly two philosophers who seem to me to attempt this kind of reconciliation.[32] The first, Spinoza, shares with

32. Kant, too, recognizes both types of ultimate causes, as I mentioned in note 25. I do not discuss him here because, first, these causes play a role in his practical philosophy. As far as his theoretical philosophy goes, Kant does balance a *transcendental* principle, the transcendental unity of apperception, against an assumption that the four groups of categories constitute a

Hegel the ideal of a single fully comprehensive system, but he also insists that the first principle is transcendent. Thus, God is the cause of himself, but because God is the only substance, God also contains and causes everything.[33] Although there is only one cause, what we actually get is two types of causality. On one hand, everything follows from the nature of substance, that is, the nature of God, and is, as such, necessary: God acts upon Himself, God is the only possible source of agency, and God acts from the necessity of His nature.[34] On the other hand, the world arranges and rearranges itself into finite modes, and it is these modes, acting on each other, that cause the next arrangement of modes. Any state of substantial modes is a consequence of the immediately preceding state. Spinoza argues that a particular arrangement of modes cannot follow from the "absolute" nature of substance because that nature is eternal and infinite, and what follows directly from this nature must also be eternal and infinite.[35] In other words, God is responsible for everything, but the particular determinations, the modes, are caused more directly by other particulars. There are, in effect, two causal tracks. Spinoza *starts* with a traditional account, in which God is the transcendent cause that explains why there is something rather than nothing; but the last three books of the *Ethics* are about modes causing other modes and the position of particular modes in respect of the whole. Hence, he *ends* with a comprehensive account. By including the transcendent cause together with everything it causes within a single substance, Spinoza should be in a good position to reconcile the opposition of the two types of ultimate causes. But he is no more able to connect these causes than anyone else.

Another philosopher who is aware of both ultimate causes is Thomas Aquinas. The transcendent cause is most prominent in his philosophy, as I have noted. But there is also evidence of the comprehensive cause.

---

comprehensive, a priori basis for all knowledge. However, inasmuch as the categories are ways of bringing cognition to the unity of apperception, the two types of principles are not opposed, and the categories are not truly comprehensive.

33. *Ethics* IP14–16 (= Book I, Propositions 14–16); Benedictus de Spinoza, *A Spinoza Reader: The "Ethics" and Other Works*, trans. E. M. Curley (Princeton, NJ: Princeton University Press, 1994).

34. God is the efficient cause acting (*Ethics* IP25), but there is only one substance on which he can act, namely, himself. Hence, everything that comes to be follows necessarily from his nature (IP29 with the Scholium).

35. *Ethics* IP28. Spinoza explains the difference between acting and being acted upon in the first three propositions of part III, and this book explores the causality of modes on other modes.

Recall the opening of the *Summa Contra Gentiles*: the first mover of the universe is intellect, and the ultimate end of the universe is the good of the intellect, namely truth.[36] That is to say the universe comes from God in order that it or, rather, *we* can attain to knowledge of God. To use Hegel's language, this is a cause that makes itself other in order to return to itself. The entire universe comes from God; but here, in contrast with Spinoza's account, God and universe are distinct. Still, the gap between the transcendent cause and comprehensive effect remains: we cannot grasp how the transcendent cause can account for the particulars, and any account of the causal mechanisms among particulars leaves out the transcendent cause and so fails to be comprehensive.

One way out of the dilemma is to accept what Aquinas calls the "two-fold truth."[37] Truths about God's nature are beyond natural reason, and they must be taken on faith; whereas we can know God's existence and unity as well as other characteristics that must be attributed to Him. The latter knowledge arises from our understanding of the sensible world. It is just this comprehensive knowledge of a whole that is unable to account for itself that leads us to posit a higher cause. But, as we saw, this higher cause is not, to us, intelligible in itself nor, consequently, can we use it to account for the specific details of the universe.[38] Aquinas holds that God's nature is revealed in Scriptures and this nature accounts for the character of the world. In effect, then, the doctrine of two-fold truth connects the transcendent God with the comprehensively caused world by religious faith. Considered from the point of view of natural reason, the doctrine constitutes an acknowledgment of the problem of reconciling the two types of ultimate causes.

We should hesitate before embracing this path, whatever its merits, in order to give due consideration to the problem it is designed to resolve and, thereby, to learn what the problem has to teach us. The transcendent ultimate cause makes possible the existence of material things as well as our ability, such as it is, to think about them. We are really talking about

36. St. Thomas Aquinas, *Summa Contra Gentiles*, Bk. I, c. 1, par. 2.

37. Ibid., Bk. I, c. 3, par. 2–3, pp. 63–64.

38. Ibid., 64, expresses the point clearly: "Those things that do not fall under the senses cannot be grasped by the human intellect except in so far as the knowledge of them is gathered from sensible things. Now, sensible things cannot lead the human intellect to the point of seeing in them the nature of the divine substance; for sensible things are effects that fall short of the power of their cause."

existence. That is why the transcendent cause is the ultimate answer to the question, why is there something rather than nothing? It is also why this type of cause falls down when we get to the "what?" question in respect of what it causes. Nor can we explain why it, perfect and self-sufficient, generates other things. The comprehensive cause, on the other hand, is fundamentally an answer to the "what?" question, especially in Hegel's hands. The presumption is that if we can answer every "what?" question, there will be no need of, and no possibility for, asking the question of existence. For even when the comprehensive cause is generating all those other things or, as Hegel might say, unfolding itself and returning to itself, it cannot account for why they exist. Thus, the distinction between these ultimate causes is, at its root, a distinction between an ultimate "what?" and an ultimate "whether?" And the dichotomy for us is our inability to answer both questions adequately together. To be sure, we may not be able to answer either question, but I have tried to show here that we certainly cannot answer both.

Faced with this choice, which ultimate cause should we choose? Or should we seek something else altogether? Why, indeed, should we seek an ultimate cause at all? Clearly, this is not like looking for a cause of cancer or of the weather. There is no practical benefit here. We can only be seeking knowledge. Ironically, though, to speak of an ultimate cause is not very helpful as far as knowledge goes—it gives us a name without much real content. Turn the question around: what is it about the world that makes us seek ultimate causes? First, things do not *exist* from themselves. They cannot be the source of their own being. Second, things are not *what* they are from themselves. Hence, we rely on external principles for a thing's nature and existence. But just what do these principles add? There is a fundamental mystery that we are seeking to explain. One way to explain it is to link things together with each other: to account for one thing through another. This path is fundamentally circular. The other way is to invoke a cause that exists on an entirely different level. Perhaps what is most interesting for us is that neither path can resolve the most fundamental mystery and that ultimately all explanations are inadequate. We can say that the ultimate cause of our seeking ultimate causes is the fundamental mystery of world, the world's not being self-sufficient. This, I propose, ought to count as the ultimate cause; for whatever other causes we posit, construct, or discover, they will not undo this ultimate cause.

Part Four

Contemporary Contributions

9 ∽ Some Contemporary Theories of Divine Creation

Conceptions of God can be classified conveniently into two rough sorts, those that conceive God as a determinate entity, and those that conceive God as the ground of being, not a determinate entity within or along-side the world.[1] The intellectual strategy of classifying conceptions is by no means innocent. Perhaps no individual thinker fits the classifications exactly, and to treat a philosopher as falling into a classification scheme is to obscure those elements of the philosophy that do not register in the scheme.[2] Nevertheless, a classification scheme can help sort out certain elements of the logic of conceptions, which is the purpose here.

The determinate-entity conceptions allow ready personifications with anthropomorphic images from popular scriptures; these conceptions are represented with extraordinary philosophical precision in our time by process theology. The ground-of-being conceptions sort into a

---

1. The classification of theologies into determinate-entity and ground-of-being conceptions has been developed recently in these terms by Wesley J. Wildman; see his "Ground of Being Theologies" in *The Oxford Handbook of Religion and Science*, ed. Philip Clayton (Oxford: Oxford University Press, 2006). This distinction in my own way of thinking was first elaborated in my *God the Creator: On the Transcendence and Presence of God* (Chicago: University of Chicago Press, 1968; revised edition with a new introduction, Albany: State University of New York Press, 1992). That book divides theories of Being-itself into those that conceive being to be determinate and those that conceive it to be indeterminate. The phrase "ground of being" derives from the extensive work of Paul Tillich.

2. The moral of this point is that the remarks about philosophers in this paper should not be taken as my serious commentary about thinkers such as Aquinas, Plotinus, Tillich, or Whitehead (whom I have discussed with my analysis of their texts in other places) but rather as illustrative of the classification logic.

further subdivision: fullness-of-being conceptions and *ex nihilo* conceptions.

Fullness-of-being conceptions, such as found in Neoplatonism and Thomism, and perhaps Kyoto School Buddhism, conceive God or the Ultimate to be beyond finite determinateness, and hence indeterminate in a strict sense by virtue of simplicity and by having no contrast term.[3] As the pure fullness of reality, God is conceived to create the world by some kind of diremption or introduction of negation that finitizes elements of the fullness of being, *creatio a deo*.[4] Although strictly speaking indeterminate, the objects of the fullness-of-being conceptions are sometimes thought to possess, in an eminent and infinite way, some characters such as goodness, unity, and beauty that apply determinately to finite things; Thomas Aquinas's theory of the analogy of being develops one logical way of attributing determinate characters (the transcendentals) to a God conceived to be intrinsically indeterminate or simple.

Ex nihilo conceptions of God as ground of being claim that God is the creative act that gives rise to the world, and also in so doing gives rise to the divine nature as creator. Apart from creating, God has no determinate nature, nor an indeterminate eminently full nature, although the act of creating itself determines a divine nature. Symbolizing the act of creation as will, it is sometimes said that the divine will determines the divine nature, a claim made about Duns Scotus in contrast to Thomas Aquinas (for whom the divine nature determines the divine will).[5] Radical Orthodox theologians such as John Milbank read this glorification of will as the root of all evil in modern thought that inevitably leads to nominalism.[6] Nevertheless, I believe the *ex nihilo* ground-of-being conceptions to be the best hypothesis in our current situation, and I do not

3. In Buddhist rhetoric, the ontological ground is absolutely full nothingness. See, for instance, Keiji Nishitani's *Religion and Nothingness,* trans. Jan van Bragt (Berkeley: University of California Press, 1982).

4. One of the most exacting discussions of diremption or contraction is by Paul Weiss, in his *Modes of Being* (Carbondale: Southern Illinois University Press, 1958), 505–6.

5. Scotus, of course, is far too subtle to be summarized adequately in a slogan about the priority of divine will or nature. He argues that God's will and nature are identical, but that the nature is of the character of an act of will intrinsically defined by a final cause. See, for instance, his *Opus oxoniense* 1, dist. 2, question 1; this is translated by Allan Wolter, O.F.M., in his *Duns Scotus: Philosophical Writings* (London: Thomas Nelson, 1962), 35–81.

6. See John Milbank's *Theology and Social Theory: Beyond Secular Reason* (Oxford: Blackwell, 1990), 14, 423–26.

think that Scotus' realistic theory of common natures, expressed in modern form by philosophers such as Charles Peirce, necessarily reduces to nominalism.[7]

Another way of distinguishing the fullness-of-being from the *ex nihilo* ground-of-being conceptions is to say that the former conceive God or the Ultimate as symmetrical, the latter as asymmetrical.[8] Symmetry symbolizes wholeness, completeness, that which is settled completely in itself, and to which reference is made in explaining other things. Mathematicians resonate with the sensibility that when you have everything in equilibrium, in balance, nothing more needs to be said. Asymmetry in this context symbolizes the arbitrariness of will, the fact that the divine act of creation produces a particular singular world, and is itself singular. The intellectual piety of symmetrical conceptions fosters a repose of mind. The intellectual piety of asymmetrical conceptions fosters a restless inquiry, an empirical questioning to find out just what world God creates, and what God as creator does and is in particular. The symmetrical views have the problem of understanding how a symmetrical ground of being can break symmetry to create an asymmetrical world. The asymmetrical views, by contrast, expect an asymmetrical world and have the problem of explaining how natural selection eliminates unreinforced elements so as to leave the vast regularity and stability that the world exhibits. As the appeal of symmetry is to mathematicians, the appeal of asymmetry is to artists and humanists for whom the thisness, the Scotistic *haecceity,* if you will, of a complex singular universe exhibits the most dense and valuable reality.

In what follows I shall remark first on process theology's conception of God as an example of the determinate-being sort, arguing against that conception. Then I shall develop the contrast between the fullness-of-being and *ex nihilo* ground-of-being conceptions, arguing for the latter conception. The *ex nihilo* conceptions need further technical development, which I shall sketch along the way. Finally I shall remark on some of the implications for spiritual life of the different conceptions.

7. See John Boler's *Charles Peirce and Scholastic Realism* (Seattle: University of Washington Press, 1963). Peirce would agree with Milbank that nominalism is a bad philosophy—in fact, the root of nearly all error in Western philosophy.

8. I owe this use of the distinction between symmetry and asymmetry to Wesley J. Wildman.

I. PROCESS THEOLOGY

Process theology is greatly to be revered in our time because it derives from the ground-breaking work of Alfred North Whitehead, who demonstrated against a powerful Kantian tradition that metaphysics is both possible and necessary in this age of modern science.[9] Although it was Charles Peirce who formulated the anti-Kantian argument that metaphysics is hypothetical, it was Whitehead who worked out a detailed system illustrating that.[10] Kant confused the valid point that metaphysics is about ontological foundations with the invalid point that metaphysics itself needs to be foundational, that is, certain and apodictic. Metaphysics needs only to be the development and defense of hypotheses about ontological foundations. This is what Whitehead did. The argument from *esse* to *posse* is a fine argument.

Whitehead conceived God to be an everlasting actual entity that prehends every finite actual entity as soon as it becomes definite, and that supplies initial aims to each emerging finite actual occasion to guide its transition from subjective unity to subjective harmony; the technical details of this conception are not germane to my present argument. An interesting contrast Whitehead saw between finite actual entities and God is that the latter is infinite in its conceptuality but finite in that all its actuality is prehended from the particular states of the world moment by moment.[11]

A difficulty was noticed in Whitehead's conception early on, namely, that because God is conceived never to finish and hence never to be definitely actual, there is no way in which finite actual entities can prehend God. Unlike finite entities, which finish their coming-to-be in order to be prehended subsequently, God never finishes coming-to-be and hence is unavailable as something actual and definite to be prehended. Less ob-

9. Whitehead's great work on God is *Process and Reality: An Essay in Philosophical Cosmology*, rev. edition, ed. David Ray Griffin and Donald Sherburne (New York: Free Press, 1978). See also his *Religion in the Making* (New York: Macmillan, 1926).

10. For both conceptual and historical analyses of this point regarding Peirce and Whitehead, see my *The Highroad around Modernism* (Albany: State University of New York Press, 1992), chs. 1–2, 6.

11. Whitehead's most succinct statement of his theology is in part 5 of *Process and Reality*, although the technical discussions of God's interactions with finite actual entities run throughout the book.

viously, God can never finish prehending one finite actual occasion so as to be able to move on to another—the order of time cannot be quite real within God.[12]

Charles Hartshorne addressed this difficulty with an alternative, though closely related, conception of God.[13] For Hartshorne, God is a society of actual entities, each of which has finite duration, and each allowing of being prehended when definite and able to pick up on the things that have occurred since the previous divine actual entity prehended its world. This neatly solves Whitehead's problem. But it occasions its own difficulty. No guarantee exists that a divine actual entity within the society will be succeeded by another divine entity. Each divine entity is conditioned by absolute metaphysical requirements, but those requirements need an actual entity within which to reside, according to process philosophy. No overarching entity holds those metaphysical requirements over the transition from an earlier to a later member of the divine society, the very point that prompted Whitehead to make everlasting the single actual entity God, so as to embrace all dates of temporal actual entities within God's absolute primordial eternal nature. It does not help to say that an emerging divine entity prehends the metaphysical requirements from its predecessor, because the prehender has the freedom to negatively prehend them.

These issues have been debated in great detail, with many imaginative variations. Lewis Ford, for instance, has altered the process view to say that God is the reality of the future, constantly framing possibilities for emerging actual entities.[14] Joseph Bracken has been perhaps the most imaginative in developing a Trinitarian process theology based on the idea of societies of Persons.[15] I want to lodge an objection to all the process theological conceptions of God as a determinate entity, however,

12. I have discussed these and other difficulties in *Creativity and God: A Challenge to Process Theology* (New York: The Seabury Press, 1980; new edition, Albany: State University of New York Press, 1995).

13. His classic statement is in *The Divine Relativity* (New Haven, CT: Yale University Press, 1948).

14. See Lewis S. Ford, *Transforming Process Theism* (Albany: State University of New York Press, 2000).

15. Joseph A. Bracken, S.J., has worked with great imagination to alter process theology to get around these difficulties. See, for instance, his *The One in the Many: A Contemporary Reconstruction of the God-World Relationship* (Grand Rapids, MI: William B. Eerdmans, 2001), or *The Divine Matrix: Creativity as Link between East and West* (Maryknoll, NY: Orbis, 1995).

and my objection is based on an argument about the one and the many.

In process thought, any complex thing, from a single actual entity to an organic society of societies of actual entities to relatively unorganized adventitious meetings of trajectories of processes, is to be understood by identifying the decision-points that have gone into their constitution. A decision-point—that is my language—is where an act of creativity adds some novelty that resolves the things prehended into a new definite actual harmony. Each emerging actual entity has its own subjective decision-point, but then each thing prehended has its own objectified subjective decision-point, and so on *ad infinitum*. Whitehead called this the "ontological principle."[16] One of its consequences is that, whereas the metaphysical *principles* of process philosophy capture the intellectual impulses of rationalism, the need to understand particular things by looking to find their salient decision-points captures the intellectual impulses of empiricism. Whitehead recognized the singularity of the universe and developed a cosmology to understand things in their singularity as well as to express the general summary patterns of our cosmic epoch.

Now, the basic metaphysical situation, according to process philosophy, is that God and the world are bound in processes of interaction governed by the metaphysical principles. The most abstract statement of this situation (prescinding from the distinction between God and world) is the Category of the Ultimate; the more fleshed out statement is the philosophical cosmology itself as detailed in *Process and Reality*.[17] This is a complex metaphysical situation, God interacting with world. Therefore, the ontological principle would oblige us to ask what decision or decisions constitute that complex situation. Whitehead did not ask that question, deferring instead to the myriad decisions of entities within the metaphysical situation.

Should we not say, to repair this lack, that there must be an ontological decision-point of creativity that constitutes the complex basic metaphysical situation? This ontological creative act must be singular, because the difference between multiplicity and unity arises only with the creation of the basic metaphysical situation. The ontological creative act must be eternal, because time and its unfolding are among the cre-

16. See *Process and Reality,* 24–26 and *passim.*
17. For the Category of the Ultimate, see *Process and Reality,* 21–22.

ated elements of the basic metaphysical situation; and it must be immense or non-spatial, because spatiality is similarly created.[18] Decision-points within the metaphysical situation can be called cosmological because they are governed by the metaphysical strictures of the philosophical cosmology; the decisive creative act of the basic metaphysical situation can be called ontological, by contrast. Whereas cosmological decision-points employ prehended antecedent actual entities and integrate them into new definite entities by adding novel elements, the ontological decision-point has no antecedents and thus creates total novelty. The ontological decision-point creates *ex nihilo*. The analogy between finite actual entities and the ontological decision-point, which I would call God, in preference to the troubling concept that process theology calls "God," is positive in that both involve the coming-to-be of definite novelty. The limit to the analogy is that finite actual entities add novelty to already actual prehended entities that function as potentials, whereas the ontological creative act is all novelty, with no antecedents and no potentials.[19] Aside from the nature the ontological act takes on in creating the basic metaphysical situation, the act is indeterminate.

Process theologians might argue that the basic metaphysical situation, although complex, is absolutely primary.[20] By definition, the ontological principle cannot demand that a creative decision is required to produce the basic metaphysical situation in which the ontological principle resides as a norm. Nevertheless, if that metaphysical situation is the ultimate context, then it does demand that all complexities be understood in reference to decision-points, and it is left with the unexplained surd of the complex situation itself. The ontological creative act does not itself have a determining structure other than the ones it establishes in

18. On the eternity of the ontological creative act, see my *Eternity and Time's Flow* (Albany: State University of New York Press, 1993).

19. This is an interesting reversal of the more common analogy drawn between human beings and God, elaborated splendidly by Keith Ward in his *Religion and Creation* (Oxford: Oxford University Press, 1996). I have discussed his analogy, and presented the one defended here, in *Symbols of Jesus: A Christology of Symbolic Engagement* (Cambridge: Cambridge University Press, 2001), chapter 1.

20. The debates discussed here occur widely in the literature of process thought. But see especially "Three Responses to Neville's *Creativity and God*" by Charles Hartshorne, John B. Cobb Jr., and Lewis S. Ford in *Process Studies* 10/3–4 (Fall–Winter 1980): 73–88; see also my follow-up, "Concerning *Creativity and God*: A Response," in *Process Studies* 11/1 (Spring 1981): 1–10.

the created basic metaphysical situation. All it has is its power of making novel things, namely, the world with its complex metaphysical situation. The rationalism of seeking explanations of complexities in decision-points comes together with the empiricism of finding the ontological decision-point in a unified dialectical inference to the ontological creative act, or ground of being.

Process theology can avoid this move simply by refusing to ask the ontological question of the complex basic metaphysical situation. This is to say, it can refuse to take the problem of the one and the many seriously beyond its theory of how emergent entities unify their prehended contents. It can affirm one or several of its conceptions of an absolute but determinate and finite God, and decline to address the question of why or how there is anything at all. But then it would have to admit to a far more profound arbitrariness than one expects from process thought. It would suffer from neglecting a helpful way to join the grand tradition of God as creator that otherwise is precluded from its conceptions of the finite determinate God who works only by lures.

Now I want to make a stronger argument against process theology, which applies more generally to all conceptions of God as a determinate being, though I will use process cosmology as illustration. What is involved in determinateness as such?[21] A thing is determinate when it is this rather than that, itself rather than some other. My hypothesis about this is that a thing is a harmony with two kinds of features. It has conditional features by virtue of which it is related to other things with respect to which it is determinate, and it has essential features by virtue of which it has its own being with existential location and in terms of which it integrates its conditional features. Both conditional and essential features are equally necessary for a harmony, and we should not be misled by language to think that the essential ones are somehow more important. For a thing to be determinate, other things must exist with respect to which it is determinate, so that determinateness requires a multiplicity of things. Process philosophy illustrates this hypothesis in that the things prehended in an actual entity are conditional features, while the subjective elements involved in integrating them, elements that are spontaneous to the emerging entity relative to what is given in the past, are

---

21. This question was answered with a complex argument in my *God the Creator*, part 1.

the essential features; the resulting definite actual entity is the harmony of both. Relative to process conceptions of God, the primordial nature is the essential element of God and the concrete nature made up of prehensions of finite entities is conditional.

Now here is the problem of the one and the many. Different harmonies are related in cosmological ways by their assorted conditional features. But each harmony requires the togetherness of both its essential and its conditional features to be itself, and thus to be able to function conditionally with respect to other things. Therefore, there must be some ontological context in which the essential features of different harmonies are together that is the ground for the possibility of things conditioning one another cosmologically. Traditionally in Western philosophy, that ground for determinateness is being, and it makes possible the relations of unity and multiplicity among the determinate beings. Obviously, this ground cannot be determinate, for then a yet deeper ground would be needed to relate it to the determinate things it grounds. If the ground were simply indeterminate, mere nothingness, it could not function as the ontological context in which harmonies are together as involving both their essential and their conditional features. My hypothesis, the classic idea of creation *ex nihilo,* is that the ground is the act of creation that immediately makes the harmonies in whatever relations they have with one another.

As illustrated in a dilemma of process theology, the essential spontaneity in finite actual occasions needs to be together with the primordial nature of God in a deeper way than can be given by the alleged prehending of God by the finite entities and vice versa. Indeed, God cannot prehend finite entities without using the eternal objects of the primordial nature, and finite entities cannot prehend other entities, including God, without the essential functions of subjective spontaneity. The ontological ground of the singular, fundamental creative act is necessary for a (Whiteheadian or Hartshornean) process God and finite actual entities to be in process relative to one another. To put the point more generally, any conception of God as a determinate being with some essential features that are not derivative from conditional relations with the world needs to be related to the world by a deeper ontological ground that creates them together so that they can interact. If it be said that the world derives wholly from a creative act of a determinate God and that no ontologically prior ground is necessary for the relation between the two, then this is to admit that the creating God is not determinate with respect to the world apart from creation, which then reduces to the creation *ex nihilo* position.

II. GROUND-OF-BEING THEOLOGIES

So far I have argued against process theology as an instance of a theological conception of God as a determinate entity, and have done so with an argument that generalizes to all or most conceptions of God as a determinate entity. For things to be determinate, they need to be grounded in an ontological act that creates them together, even when their togetherness is a matter of unfolding through time. Now I want to consider the distinction between fullness-of-being and *ex nihilo* conceptions of the ontological ground.

A distinct advantage of the fullness-of-being conceptions is that the created world participates in finite ways in the reality (which usually also means the value) that the full-being God has. This is so, for instance, on Neoplatonic conceptions, Thomistic conceptions, and even on the Buddhist conception of non-being as pure fullness developed by thinkers such as Nishitani. The world thus has divine being and value, however limited that is in finite form. In Neoplatonic and perennial philosophy conceptions, there are levels of reality, and yet even the levels most distant from the transcendent fullness of being have some derivative positive reality and worth.

The chief difficulty with the fullness-of-being conceptions as a class, however, comes in the interpretation of how God so conceived can create or ground the determinate multiplicity in the world. It would seem that creation would consist in making only negations or limitations so as to break up portions of the fullness of being into finite bits. Any positive reality in the finite world could not be new at all, since it is part of the original fullness of being. The only novelty in creation must be the negations that delimit the infinite into the finite. But what could it mean to create a pure negation? The negation must be pure, because any mixed-in positive reality would be antecedent within the fullness of being and therefore could not be created. Even more puzzling is the question of how pure negation plus pure being give rise to determinate being at all. Pure negation is as utterly indeterminate as pure being. Hegel knew this at the beginning of his *Lesser Logic* when he said that to get determinate being out of being and non-being, one has to postulate becoming as well.[22] Yet the world of becoming is precisely what requires determinateness in the first place: to become is to move from one determinate situation to another, as process philosophy has so exquisitely shown.

So I suggest that the fullness-of-being conceptions have a general flaw in intelligibility: they cannot account for how God as the fullness of being creates something determinate. This is to say, a situation of pure symmetry, to use the earlier language, cannot account for how symmetry can be broken into something asymmetrically particular that derives from symmetry. Symmetrical processes within time's flow can give rise to asymmetrical results sometimes because those processes are always within a larger context that is asymmetrical with respect to the symmetrical processes.[23] But it is difficult to see how ontological grounding by a symmetrical source can introduce asymmetries that constitute a particular determinate world. To conceive of creation *a deo* is to suggest that the only thing that distinguishes the fullness of divine being from the created finite world is newly made nothings.

By far the simpler hypothesis is that divine creating gives rise to determinate things that have positive being and definite negations or limitations together. In fact, to make something new is to make something determinate, which involves a determinate mixture of being and non-being. If one allows the notion of making novel things, then creation of something determinate out of nothing is the simplest way to go. To disallow the notion of making something new, to say that out of nothing, nothing comes, is to deny divine creation, and is to be stuck with surd novel pure negations that somehow are supposed to delimit the fullness of being into finite chunks. Therefore, the creation *ex nihilo* conception of God as ground of being is preferable to the fullness-of-being conceptions.

The creation *ex nihilo* conception is hard to swallow, I admit, because we have a kind of elementary folk-psychology assumption that only determinate agents can do things such as create novel worlds. Perhaps

22. *The Logic of Hegel, translated from The Encyclopedia of the Philosophical Sciences,* by William Wallace. (Second edition, revised and augmented; Oxford: Oxford University Press, 1892), chapter 7.

23. See Joe Rosen's "The Primacy of Asymmetry over Symmetry in Physics," in *Physics and Whitehead: Quantum, Process, and Experience,* ed. Timothy E. Eastman and Hank Keeton (Albany: State University of New York Press, 2004).

you follow my arguments for rejecting a straightforward conception of God as determinate, but something of the determinate agent notion still seems to attach to the fullness-of-being conceptions of God as ground of being. Although not exactly determinate, because literally not finitely this rather than that, the fullness of being can be conceived as really real, purely good, unified with pure simplicity, and so forth. Although God so conceived is understood to be the ground of determinate being, to God so conceived are also attributed those virtuous traits in infinite form apart from creation. So we sometimes think, when we try to rationalize our folk psychology, that God can be worshipped as really real, purely good, simply unified, etc., without reference to creation. Actually, however, the fullness of being can be conceived to have those determinate traits only by extrapolation from the finite determinate versions of those traits in the world. God cannot be conceived to be apart from creation and still have those infinite full traits, because the trajectory of moving from the finite to the infinite is not a finite continuum. The trouble with all analogies of proportion or proper proportionality is that the distance between the infinite and finite is infinite, and therefore breaks all continuity of extrapolating from the finite. To give teeth to the claim that the fullness of being is really real, purely good, simply unified, etc., apart from creation, it would be necessary to sneak back in some notion of God as a determinate being apart from creation.

So I appeal for a serious consideration of the primitive notion of making, of creating, wherein something determinate arises that is new relative to what existed before. In the instance of ontological divine creation, the creative act starts from nothing and gives rise to all determinate things, including the determinate indeterminacies of time's flow and human freedom. We can understand this by analogy with human beings, yet with a different analogy from that which says that God as an agent must have a nature with which to act, just as human beings have a nature with which they act. The analogy I propose, and mentioned earlier, is that, in human affairs, what is most interesting about us is not what is given us in our environment, and in our biological and social heritage; what is most interesting is what we do with all that is given. Our moral character develops over time through the countless decisions, mostly small but some big, that are our novel contributions to the given elements of our lives. Although we finite human beings make only very

small advances *ex nihilo* on what is given, God as the ontological creator of the entire metaphysical situation has nothing given and makes
the positive reality of the entire cosmos. Whereas our freedom of creative making is extremely constrained by given elements, God's is wholly
unconstrained because it has nothing given. God the creator *ex nihilo* is
the creative act whose terminus is the singular world, whatever that is.
To know God's nature, then, requires knowing the world created. To understand the world, not only in its determinate nature, but as created out
of nothing, is to understand God in the act of creation.

The radical character of the eternity and immensity of the ontological creative act needs to be underscored. We see from the world that time
does flow, for instance. Therefore, the divine creative act terminates in a
metaphysical situation in which every date has a present emergent reality,
a past fixed reality, and a future reality whose formal structure as possibility shifts with every present change that affects the future. Eternity is the
togetherness of the past, present, and future, and that togetherness is not
temporal. God is never only at a "now." The dynamism of the divine life is
not temporal, like the dynamism of our lives. Rather it consists in the fact
that in eternity every date is in the mode of present creativity, every date is
in the mode of past fixedness, and every date is in a kaleidoscope of structural possibilities relative to the changes of present emergence. To get our
minds around that dynamism of eternity is extremely difficult, and it is
easier to imagine God as a determinate temporal being who might interact with us like other temporal beings do. Nevertheless, for the metaphysically minded, the complex theory of God as the act of ontological creation
ex nihilo can serve as a sign for engaging God. That engagement embraces
both the delight in divine presence found in each determinate thing and
the mystic's awe at the act itself that makes ontological novelty.

III. CONCEPTIONS OF GOD AND PIETY

I suggested just now that conceptions of God can be used as signs by
which we engage God. This is no innocent suggestion, but this is not the
place to defend it.[24] I wish to conclude with some observations about the

24. See my *On the Scope and Truth of Theology: Theology as Symbolic Engagement* (New York and London: T & T Clark, 2006).

piety or mode of engagement of God that is associated with each of the kinds of conceptions of God mentioned here.

Determinate entity conceptions lend themselves to pieties of justice and righteousness, supposing that the world has something of the divine intent or nature inscribed within it but also has serious problems of being out of alignment. So, piety is ordered toward bringing the world, at least in our neighborhood, into closer alignment. Process theology is a paradigmatic example of this, with its emphasis on God's struggles with the evils of the world, limited to offering remedial lures but without the power to zap the evil directly. Human beings in their piety are co-workers, co-creators with God of a world that might be improved.[25]

Fullness-of-being conceptions of God lend themselves to a piety of appreciation of divinity throughout all the world, in nature and in individual human beings, for everything in the world is a dirempted version of God's fullness. At the same time, this piety longs for the greater richness of the fullness in God, and hence is a bit impatient with the determinately limited reality and value of finite things. Mysticism in this kind of conception of God, as the fullness of being, tends toward the merging of the finite into the infinite. Perhaps Plotinus' flight of the alone to the Alone is a bit dramatic, but it points to the piety of repose in divine fullness.

Creation *ex nihilo* conceptions also lead to a piety of appreciation of beauty, value, and even divinity in the world, but not as derived from a purer, fuller version of those elements in God apart from the world. Rather, the piety of this conception is marked by wonder and surprise at the world God creates. God creates a world of determinate harmonies, which are valuable and beautiful. This piety takes quite seriously the observation in Genesis that God creates this and that and sees that they are good. They do not have to be good because of some antecedent divine nature. In fact, God makes the divine nature good by creating a good world. That the world is not entirely good also has implications for the divine nature. The piety of creation *ex nihilo* theologies is not oriented to repose so much as to inquiry into what world God actually grounds,

---

25. On the piety toward justice in process theology, see Marjorie Hewitt Suchocki's *The End of Evil: Process Eschatology in Historical Context* (Albany: State University of New York Press, 1988) and *God Christ Church: A Practical Guide to Process Theology* (new rev. ed.; New York: Continuum, 1995).

and the celebration of it. Because the divine nature is constituted by the product of the divine act, this is a radically incarnationalist theology. The mysticism in this piety is awe at the power of making, at the ontologically creative decision itself, at the vast togetherness of all the parts of creation in the divine eternity and immensity, and at the singularity of each thing as a part of the terminus of the divine creative act.

I confess that I worry about whether these fundamentally different pieties might be more determinative of the theologies we hold than the arguments we give for the different conceptions. For argument's sake, I hope that the arguments lead us to develop pieties rather than the other way around.

Permit me to conclude by offering an answer to the question why there is anything at all rather than absolutely nothing. Part of the answer has to do with interpreting the question. It cannot mean to ask for what purpose the world is created, because purposes are among the things created, being determinate. I take it that the question asks what makes the difference between absolutely nothing and the world of somethings. The answer I would give is that the divine creative act is what makes the difference.

Brian Martine

---

10 ✐ Pragmatic Reflections on Final Causality

Setting out to write a little paper on "the ultimate why question" is the
sort of thing that only philosophers would do—at least as anything more
than a joke. In fact, one fears that it is just the kind of thing that has
made people in our very practical age turn away altogether from philosophy as what seems to many if not most of them a perfectly useless
pursuit. What on earth can one mean by asking "why?" independently of
some particular context? Can such a question mean anything at all? Far
from considering this a naïve response, I rather think it a sensible one. If
the "ultimate why question" is taken to mean asking why there is something rather than nothing, where the expression 'nothing' is supposed to
mean "nothing at all" or "absolutely nothing," I don't think the question
is worthy even of being called useless. It is simply meaningless. Proposing "absolutely nothing" as the alternative to "something" is the same
as saying that there is no alternative to "something." And this whether
the expression 'something' is taken to refer to something in particular or
something in some cosmic sense—that is, "anything at all." In order for
the question "why is there something rather than nothing" to mean anything, there has to be at least in principle an alternative proposed to the
existence of something. Where no alternative is proposed—as is certainly the case when one suggests that the alternative is absolutely nothing—
what was formulated as a question turns out to be an assertion, the assertion of something or other. What exactly is being asserted, of course,
remains rather mysterious.

I do not mean to propose these remarks as news—at least not to anyone acquainted with the philosophical tradition. It is with this little logi-

cal puzzle, after all, that Western logic begins. Having begun by articulating this problem, Parmenides concludes that philosophy stops as soon as it starts, trapped inescapably within the "well-rounded sphere" of immutable Being. Logic appears to have doused Becoming as he puts it, and with it, unhappily, the world of ordinary experience, including the experience of the philosopher who thought up this question, and hence presumably the question itself. One might well ask where exactly one is meant to go from here. Well, Parmenides, as we know, went merrily on his way speculating about the nature of the changeable world, the fundamental nature of which, that is, change, he had just shown to be impossible. And he had the happy fortune of being able to feel quite free in his speculation, since his logical analysis of Being had shown that if there were such a world, we could not actually know anything about it anyway. Having excluded the possibility of determinate being by showing that being has no alternative, and hence cannot be bounded or defined, he had also succeeded (willy nilly) in excluding the possibility of any of the usual things we mean by "meaning." Meaning, after all, seems always to have to mean this or that, as Aristotle was pleased to tell us after another couple of generations of this sort of talk. (I suppose one should also note that he also told us that *ousia* has no contrary, placing *ousia* in exactly the same trackless logical waste that Parmenides had marked out for his own notion of Being—or would have if he had left open the possibility of [legitimately] marking out anything at all.)

Back to our original question then—or to what sounded like a question: "Why is there something rather than nothing?" And back likewise to the attendant question: "What can this possibly mean?" If it is actually the assertion of something—the sort of something that philosophers call Being—then it seems we need to ask just what the assertion of Being is supposed to mean. It cannot mean Being in its simple immediacy, because such expressions, indistinguishable as they are from expressions like "absolutely nothing," turn out to mean nothing at all. No term expressed in simple immediacy, that is, out of relation to anything else, can mean anything. Certainly, there is the possibility of thinking of something like immediate Being by contrast with mediated (that is, related) Being, but in order to do that, we have to think two terms, not just one— immediate Being or Being out of relation on the one hand, and mediated Being, or Being in relation on the other. Or to put this in more familiar terms, we have to think of Determinate Being as that by contrast with which it might be possible to make sense of—Being *simpliciter*. (Personally, I think it wise to reserve judgment about whether this expression can mean anything even when drawn into relation with Determinate Being.)

Since one cannot meaningfully assert just one thing, the "something" that is asserted by the "ultimate why question" has to be plural—it is actually the assertion of some things, that is, of Determinate Being. It is in one sense a rather bald assertion, inasmuch as no argument is proposed in the way of a demonstration. On the other hand, it seems fair to suggest that no such demonstration is really required, since the assertion is itself undeniably something. Something is after all on the ground as soon as the assertion is made. Moreover, while forming this assertion as a question might be regarded as deceptive in one sense, there is nonetheless another and an important sense in which it is certainly a genuine question. The assertion of something is implied if the question is to mean anything at all. The actual question, then, is this: "Why is there *this* something rather than some other something?" Why is there this world rather than another? Why is Being defined along these lines rather than others? Now the game begins in earnest. Which lines do you have in mind? What makes you think your lines are better than mine? And philosophy is off and running.

But still the question is puzzling. I do not mean that it is puzzling just because the answer is obscure inasmuch as there are too many answers and no clear set of criteria for deciding among them, though this is certainly true. I mean that what is being asked is still unclear. The ancients seem to have imagined the question to mean one thing, the medievals on the whole follow them, and the moderns take it to mean something else altogether—or so we have been in the habit of saying to ourselves for several centuries now.

Socrates smiles condescendingly as he sits in his cell awaiting his death, pointing out that what the materialists consider an adequate answer to the question of why he is sitting there is hopelessly inadequate. No description of how his bones and sinews are knitted together can explain what he is doing there, however useful such a description might be in explaining what is at the moment propping him up. No, to answer the question of why he is sitting there in the prison, that is, to answer the question "why this state of affairs rather than some other?" we must transcend the immediate state of affairs and seek our answer among the forms of justice and goodness and his attempt to align his decisions with them. Considered in its simple immediacy, any immediate state of affairs must remain darkly mysterious, and empirical description, however elaborate, does nothing to penetrate the darkness, though it does give us something to do while waiting for whatever might happen next.

Or so Plato suggests as he launches the Doctrine of the Ideas. If we are to make sense of things at all, he assumes we have to move beyond things in what I have been calling their simple immediacy, teaching ourselves to think beyond our direct confrontation with a particular state of affairs by considering its relation to other actual and possible states of affairs. The commonalities detected in or assigned to (or both) such states can be elevated into beings or meanings (or both) taken to have a status independent of particular states of affairs, and, considered in a certain way, can be used to provide answers to the question, "Why this state of affairs rather than some other?" Ideas like Justice itself and The Good itself swim into view, albeit rather vaguely, and along with them the notion of an end with causal significance. Socrates' question now has an answer that he considers much more to the point: he is there in the prison because his being there is required by justice itself, that is, required by his responsibility as a rational being to align his actions insofar as he can with the form of justice.

Considered in this way, the Doctrine of the Ideas and its many descendants emerge as responses to the reformulated why question. Particular states of affairs come to be as they are (to the extent that they are intelligible) through forming themselves in accord with meanings thought to transcend the immediacy of direct experience thereby escaping the logical recalcitrance of simple immediacy. Now we can speak about these states of affairs. By virtue of its relation to ideas that stretch beyond the immediate character of the state we are trying to understand, that state is reconsidered as something drawn into a web of mediated relation, and philosophy finds its voice.

More than that, another problem seems to be solved. The restless movement typical of the practical world as one state of affairs is transformed into another can now be corralled and drawn into meaningful discourse. The movement from one state to another takes on a direction as it comes to be seen as a movement toward an end whose qualitative character draws a series of immediate moments together into a progression. Meaning stretches backward from the end through the series of moments, illuminating each of them now as something purposive, a state of affairs meaningful both as itself directed toward some ultimate end and as the issue of similarly directed states. The merely mechanical description of the materialist is superseded by a conception of meaning as extending from the ends toward which immediate states of affairs can be conceived as developing. This particular man seated on this particular prison bench awaiting his death escapes the ineffable simple immediacy of the moment by thinking it in relation to other such moments, and ultimately in relation to a cosmic order constituted by what now comes to be seen as meaning itself. Why not think all simple states of affairs in these terms? Each rises out of the mystery of immediate experience newly clothed in the meanings contributed to it by a set of ideas considered to be meanings-in-themselves. An answer is proposed to the question, "Why this state of affairs rather than some other?" It is as it is because it is informed by the end toward which it is directed.

This is of course only one way of tracing the genesis of Plato's cosmic schema, a schema which provides the underlying logical template for at least the next two millennia, and arguably for the entire development of the tradition. I have chosen it because it exposes its relation to practical experience, a relation that is too often obscured when Plato and his descendants are thought of chiefly as metaphysicians elaborating a fundamentally static view of Being. The Doctrine of the Ideas, I believe, originally presented a compelling ontology not least because it was one tied to our direct natural experience. We live the world—at least when we live it successfully—as a place animated by purpose. Driven by the ordinary requirements of natural being, we direct ourselves toward ends identified straightforwardly by our basic needs. As we find ways of satisfying the most basic of those needs, it becomes possible to turn our attention to questions increasingly wide in scope, but the habits formed in the early stages of this process are never really left behind. The activity that directed itself toward food or shelter was made meaningful quite straightforwardly by the end it sought, an end whose meaning and value could be taken for granted as something in itself. Struggling through the forest in search of food, or chopping bits of it down to provide ourselves with shelter from the cold and wet, the meaning of our labor is obviously in-formed by the ends in view. Those ends are not open to any meaningful question.

Having provided ourselves with sufficient food and shelter, it is not surprising to find the same general thinking applied to the more com-plex questions with which we now have the luxury of concerning our-selves. Is it not reasonable to suppose that the moments of a more elabo-rate experience should in the same sense draw their meanings from ends which are similarly meaningful in themselves? Socrates contemplates his immediate situation and tells his friends that it is caused by such an end, and in being so caused, he supposes that it is informed by the mean-ing and value that defines the end. It is justice itself that makes sense of this moment in his personal and particular history, as it has been oth-er meanings in themselves that have made sense and continue to make sense of the other moments of his particular history. The world of prac-tical experience takes on form and meaning as something shaped by an array of ends-in-themselves, of finalities whose own meaning and value is taken to stand beyond question.

There is much to admire in this view, as scarcely needs saying, but unhappily, a host of problems begin to emerge as it is fully articulated. Plato himself points to many of the serious problems with his version of it, gradually modifying the original schema to try to take account of them. As he does so, first in the *Symposium* and the *Phaedrus,* and then later in the *Parmenides* and the *Sophist,* what seems to me to be the most serious of its drawbacks becomes increasingly clear. And this is a prob-lem tied directly to thinking of the Ideas as finalities whose meanings are supposed to imbue the world of practical experience with its mean-ing—which world is of course now seen as derivative. From a perspective generated in the first place by the needs of practical experience, the ends of that experience do indeed seem to be inherently meaningful. We need not ask whether the food we seek has a meaning or a value—its mean-ing and value is obvious as is the sense in which it makes the seeking of it meaningful. But practical ends also always appear in contexts in which their relation to the activity of seeking them is bound to their own mean-ing. Something becomes food directly in relation to the being that seeks it; while all living beings seek nourishment, what nourishes one being might well kill another. When we lift the idea nourishment out of the context in which it became meaningful in the first place, imagining that we can attach the same inherent meaning and value it had in the practical context to the abstraction "nourishment in itself" or something of the sort, we set out on a course that endangers the groundwork of the meaning we should like to ascribe to our abstraction.

As soon as we begin to imagine that an end should be considered as something in itself, thereby divorcing it from the experience that directs itself toward it, we interrupt the web of relations that made sense of considering the end inherently meaningful. Its meaning after all was not really inherent in the end alone; it was always something that emerged from a certain ordering of experience which was itself driven by various other factors both clear and obscure. Once identified as an end, it does indeed seem to return to the experience leading up to it, lending meaning to what would otherwise be a series of individually immediate and hence ineffable states of affairs. But the meaning contributed by the end (when we think of it in such a fashion) continues to depend upon the experience which originally brought it into focus. The meaning of the practical states of affairs, now organized and made meaningful as directed toward an identifiable end, is no more derivative than is the meaning of the end itself. Reasonable as it might seem to elevate the end to a position independent of practical experience, doing so can only result in isolating the end, thereby depriving it of the very relation to practical experience upon which it depends for its meaning. If we do not resist this temptation (and we have on the whole been no more successful than Plato was at resisting it) we find ourselves (as he did) unhappily confronted by an end whose basic nature is as ineffable as were the immediate states of affairs we had hoped to understand in terms of it.

Viewed as meanings or beings in themselves, Plato's Ideas (just as the various abstractions that follow them in the metaphysical tradition) quickly disappear from view. In any case, they disappear from the view of discursive reason, inasmuch as discursivity depends upon relation, and things imagined to exist in themselves, whatever else might or might not be true of them, are imagined to exist out of relation. It's possible of course to propose some special capacity that affords access to such things, (*noesis,* for example), but even if one is inclined to accept the bald assertion of such a capacity, the difficulty is not overcome. The meanings (or beings) in themselves supposed to be intuited by such a capacity as things standing somehow altogether out of relation, are cut off thereby from any possible relation to the practical experience they are supposed to inform, to shape into something meaningful. The prototype of the many dualisms of the tradition appears, befuddling the attempt to make sense out of the very experience that originally gave rise to it. The "why question" we had hoped to answer appears to have led to the conclusion that no such question can really mean anything as soon as we persuade ourselves that meaning itself stands apart from the experience from which the question emerged in the first place.

Once again we ask, "Where do we go from here?" We can of course choose to content ourselves with a diremption between reality and appearance, reconciling ourselves thereby to the view that the world in which we actually live out our lives is a poor and tawdry thing, at its best a cheap imitation of transcendent meanings in themselves. But just to the extent that such meanings, considered in such a way, are logically inaccessible, there is no way even to determine whether this makes sense.

Or, there is the option of following Parmenides down the path he abjures and then sets out upon, diving into the world of not-being, the world of movement and becoming, supposing that if we busy ourselves with how things seem to work, the ends that we had hoped to understand will somehow take care of themselves. We can smile back at Socrates as he maunders away about why he is sitting there on the prison bench, and in the meantime occupy ourselves with poking and prodding at him to try to figure out how exactly it is that he is able to sit up straight. There is no point in asking where the electrons came from, or why there are such things in the first place. It is enough to come to what we now call an "understanding" of how they are related to each other—thereby providing what we now call an "explanation" of the immediate state of affairs.

Mind you, after enough poking and prodding, we still present ourselves with indiscernible entities supposed to provide the real truth about things, and still (until very recently at least) are inclined to imagine that their immediate relations to one another can be ascribed to laws every bit as distant (and for many of the same reasons) from practical experience as Plato's Ideas were, but at least reality is not split in two. Instead, the divide opens between a world which is imagined to be all of a piece on the one hand and our appraisal of it on the other. Knowing, unhappily, is divorced once again from the known, but now in a way that leads us to suggest with Hume, for example, that we just have to pull up our socks and accept it. We have learned that there is not really any answer to the why question, not so much because meaning lies beyond our grasp as because the sort of meanings our benighted ancestors sought turn out to be entirely too much in our own hands. We persuade ourselves on the basis of a diremptive bivalent logic (not at all unlike that of our sadly misguided ancestors) that our willful and feckless consciousness ghosts over the surface of the world as it is in itself, succeeding, if only occasionally, in making sufficient contact to be able to discern its mechanical workings.

We further persuade ourselves that if we describe those workings in terms sufficiently abstract, we are certainly nearing the truth of the matter. New abstractions emerge, which, while not exactly replete with human significance, have on exactly those grounds the merit of evading the ambiguity inherent in the old ones. These abstractions might not tell us why things are as they are, but they do seem to tell us how things are as they are. All the prodding and poking turns out to have been worthwhile. We have not only come considerably closer to telling poor old Socrates just how it's possible for him to sit up straight on the bench, we have also discovered that the only questions that make any sense are questions with instrumental answers. He can justifiably put aside his worries about justice. We've learned a new trick of abstraction, and this one abstracts us from the notion of there being such a thing as an independent ground of meaning and value. Whether they're the rather outsized heads of modern rationalists, or the more modest ones of modern empiricists, it's all just in our heads. Sit back against the prison wall. The electrons will tell us how to do things, if not perhaps exactly what things to do.

Still, we find ourselves asking, "Why?" Why this world instead of some other? More importantly, and most fundamentally (for us), why this course of action instead of some other? The electrons cannot answer this question any more than our equally abstract ideas of meanings-in-themselves could. Perhaps it is time to become a bit more chary of abstractions than we've been on the whole inclined to be. Oh, we have had warnings enough. Nietzsche (of all people!) warned us. The pragmatists warned us. Whitehead warned us. All, so far, it seems, to no end. And the end, after all, is our question. Is there such a thing? I want to recommend a return to the beginning of all of this. What made us ask the question in the first place? What made us think that there could be a meaning beyond the immediate state of affairs in which we find ourselves blindly grasping for a way to make sense out of things? The answer to this question, considered naturally, seems fairly straightforward. We reach for things that we need, at first quite simple things, and gradually, as our experience expands beyond the concerns of mere survival, toward reasons that make sense of bothering to survive.

When we have time to take a breath and consider things, we ask ourselves whether it is worth the trouble—at least, we beings capable of abstraction ask such questions. But there is really no question here; there is just a natural drive put in the form of a question. Should we suppose that because the question's genesis can be ascribed to a natural drive that it is not an important one? Thinking this makes sense only if we separate ourselves from the rest of what there is. We have been so long in the habit of doing so—based on the analysis peculiar to "modern" thought—that it continues to seem a sensible thing to do, warnings to the contrary notwithstanding. But this is only a function of the peculiarly modern form of abstraction. The question we mean to address in asking the "ultimate why question" comes to life at the moment that beings like us come to life and ask it. The world comes to be filled with meaning as soon as there are beings who wonder about meaning and whose natural drives invest the world with the meanings toward which those drives direct themselves.

Do we merely invent these meanings then? Do we make them up out of whole cloth as we might a figment of the imagination assigned to some arbitrary activity of consciousness? No more, I think, than I invented the floor beneath my feet. It is there all right, and I haven't the smallest question about whether I am standing on it, however much Descartes might like to warn me to be cautious about such a claim. So is the river there a few miles away from us and the sea it empties into, and neither of them dependent on my fancy. So, equally, I believe are the meanings that we find in our lives, including those that draw us together in asking these questions, meanings that we have not invented out of whole cloth, but meanings that we discover as a part of the world in which we participate. They are as real as we are real. The meanings that we bring into the world return to our experience of it and contribute to the developing meaning of Being itself. But this use of the expression "Being itself" is not in the least intended to lift Being out of relation to the world of practical experience. That abstract notion of Being is merely abstract and it is abstracted from the unfolding evolution of meaning generated by the constant play of Being and Becoming. Meaning and Being come to be. Parmenides' notion, that abstract idea of Being, finds its origin in this play between what is and what is not yet, and even as an abstraction, can make sense only by virtue of a defining contrast with what is not, with what is Becoming.

Similarly, when we take the modern turn and separate reason or consciousness or mind or spirit (or whatever one chooses to call this dimension of being) from the practical ground out of which it arises, we can choose to puzzle ourselves about how this activity of being is related to its own ground. We can propose that it is hopelessly separate and cannot ever assure itself that it knows anything, or that there is nothing to know but itself thereafter holding that whatever there can be devolves into its own activity, or that it is so hopelessly isolated as to empty itself of all content, becoming a nothingness engaged in the futile search for a something. But all of these proposals result from the same sort of overweening pride in our ability to abstract ourselves from the immediate state of affairs which gives rise to all of this in the first place. Proud of our theories, we consider the practice from which they emerge as a degraded, paltry thing not worthy of our regard. It has none of the clarity and precision our age-old theoretical practice has been in the habit of demanding. Theory is, however, just another kind of practice, meaningful only to the extent that it is practical, that is, only to the extent that it can return to Socrates' prison bench and make sense out of what he is doing there.

Should we tell Socrates that there is no point in trying to identify his reason for being there? That he should abandon the search for a final cause that can make sense out of his decision to be there? Of course not. He is quite right to tell the materialists that their theoretical practice is inadequate. He is also quite wrong to suppose that there is no point in poking and prodding around in the world of direct experience, opting instead in favor of leaving that world behind and seeking its ultimate meaning in some notion of an end-in-itself. Ends make sense only when drawn into relation with the practice which gives rise to them. Being makes sense only when drawn into relation with Becoming. Theory becomes meaningful only when drawn into relation with the practice of which it is a part and to which it must return in order for there to be any possible answer to the ultimate why question.

Nicholas Rescher

11 ∽ Optimalism and the Rationality of the Real

On the Prospects of Axiological Explanation

I. IS THE REAL RATIONAL?

Is the real ultimately rational? Can we ever manage to explain the nature of reality—the make-up of the universe as a whole? Is there not an insuperable obstacle here—an infeasibility that was discerned already by Immanuel Kant, who argued roughly as follows: The demand for a rationale that accounts for reality-as-a-whole is a totalitarian demand. As such it is illegitimate. All explanations require inputs. Explanation always proceeds by explaining one thing in terms of something else. There thus is no way to explain Reality, to give an account of everything-as-a-whole. For this sort of thing would evade neither a vitiating regress nor a vicious circle.

So goes Kant's reasoning. And there is much to be said for it. After all, in the realm of a factual explanation we always have recourse to factual premises to substantiate our factual conclusions. And so an all-encompassing explanation of the facts is clearly impossible—or so it seems. But here appearances are deceiving. In the present, genuinely extraordinary case of totalitarian explanation, another very different option stands before us. For here we can—and in the final analysis must—shift the framework of explanation from the descriptive/factual order of explanation to the normative/axiological order. But what would such an explanation look like?

This essay served as my March 2005 presidential address to the Metaphysical Society of America. On relevant issues see also my books *The Riddle of Existence* (Lanham, MD: University Press of America, 1984), and *Nature and Understanding* (Oxford: Clarendon Press, 2000).

II. THE TURN TO AXIOLOGY

From its earliest days, metaphysics has been understood also to include "axiology," the evaluative and normative assessment of the things that exist. And just here lies the doorway to another mode of explanation—an explanation of facts in terms of values, and of reality in terms of optimality.

Accustomed as we are to explanations in the mode of efficient causality, this idea of an axiological explanation of existence on the basis of an evaluative optimalism has a decidedly strange and unfamiliar air about it. Let us consider more closely how it is supposed to work.

The approach rests on adopting what might be called an *axiogenetic optimality principle* to the effect that value represents a decisive advantage in regard to realization, in that in the virtual competition for existence among alternatives it is the comparatively best that is bound to prevail.[1] Accordingly, whenever there is a plurality of alternative possibilities competing for realization in point of truth or of existence, the (or an) optimal possibility wins out. (An alternative is *optimal* when no better one exists, although it can have equals.) The result is that things exist, and exist as they do, because this is for the (metaphysically) best.

No doubt it will be a complicated matter to appraise from a metaphysical/ontological standpoint that condition X is better (inherently more meritorious) than condition Y. But, so optimalism maintains, once this evaluative hurdle is overcome the question "Why should it be that X rather than Y exists?" is automatically settled by the circumstance of X's superiority, via the ramifications of optimality. In sum, a Law of Optimality prevails: value (of a suitable—and still unspecified—sort) enjoys an existential bearing, so that it lies in the nature of things that (one of) the best of available alternatives is realized.[2]

---

1. The prime spokesman for this line of thought within the Western philosophical tradition was G. W. Leibniz. A present-day exponent is John Leslie for whom see especially his *Value and Existence* (Totowa, NJ: Rowman & Littlefield, 1979). See also the present author's *The Riddle of Existence* (Lanham, MD: University Press of America, 1984).

2. To make this work out, the value of a disjunctive-alternative has to be fixed at the value of its optimal member, lest the disjunctive "bundling" of a good alternative with inferior rivals so operate as to eliminate the good alternative from competition.

III. ABANDONING CAUSALITY

Optimalism is certainly a *teleological* theory: it holds that reality's *modus operandi* manifests a tropism toward a certain end or *telos*, namely optimalization. Such an axiology represents a doctrine of "final causes" in Aristotle's sense, but it is emphatically not a *causal* theory in the nowadays standard sense of efficient causation. It does not—and does not need to—regard value as a somehow efficient cause, a productive agency.

On the contrary—value is not *productive* at all, but merely *eliminative* in so functioning as to block the way to availability of inferior productions. It does not drive causal processes but only channels or delimits them by ruling certain theoretical (or logical) possibilities out of the realm of real possibility. Consider an analogy. The English language allows double letters in its words, but not triple letters. But that does not mean that the double "L" of "follow" *causes* that "LL" successive lettering to be something different from "L." The principle explains without causality. It merely imposes a structural constraint of possibility. The lawful principle at issue explains the factual situation without any invocation of causality, since an explanation via inherent constraints on possibility is not a causal explanation at all.

It would be a deeply mistaken idea to see value as a somehow actively productive agency. Values play an explanatory role alright, but not in the causal mode. Causality is, after all, not our only explanatory resource. For example, when natural laws obtain, there is, no doubt, a *reason* for their obtaining (an axiological reason, as we ourselves see it). But this reason can presumably be provided by an explanatory principle that need not carry us into the order of *efficient* causality.

Optimalism readily concedes that value does not engender existence in the mode of efficient causation and that it would indeed be rather mysterious if values were asked to do so. But this concession is to be seen as irrelevant. The fact is that the complaint "How can values possibly operate causally?!" simply confuses axiological explanation with productively efficient explanation.

Only with explanations of why physical objects and events are realized need we involve causes and effects. But laws of nature themselves do not "exist" as constituents of the physical realm—they just *obtain*. They don't have causes—and don't need them. It would be inappropriate to ask for their explanation in the order of efficient causation. And so the fact that axiology does not provide such an explanation is not an occasion for appropriate complaint. It does not stop value-explanations from qualifying as explanations. Value-explanations present perfectly good answers to "Why is something-or-other so?" type questions. It is just that in relation to laws, values play only an *explanatory* role through possibility elimination and not a causally *productive* role through actual creation. And this is no defect, because a productive process is simply not called for.

And so, to inquire into how values operate causally in law-realization is simply to adopt an inappropriate model for the processes involved. Value explanation just is not causal: values do not function in the order of efficient causality at all.

IV. WHY OPTIMALISM?

But why should it be that optimalism obtains? Why should what is for the best be actual? What sort of possible argument can be given on this position's behalf? That Law of Optimality to the effect that "whatever possibility is for the best is *ipso facto* the possibility that is actualized" is certainly not a logico-conceptually *necessary* truth. From the angle of theoretical logic it has to be seen as a contingent fact—albeit one not about nature as such, but rather one about the manifold of *real* possibility that underlies nature. As a predominately contingent fact, it obtains as a matter of ontological rather than logico-conceptual necessity, while the realm of possibility as a whole is presumably constituted by considerations of logical-metaphysical necessity alone.[3]

To be sure, optimalism itself presumably has an explanation, since one can and should maintain the Leibnizian Principle of Sufficient Reason to the effect that for every contingent fact there is a reason why it is so rather than otherwise. But with the Law of Optimality this explanation resides in itself—in its own nature. For it is, in the final analysis, for the best that the Law of Optimality should obtain. After all, there is no

---

3. The operative perspective envisions a threefold order of necessity/possibility: the logico-conceptual, the ontological or proto-physical, and the physical. It accordingly resists the positivistic tendency of the times to dismiss or ignore that second, intermediate order of considerations. And this is only to be expected, since people nowadays tend to see this intermediate realm as predicated in value considerations, a theme that is anathema to present-day scientism.

decisive reason why that explanation has to be "deeper and different"—that is, no decisive reason why the prospect of *self-explanation* has to be excluded at this fundamental level.[4] After all, we cannot go on putting the explanatory elephant on the back of the tortoise on the back of the alligator *ad infinitum:* as Aristotle already saw, the explanatory regress has to stop somewhere at the "final" theory—one that is literally "self-explanatory." What better candidate could there be than the Law of Optimality itself, with the result that the division between real and merely theoretical possibilities is as it is (i.e., value based) because that itself is for the best?[5]

Optimalism has many theoretical advantages. Here is just one of them. It is conceivable, one might contend, that the *existence* of the world—that is to say, of *a* world—is a necessary fact while nevertheless its *nature* (i.e., of *which* world) is contingent. And this would mean that separate and potentially different answers would have to be provided for the questions "Why is there anything at all?" and "Why is the character of existence as it is?—why is it that this particular world exists?" However, an axiogenetic approach enjoys the advantage of rational economy in that it proceeds uniformly here. It provides a single uniform rationale for both answers—namely that "this is for the best." It accordingly also enjoys the significant merit of providing for the rational economy of explanatory principles.

In the end, we must expect that any ultimate principle must explain itself and cannot, in the very nature of things, admit of an external explanation in terms of something altogether different. The impetus to realization inherent in authentic value lies in the very nature of value itself. A rational person would not favor the inferior alternative: and a rational reality cannot do so either.

To be sure, the Law of Optimality presupposes a manifold of suitable value parametrics that relate to various physically relevant features

---

4. After all, there is no reason or logico-theoretical principle why propositions cannot be self-certifying. Nothing vicious need be involved in self-substantiation. Think of "Some statements are true" or "This statement stakes a particular rather than a universal claim."

5. Optimalism is closely related to optimism. The optimist holds that "Whatever exists is for the best," while the optimalist maintains the converse that "Whatever is for the best exists." However, when we are dealing with exclusive and exhaustive alternatives the two theses come to the same thing. If one of the alternatives $A, A_1, \ldots A_n$ must be the case, then, if what is realized is for the best, it follows automatically that the best is realized (and conversely).

(symmetry, economy, regularity, or the like) as merit-manifesting factors. It should be acknowledged that the optimization at issue is—and should be—geared to a "scientifically reputable" theory of some suitable kind, coordinate with a complex of physically relevant factors of a suitable kind. After all, many a possible world will maximize a "value" of *some* sort (confusion and nastiness included). For present purposes, value will have to be construed in its positive sense—of being valuable by worthiness of positive appraisal.

The manifold of logical possibility is subject to various reductions. Conformity with the laws of nature induces a reduction to physical possibility. Conformity with the principles of metaphysics induces a reduction to metaphysical possibility, and conformity to considerations of value induces a reduction to axiological possibililty—which is perhaps the most stringent of these. Thus along these lines, as Leibniz sees it, the value of a system is determined by an optimal balance of procedural order (uniformity, symmetry) and phenomenal variety (richness, plenitude)—both reflected in such cognitive features as intelligibility and interest. It is its (presumed) gearing to a positive value which like elegance is plausibly identifiable as physically relevant—contingently identifiable as such subject to scientific inquiry—that ultimately prevents the thesis "optimalism obtains because that's for the best" from declining into vacuity. And this of course means that optimalism is not so much a practice as a program.

V. IS OPTIMALISM THEOCENTRIC?

"Yet what if one is skeptical about theism? Would one then not have to reject optimalism?" Here the optimalist replies: "Not at all. Optimalism does not require theism—it need not call upon God to institute optimalism. The doctrine is perfectly self-supportive: it obtains on its own basis, not necessarily because God willed it so, but just simply because that's for the best."[6]

The fact of the matter is that optimalism does not require a creator to provide for the productive efficacy of value. The insistence upon the need

---

6. Indeed, an over-enthusiastic optimalist could take the line that theism hinges on optimalism rather than the reverse because: "God's own existence issues from optimalism: he exists because that's for the best."

for productive agency is based on the mistaken idea that an explanation in the mode of *efficient causality* as nowadays understood is required. For, as indicated above, an operative principle can require conformity without any sort of productive action.

A word of caution at this point. One of the prime motives for taking axiological explanation seriously is that it enables us to avert the temptations and difficulties of theological explanation. But the rationale for this is not an *odium theologicum*—an aversion to theological considerations as such. It is rather the idea of the medieval dictum *non in philosophia recurrere est ad deum*—that we should not ask God to pull our philosophical chestnuts out of the fire. Synoptic questions like "Why is there anything at all?" are philosophical questions and they ought ideally to be answered by philosophical means.

On the other hand, it must be stressed that axiological explanation is altogether congenial to theism although it does not require it. After all it is only to be expected that if the world is created by a God of the sort that the tradition encourages us to accept, then the world that such a God creates should be one in which values play a role. And so it would seem that theism requires axiological explanation even more than axiological explanation requires theism.[7]

All the same, the present approach differs decisively from that of Leibniz. He proposed to answer the question "Why is it that the value-optimizing world should be the one that actually exists?" with reference to the will of a God who chooses to adopt value optimization as a creative principle. Thus Leibniz was committed to an idea that it is necessary to account for the obtaining of a principle in terms of the operation of an existing entity (specifically the agency of an intelligent being, namely, God). Instead, an axiological approach sees the explanatory bearing of a principle of value as direct, final, and fundamental, without mediation through the agency of a substantial being (however extraordinary).[8] On

---

7. Would such argumentation *subordinate* God to a Principle of Optimality? Not at all! The theistic optimalist can take the following stance in the interests of orthodoxy: In the order of beings (or entities or substances) God has absolute primacy. In the order of principles (of factual propositions or truths) the Principle of Optimality is paramount. And neither order is subordinate to the other; rather, they are coordinated via God's knowledge of the truth.

8. Our metaphysical invocation of a principle of value is akin to A. C. Ewing's theological application of similar ideas in his interesting article "Two 'Proofs' of God's Existence," *Religious Studies* 1 (1961): 29–45. Ewing there propounds the argument that God's existence is to be

the grounds of explanatory economy, at least, purpose is thus something that we would be well advised to forego if we can actually manage to do so. Let us have a closer look at this issue of purposes.

VI. IS OPTIMALISM PURPOSIVE?

In taking the axiological route, one is not saying that the realization of value is reality's purpose. We need not personify nature to account for its features. To say that nature embodies value is a very far cry from saying that the realization of value is one of nature's purposes. That reality operates in a certain manner—that its *modus operandi* follows from certain laws and principles—is in principle a non-theological thesis. The values involved in axiological explanation need not be *somebody's* purpose. No element of personification, no reference to anyone's aims or purposes, need be involved in axiological explanation. Purpose, on the other hand, necessarily requires a purposer—it must be *somebody's* purpose. In this regard, value stands with order rather than with purpose. Order "seeking" in nature does not presuppose an orderer, nor value "seeking" a valuer. The maintenance of enhancement of a value can be a matter of "blind" operation of impersonal optimific forces.

Let us return to the idea of purposiveness and consider the objection "It is only by constituting the motives of agents that wishes can obtain explanatory efficacy. Only by serving as some deliberate agent's motivational repertoire can a value come into effective operation." Such a view of value-explanation is nothing new: it has existed in embryo since Plato's day thanks to his conception of demiurge. The guiding idea has generally been that the only way in which values can be brought to bear in the explanation of phenomena is through the mediation of a creative agent.

Accordingly, thinkers from classical antiquity onward have defended (or attacked) the principle that explaining the presence of order in nature—the fact that the world is a cosmos—requires postulating a creative intelligence as its cause. That nature manifests and exemplifies such cognitive values as order, harmony, uniformity was thus explained by

---

accounted for axiologically: that he exists "because it was supremely good that God should exist" (p. 35). This approach, by contemplating the aspect that value is so fundamental that the deity itself can be accounted for in its terms, has the substantial merit of avoiding Leibniz's tactic of presuppositionally grounding the efficacy of value in a preexisting deity.

regarding these as marks of purpose. On this basis, the mainstream of Western thought regarding axiological explanation has taken the line that there is a supernatural agent (God, demiurge, spirit), and the values obtain their explanatory bearing by influencing the state of mind which governs his creative endeavors.

This essential purposive approach characterizes the traditional "argument from design," which explains the creation with reference to a creator (as its *ratio essendi*) and infers the existence of this creator from the orderly structure of created nature (as his *ratio cognoscendi*).[9] The sequential explanatory slide from design to value to purpose to intelligence was historically seen as inexorable. And so the recourse to an explanatory principle that is geared to values without any such mediation represents a radical departure. The guiding conception of the present deliberations—that value is the natural place to sever this chain—reflects a break with a longstanding tradition.

The justification of this break with the tradition of design explanation lies in observing the important distinction between values and purposes. Granted, a purpose must be *somebody's* purpose: it must have some intelligent agent as its owner-operator. It lies in the very nature of the concept that purposes cannot exist in splendid isolation: they must, in the final analysis, belong to some agent or other. For purposes as such, to be is to be adopted. Purposive explanations operate in terms of why conscious agents do things, and not in terms of why impersonal conditions obtain.

A value, however, can be altogether impersonal. And this means that value explanation is not necessarily purposive. Being a value does not require that somebody actually values it (any more than being a fact requires that somebody actually realizes it). A person can certainly hold a certain value dear, but if it is indeed a value, then its status as such is no more dependent on its actually being valued than the symmetry of a landscape depends on its actually being discerned. Values admit of being prized, but that does not mean that they actually are, any more than a task's being difficult means that anyone actually attempts it.

9. For a useful collection of relevant texts see Donald R. Burrill, *The Cosmological Arguments: A Spectrum of Opinion* (Garden City, NY: Anchor Books, 1967). Two interesting recent accounts of the issues and their historical ramifications are William L. Rowe, *The Cosmological Argument* (Princeton: Princeton University Press, 1975), and William L. Craig, *The Cosmological Argument from Plato to Leibniz* (London: Macmillan, 1980).

To be of value is to *deserve* to be valued, but that of course need not actually happen: the value of things can be underestimated or overestimated or totally overlooked. Neither the items that have value nor the fact of their being of value depend on apprehending minds for their reality. And this holds in particular for "ontological" values like economy, simplicity, regularity, uniformity, and so forth, which figure in the axiological explanation of laws. In sum, the being of values does not consist in their being valued, any more than does the being of most other sorts of things demand their being perceived. We surely do not need to anthropomorphize here, even as a claim to end-directed transactions in the world ("Nature abhors a vacuum") is without any implications about a purposively operating mind. A system can be goal-directed through its inherent natural "programming" (e.g., heliotropism or homeostasis) without any admixture of purpose, even as a conservation of energy principle need not be held on the basis of nature's "seeking" to conserve energy.

And so, though axiological explanations fail to address a question for which design explanations have an answer—namely the causal question "How do values operate productively so as to bring particular laws to actualization?"—this reflects no demerit. For it seems plausible to see this question as simply inappropriate. Values don't "operate" in the purposively causal order at all. Value considerations render certain law possibilities real in somewhat the same way that law conformity renders certain event possibilities real. The issue of a specifically purposive efficacy simply does not arise.

VII. FURTHER DIFFICULTIES

However, the threat of a difficulty seems to arise in the form of a possibility range that is evaluatively "topless"—that is, a range that does not have some alternatives that are optimal in the sense of not being bettered by any others.[10] In such a range, each alternative is surpassed by yet another that is better. And so on optimalistic principles it would transpire that there are no real possibilities at all. Within such a range there will be no optimum and thus no possibility of actualization. Here optimalism must

10. Leibniz saw the existence of the actual world as a decisive argument against hopelessness, since existence could not be realized in a realm of topless meritoriousness. Here a benevolent creator would be effectively paralyzed.

take the bull by the horns. Insofar as situations can be imagined which—like that of a "topless" infinite alternative spectrum—could raise difficulties for the theory, it could and should simply be seen as part and parcel of optimalism to assert that such situations cannot actually arise: that a reality that is benign all the way through is thereby such that it excludes such a problematic situation with respect to what is really possible. As optimalism sees it, the very fact that toplessness conflicts with optimalism excludes toplessness from the range of real possibilities.

But what if there is a plurality of perfection-contributory features so interrelated that more of the one demands less of the other? Here everything is bettered in some respect by something else, so that to all appearances it would result that nothing is synoptically and comprehensively all-in best.

In such cases, however, one can—and should—resort to a function of combination that allows for the interaction of those different value parameters. For example, with two operative value-making factors, say cheapness (that is, inverse acquisition cost) and durability in the case of a 100-watt light bulb, one will use the ratio of (cost of purchase) to (hours of usability) or equally cost/hour of service as a measure of merit. In this way, the multi-factor case can be reduced to the situation of a single compound and complex factor, so that optimization is once again possible. And that this should obtain is guaranteed by optimalism itself: it is part and parcel of the best possible order of things that optimalism should be operable within it.

VIII. VIOLATING COMMON SENSE

To anyone who is minded to object to optimalism as somehow violating common sense, I have only one thing to say: "Where have you been recently and what have you been doing?" One thing you certainly have not been doing is keeping track of the expository literature of contemporary microphysics and cosmology, and one place you have certainly not been is at your television set watching any of the recent science channel programs on string theory. Surely common sense no longer qualifies as a club for any explanatory theorizing on reality's fundamentals. Insofar as common sense is to be used as a yardstick, it is surely not optimalism but contemporary cosmology that falls short.

Nonetheless, how can sensible people possibly embrace the conception that the inherently best alternative is thereby automatically the actual (true) one? Does not the world's all-too-evident imperfection stand decisively in the way here?

The matter is not all that simple, however. For the issue is going to pivot on the question of what "inherently best" means. If it means "best" from the angle of your desires, or of my interests, or even of the advantage of *homo sapiens* in general, then clearly the thesis loses its strong appeal. For the sake of plausibility, that "best" should be construed as looking to the condition of existence-as-a-whole rather than to the condition of one particular privileged individual or group. Optimality in this context is clearly not going to be a matter of the affective welfare or standard of living of some particular sector of existence; it is going to have to be a metaphysical good of some synoptic and rather abstract sort that looks to the condition of the whole.

Yet is such a theory of axiological ontogenesis not defeated by the objection: If it really were the case that value explains existence, then why isn't the world altogether perfect?

The answer lies in the inherent complexity of value. An object that is of any value at all is subject to a complex of values. For it is the fundamental fact of axiology that every evaluation-admitting object has a plurality of evaluative features. Take a car—an automobile. Here the relevant parameters of merit clearly include such factors as speed, reliability, repair infrequency, safety, operating economy, aesthetic appearance, road-handling ability. But in actual practice such features are interrelated. It is unavoidable that they trade off against one another: more of A means less of B. It would be ridiculous to have a supersafe car with a maximum speed of two miles per hour. It would be ridiculous to have a car that is inexpensive to operate but spends three-fourths of the time in a repair shop. But perfection—maximum realization of every value dimension all-at-once—is simply unrealizable. And of course it makes no sense to ask for the impossible.

Thus the objection "If value is the key to existence, the world would be absolutely perfect" proves to be untenable. All that will follow on axiogenetic principles is that the world will exemplify an optimal balance of the relevant evaluative factors. An optimally realizable best need not be "perfect" in the normal sense of that term, which unrealistically demands value maximality in every relevant respect.

Because some desiderata are in conflict and competition with others, it is an inherently inevitable feature of the nature of things—an inevitable "fact of life"—that value resolution is always a matter of balance, of trade-offs, of compromise. Value factors always compete in matters of realization. A concurrent maximum in every dimension is simply unavailable in this or indeed any other conceivably possible world. All that one can ever reasonably ask for is an auspicious combination of values. And here optimalism can take comfort in the view that indeed there is just exactly one overall optimal alternative, just exactly because that's for the best.

IX. WISHFUL THINKING?

But is not optimalism merely a version of wishful thinking? Not necessarily. For even as in personal life what is best for us is all too often not at all what we individuals want, so in metaphysics what is abstractly for the best is very unlikely to bear any close relationship to what we would want to have if we humans could have things our way.

What prevents optimalism from being too Pollyanna-ish to be plausible is the deeply pessimistic acknowledgment that even the best of possible arrangements is bound to exhibit very real shortcomings. The optimalist need not simply shut his eyes to the world's all-too-evident parochially considered imperfections. For what the optimalist can and should do is to insist that, owing to the intricate inherent interrelationships among value parameters, an "imperfection" in this or that respect must be taken in stride because "imperfections" have to be there for an optimal overall combination of value to be realized. Leibniz took the right approach here: optimalism does not maintain that the world is absolutely perfect but just that it is the best that is possible—that all things considered, the world as it is outranks the available alternatives. There is, in fact, a point of view from which optimalism is a position that looks to be not so much optimistic as deeply pessimistic. For it holds that even the best of possible arrangements is bound to exhibit very real imperfections from the angle of narrowly parochial concerns or interests.

X. CONCLUSION

The upshot of these deliberations is that, once one is willing to have recourse to axiological explanation, there no longer remains any good reason to think that the existence and nature of the real is something so deeply problematic as to remain inexplicably unintelligible—an issue which—on Kantian or other principles—we ought not to inquire into. The axiological approach to explanation represented by optimalism is, to be sure, a drastically unusual and extraordinary one. But then, of course, the question of why Reality should be explicable is a highly unusual and extraordinary question, and it is a cardinal principle of cognitive sagacity that if one is asking an extraordinary question, one must expect an extraordinary answer.

Bibliography

Acar, Rahim. "Reconsidering Avicenna's Position on God's Knowledge of Particulars." In *Interpreting Avicenna: Science and Philosophy in Medieval Islam*, edited by J. McGinnis, 142–56. Leiden: E. J. Brill, 2004.

———. *Talking about God and Talking about Creation: Avicenna's and Thomas Aquinas' Positions*. Leiden: E. J. Brill, 2005.

Adams, Robert Merrihew. "Leibniz's Theories of Contingency." In Chappell, vol. 12, pt. I, 1–41.

Adamson, Peter. "On Knowledge of Particulars." *Proceedings of the Aristotelian Society* 105 (2005): 257–78.

Allen, Reginald E. *Plato's Parmenides: Translation and Analysis*. Minneapolis: University of Minnesota Press, 1983.

Ameriks, Karl, ed. *The Cambridge Companion to German Idealism*. Cambridge: Cambridge University Press, 2000.

Aristotle. *Aristotle's Metaphysics*. Edited by W. D. Ross. Oxford: Clarendon Press, 1981.

———. *Opera: ex recensione Immanuelis Bekkeri, edidit Academia regia borussica*. Berlin: Walter de Gruyter, 1960–87.

———. *Metaphysics: Books I–IX*. Translated by Hugh Tredennick. Loeb Classical Library. Cambridge, Mass.: Harvard University Press, 2003.

Averroës. *Faith and Reason in Islam: Averroes' Exposition of Religious Arguments*. Translated by Ibrahim Najjar. Great Islamic Writings. Oxford: Oneworld, 2001.

Avicenna. *Al-Isharāt wa-t-tanbīhāt*. Edited by J. Forget. Leiden: E. J. Brill, 1892.

———. *Commentary on Lambda*. In *Arisṭū 'inda l-'Arab*, edited by 'A. Badawi. Cairo: Maktabat an-naḥda al-miṣrīya, 1947.

———. *Liber de Philosophia Prima sive Scientia Divina I–IV*. Edited by Simone Van Riet. Louvain Peeters-Leiden: Brill, 1977.

———. *Najāt, Ilāhīyāt*. Edited by M. T. Danish'pazhuh. Tehran: Danishgah-i Tihran, 1985–86.

———. *Shifā', al-Burhān*. Edited by 'A Badawi. Cairo: Association of Authorship, Translation and Publication Press, 1966.

———. *Shifā', al-Ilāhīyāt*, in *The Metaphysics of 'The Healing'*. Translated by Michael E. Marmura. Islamic Translation Series. Provo, UT: Brigham Young University Press, 2005.

———. *Shifā', al-Qiyās*. Edited by S. Zayed. Cairo: Wizārat-al ma'ārif, 1964.

———. *Shifā', aṭ-Ṭabī'īyā*. Edited by S. Zayed. Cairo: General Egyptian Book Organization, 1983.

———. *Ta 'līqāt*. Edited by 'A Badawi. Cairo: Maktabat al-'Arabīya, 1973.

Beiser, Frederick C. *The Fate of Reason: German Philosophy from Kant to Fichte*. Cambridge, Mass.: Harvard University Press, 1987.

Behler, Ernst, ed. *The Philosophy of German Idealism*. New York: Continuum, 1987.

Bennett, Jonathan. "Descartes's Theory of Modality." *Philosophical Review* 103, no. 4 (1994): 639–67.

Berthrong, John H. *Concerning Creativity: A Comparison of Chu Hsi, Whitehead, and Neville*. Albany: State University of New York Press, 1998.

Blankenhorn, Bernhard. "The Good as Self-Diffusive in Thomas Aquinas." *Angelicum* 79 (2002): 803–37.

Boler, John. *Charles Peirce and Scholastic Realism*. Seattle: University of Washington Press, 1963.

Bracken, Joseph A. *The Divine Matrix: Creativity as Link between East and West*. Maryknoll, NY: Orbis, 1995.

———. *The One in the Many: A Contemporary Reconstruction of the God-World Relationship*. Grand Rapids, MI: William B. Eerdmans, 2001.

Buchheim, Thomas. *Eins von Allem. Die Selbstbescheidung des Idealismus in Schellings Spätphilosophie*. Hamburg: Felix Meiner, 1992.

Burrill, Donald R. *The Cosmological Arguments: A Spectrum of Opinion*. Garden City, NY: Anchor Books, 1967.

Buschmann, Elisabeth. *Untersuchungen zum Problem der Materie bei Avicenna*. Frankfurt am Main: Peter Lang, 1979.

Carraud, Vincent. *Causa sive ratio: La raison de la cause, de Suarez à Leibniz*. Paris: Presses Universitaires de France, 2002.

Cassirer, Ernst. *Leibniz' System in seinen wissenschaftlichen Grundlagen*. 1902. Reprint, Hildesheim: Olms, 1962.

Chan, Wing-Tsit. *A Sourcebook in Chinese Philosophy*. Princeton: Princeton University Press, 1963.

Chappell, Vere, ed. *Gottfried Wilhelm Leibniz*. Vol. 12, pts. I–II. *Essays on Early Modern Philosophers from Descartes and Hobbes to Newton and Leibniz*. New York: Garland, 1992.

Cheng Chungying. "Reality and Divinity in Chinese Philosophy." In *A Companion to World Philosophies*, edited by Eliot Deutsch and Ron Bontekoe, 185–200. Oxford: Blackwell Publishers, 1997.

Clarke, W. Norris. *Explorations in Metaphysics: Being, God, Person*. Notre Dame, IN: University of Notre Dame Press, 1994.

Confucius. *The Analects of Confucius: A Philosophical Translation*. Translated and edited by Roger T. Ames and Henry Rosemont, Jr. New York: Ballantine Books, 1998.

Corrington, Robert S. "Neville's 'Naturalism' and the Location of God." *American Journal of Theology and Philosophy* 18 (1997): 257–80.

Couturat, Louis. *La logique de Leibniz d' après des documents inédits*. Paris: Alcan, 1901.

Craig, William L. *The Cosmological Argument from Plato to Leibniz*. London: Macmillan, 1980.

Cristin, Renato, and Kiyoshi Sakai, eds. *Phänomenologie und Leibniz*. Freiburg: Alber, 2000.

Davidson, Herbert A. *Proofs for Eternity, Creation, and the Existence of God in Medieval Islamic and Jewish Philosophy*. New York: Oxford University Press, 1987.

Denker, Alfred. "Freiheit ist das höchste Gut des Menschen. Schellings erste Auseinandersetzung mit der Jenaer Wissenschaftslehre Fichtes." In *Sein—Reflexion—Freiheit. Aspekte der Philosophie Johann Gottlieb Fichtes*, edited by Christoph Asmuth, 35–68. Amsterdam: B. R. Grüner, 1997.

————. "Schelling und Aristoteles." In *Das antike Denken in der Philosophie Schellings*, edited by Rainer Adolphi and Jörg Jantzen, 305–20. Stuttgart–Bad Cannstatt: Frommann-Holzboog, 2004.

Descartes, René. *Oeuvres de Descartes*. Edited by Charles Adam and Paul Tannery. 11 vols. Paris: J. Vrin, 1996.

Desgabets, Robert. *Dom Robert Desgabets: Oeuvres philosophiques inédites*. Edited by J. Beaude. Amsterdam: Quadratures, 1983–85.

Dewan, Lawrence. "St. Thomas and the Possibles." *The New Scholasticism* 53 (1979): 76–85.

di Giovanni, George, and Harris, H. S., trans. *Between Kant and Hegel: Texts in the Development of Post-Kantian Idealism*. Albany: State University of New York Press, 1985.

Distaso, Leonardo V. *The Paradox of Existence: Philosophy and Aesthetics in the Young Schelling*. Dordrecht: Kluwer Academic Publishers, 2004.

Ehrhardt, Walter E. "'Freiheit ist unser und der Gottheit Höchstes'—ein Rückweg zur *Freiheitsschrift?*" In *Schellings Weg zur Freiheitsschrift. Legende und Wirklichkeit*, edited by Hans Michael Baumgartner and Wilhelm G. Jacobs, 240–51. Stuttgart–Bad Cannstatt: Frommann-Holzboog, 1996.

————. "Nur ein Schelling." *Studi Urbinati di Storia, Filosofia e Letteratura*, Anno LI, Nuova Serie B, N. 1–2 (1977): 111–22.

————. "Schelling's Gottesbegriff." In *Religion und Gott im Denken der Neuzeit*, edited by Albert Franz and Wilhelm G. Jacobs, 126–35. Paderborn: Ferdinand Schöningh, 2000.

Ewing, A. C. "Two 'Proofs' of God's Existence." *Religious Studies* 1 (1965): 29–45.

Fichte, Johann Gottlieb. *Early Philosophical Writings*. Translated and edited by Daniel Breazeale. Ithaca and London: Cornell University Press, 1988.

————. *Science of Knowledge (Wissenschaftslehre) with the First and Second introductions*. Edited and translated by Peter Heath and John Lachs. New York: Appleton-Century-Crofts, 1970.

Ford, Lewis S. *Transforming Process Theism*. Albany: State University of New York Press, 2000.

Frankfurt, Harry. "Descartes on the Creation of the Eternal Truths." *Philosophical Review* 86 (1977): 36–57.

Franz, Albert. *Philosophische Religion: Eine Auseinandersetzung mit den*

Grundlegungsproblemen der Spätphilosophie F. W. J. Schellings. Amsterdam: Rodopi, 1992.

Gardner, Daniel K. "Attentiveness and Meditative Reading in Cheng-Zhu Neo-Confucianism." In *Confucian Spirituality,* vol. 2, edited by Tu Weiming and Mary Evelyn Tucker, 99–119. New York: Crossroad Publishing Company, 2004.

Gerhard, Myriam. *Von der Materie der Wissenschaft zur Wissenschaft der Materie: Schellings Naturphilosophie im Ausgang der Transzendentalphilosophie Kants und Fichtes und ihre Kritik einer systematischen Bestimmung des Verhältnisses von Natur und Vernunft.* Berlin: Duncker & Humblot, 2002.

Gerson, Lloyd P. *Aristotle and Other Platonists.* Ithaca, NY: Cornell University Press, 2005.

———. "Plotinus' Metaphysics: Creation or Emanation?" *Review of Metaphysics* 46 (1993): 559–74.

Gloyna, Tanja. *Kosmos und System: Schellings Weg in die Philosophie.* Stuttgart–Bad Cannstatt: Frommann-Holzboog, 2002.

Gutas, Dimitri. *Avicenna and the Aristotelian Tradition: Introduction to Reading Avicenna's Philosophical Works.* Leiden: E. J. Brill, 1988.

Hacking, Ian. "Infinite Analysis." *Studia Leibnitiana* 6 (1974): 126–30.

Hall, David. "The Culture of Metaphysics: On Saving Neville's Project (from Neville)." In *Interpreting Neville,* edited by J. Harley Chapman and Nancy K. Frankenberry, 271–90. Albany: State University of New York Press, 1999.

———. "On Looking Up 'Dialectics' in a Chinese Dictionary." In *Being and Dialectic: Metaphysics and Culture,* edited by William Desmond and Joseph Grange, 197–212. Albany: State University of New York Press, 2000.

———. "The Way and the Truth." In *A Companion to World Philosophies,* edited by Eliot Deutsch and Ron Bontekoe, 214–24. Oxford: Blackwell Publishers, 1997.

Halper, Edward C. "The Idealism of Hegel's System." *The Owl of Minerva* 34 (2002): 19–58.

———. "The Logic of Hegel's *Philosophy of Nature:* Nature, Space and Time." In *Hegel and the Philosophy of Nature,* edited by Stephen Houlgate, 29–49. SUNY Series in Hegelian Studies. Albany: State University of New York Press, 1998.

———. "A Tale of Two Metaphysics: Alison Stone's Environmental Hegel." *Bulletin of the Hegel Society of Great Britain,* no. 51/52 (2005): 1–12.

Hartshorne, Charles. *The Divine Relativity.* New Haven, CT: Yale University Press, 1948.

Hartshorne, Charles, John B. Cobb, Jr., and Lewis S. Ford. "Three Responses to Neville's *Creativity and God." Process Studies* 10, nos. 3–4 (1980): 73–88.

Hasler, Ludwig, ed. *Schelling. Seine Bedeutung für eine Philosophie der Natur und der Geschichte: Referate und Kolloquien der Internationalen Schelling-Tagung 1979.* Stuttgart–Bad Cannstatt: Frommann-Holzboog, 1981.

Hegel, Georg Wilhelm Friedrich. *Enzyklopädie der philosophischen Wissenschaften im Grundrisse (1830).* Vol. 20 of *Gesammelte Werke.* Edited by Wolfgang Bonsiepen and Hans-Christiane Lucas. Hamburg: Felix Meiner, 1992.

————. *Hegel's Philosophy of Mind: Being Part Three of the 'Encyclopaedia of the Philosophical Sciences' (1830)*. Translated by A. V. Miller. Oxford: Clarendon Press, 1971.

————. *Hegel's Philosophy of Nature: Being Part Two of the Encyclopaedia of the Philosophical Sciences (1830)*. Translated by Arnold V. Miller. Oxford: Clarendon Press, 1970.

————. *Hegel's Science of Logic*. Translated by A. V. Miller. Muirhead Library of Philosophy. London: Allen & Unwin, 1969.

————. *Lectures on the History of Philosophy*. Translated by E. S. Haldane. Lincoln: University of Nebraska Press, 1995.

————. *The Logic of Hegel*. In *The Encyclopedia of the Philosophical Sciences*. Rev. ed., translated by William Wallace, c. 7. Oxford: Oxford University Press, 1892.

————. *Wissenschaft der Logik. Erster Teil. Die Objektive Logik. Erster Band. Die Lehre Vom Sein (1832)*. Vol. 21 of *Gesammelte Werke*. Edited by Friedrich Hogemann and Walter Jaeschke. Hamburg: Meiner, 1985.

————. *Wissenschaft der Logik. Zweiter Band. Die Subjektive Logik (1816)*. Vol. 12 of *Gesammelte Werke*. Edited by Friedrich Hogemann and Walter Jaeschke. Hamburg: Meiner, 1985.

Heidegger, Martin. *Beiträge zur Philosophie (Vom Ereignis)*. Edited by Friedrich-Wilhelm von Herrmann. Gesamtausgabe Band 65. Frankfurt am Main: Klostermann, 1989.

————. *Einführung in die Metaphysik*. Edited by Petra Jaeger. Frankfurt am Main: Verlag Vittorio Klostermann, 1983.

————. "Einleitung zu, 'Was ist Metaphysik?'" In *Wegmarken*, edited by Friedrich-Wilhelm von Herrmann, 365–83. Frankfurt am Main: Verlag Vittorio Klostermann, 1976.

————. *Die Grundprobleme der Phänomenologie*. Edited by Friedrich-Wilhelm von Herrmann. Gesamtausgabe Band 24. Frankfurt am Main: Klostermann, 1975.

————. *Der Satz vom Grund*. Pfullingen: Neske, 1957.

————. *Schelling: 'Vom Wesen der menschlichen Freiheit (1809).'* Edited by Ingrid Schüßler. Frankfurt am Main: Vittorio Klostermann, 1988.

Heine, Heinrich. "Zur Geschichte der Religion und Philosophie in Deutschland." In *Über Deutschland 1833–1863: Aufsätze über Kunst und Philosophie*, edited by Renate Francke. Berlin und Paris: Akademie-Verlag, 1972.

Hemmerle, Klaus. *Gott und das Denken nach Schellings Spätphilosophie*. Freiburg i. Br.: Verlag Herder, 1968.

Hennigfeld, Jochem. *Friedrich Wilhelm Joseph Schellings, Philosophische Untersuchungen über das Wesen der menschlichen Freiheit und die damit zusammenhängenden Gegenstände*. Darmstadt: Wissenschaftliche Buchgesellschaft, 2001.

Henrich, Dieter. *Between Kant and Hegel: Lectures on German Idealism*. Edited by David S. Pacini. Cambridge, Mass.: Harvard University Press, 2003.

————. *Grundlegung aus dem Ich: Untersuchungen zur Vorgeschichte des Ide-*

alismus. Tübingen—Jena (1790-1794). 2 vols. Darmstadt: Wissenschaftliche Buchgesellschaft, 2004.

Holz, Harald. *Die Idee der Philosophie bei Schelling: Metaphysische Motive in seiner Frühphilosophie*. Freiburg-Munich: Verlag Karl Alber, 1977.

Hourani, George F. "Ibn Sīnā on Necessary and Possible Existence." *The Philosophical Forum* 4 (1972): 74–86.

Hyman, Arthur. "Aristotle's 'First Matter' and Avicenna's and Averroes' 'Corporeal Form.'" In *Essays in Medieval Jewish and Islamic Philosophy*, edited by A. Hyman, 335–406. New York: KTAV Publishing House, 1977.

Jacobs, Wilhelm G. *Gottesbegriff und Geschichtsphilosophie in der Sicht Schellings*. Stuttgart–Bad Cannstatt: Frommann-Holzboog, 1993.

———. *Schelling lesen*. Stuttgart–Bad Cannstatt: Frommann-Holzboog, 2005.

———. *Zwischen Revolution und Orthodoxie? Schelling und seine Freunde im Stift und an der Universität Tübingen: Texte und Untersuchungen*. Stuttgart–Bad Cannstatt: Frommann-Holzboog, 1989.

Jamme, Christoph, ed. *Mythologie der Vernunft. Hegels 'ältestes Systemprogramm des deutschen Idealismus'*. Frankfurt am Main: Suhrkamp, 1984.

Jähnig, Dieter. *Schelling. Die Kunst in der Philosophie. Erster Band: Schellings Begründung von Natur und Geschichte*. Pfullingen: Neske, 1966.

Jaspers, Karl. *Schelling: Größe und Verhängnis*. München: Piper, 1986.

John Duns Scotus. *Duns Scotus: Philosophical Writings*. Translated by Allan Wolter. London: Thomas Nelson, 1962.

Johnson, A. H. "Leibniz's Method and the Basis of his Metaphysics." In *Metaphysics and its Foundations 1: Sufficient Reason, Truth, and Necessity*. Vol. 1, *Gottfried Wilhelm Leibniz: Critical Assessments*, edited by R. S. Woodhouse, 20–30. London: Routledge, 1994.

Johnson, S. A. "Ibn Sīnā's Fourth Ontological Argument for God's Existence." *Muslim World* 74 (1984): 161–71.

Jones, John D. "An Absolutely Simple God? Reading Pseudo-Dionysius Areopagite." *The Thomist* 69 (2005): 371–406.

Kant, Immanuel. *Critique of Practical Reason*. Translated by Lewis White Beck. New York: Macmillan, 1993.

———. *Critique of Pure Reason*. Translated and edited by Paul Guyer and Allen W. Wood. Cambridge: Cambridge University Press, 1998.

———. *Theoretical Philosophy 1755-1770*. Translated and edited by David Walford with Ralf Meerbote. Cambridge: Cambridge University Press, 1992.

Kasper, Walter. *Das Absolute in der Geschichte: Philosophie und Theologie der Geschichte in der Spätphilosophie Schellings*. Mainz: Matthias Grünewald, 1965.

Kinlaw, Jeffrey. "Schellings ursprüngliche Einsicht: Das ontologische Argument und die Aufgabe der Philosophie." In *System—Freiheit—Geschichte: Schellings Einleitung in die Philosophie (1830) im Kontext seines Werkes*, edited by Holger Zaborowski and Alfred Denker, 123–60. Stuttgart: Frommann-Holzboog, 2004.

Krämer, Hans Joachim. *Plato and the Foundations of Metaphysics: A Work on the Theory of the Principles and Unwritten Doctrines of Plato with a Collec-tion of the Fundamental Documents.* Translated and edited by John R. Catan. Albany: State University of New York Press, 1990.

Kreiml, Josef. *Die Wirklichkeit Gottes: Eine Untersuchung über die Metaphysik und die Religionsphilosophie des späten Schelling.* Regensburg: S. Roderer Verlag, 1989.

Kremer, Klaus. "Bonum est diffusivum sui: Ein Beitrag zum Verhältnis von Neuplatonismus und Christentum." In *Aufstieg und Niedergang der Römischen Welt,* edited by Wolfgang Haase and Hildegard Temporini, Part II, vol. 36.2, 994–1032. Berlin: Walter de Gruyter, 1987.

Kretzmann, Norman. "A General Problem of Creation: Why Would God Cre-ate Anything at All?" In *Being and Goodness,* edited by Scott MacDonald, 208–28. Ithaca: Cornell University Press, 1991.

———. "Goodness, Knowledge, and Indeterminacy in the Philosophy of Thom-as Aquinas." *The Journal of Philosophy: Supplement* 80, no. 10 (1983): 631–49.

———. *The Metaphysics of Creation: Aquinas's Natural Theology in "Summa contra Gentiles II."* Oxford: Clarendon Press, 1999.

———. *The Metaphysics of Theism: Aquinas's Natural Theology in "Summa contra Gentiles I."* Oxford: Clarendon Press, 1997.

Krings, Hermann. "Genesis und Materie—Zur Bedeutung der 'Timaeus'—Handschrift für Schelling's Naturphilosophie." In Schelling, "Timaeus" (1794), 115–55.

Laozi. *The Daodejing of Laozi.* Translated by P. J. Ivanhoe. Indianapolis-Cambridge: Hackett, 2003.

Leibniz, Gottfried Wilhelm. *Confessio Philosophi.* Edited by Otto Saame. Frankfurt am Main: Klostermann, 1967.

———. *Discourse on Method and Other Essays.* Edited and translated by Daniel Garber and Roger Ariew. Indianapolis: Hackett Pub. Co., 1991.

———. *Monadologie.* Edited by André Robinet. Paris: PUF, 1954.

———. *Nouvelles Lettres et Opuscules inédits de Leibniz.* Edited by Foucher de Careil. Paris: Durand, 1857.

———. *Opuscules et fragments inédits de Leibniz.* Edited by Louis Couturat. Paris: Alcan, 1903.

———. *Die philosophischen Schriften von Gottfried Wilhelm Leibniz.* Vol. 4. Edited by G. I. Gerhardt. Hildesheim: Olms, 1965.

———. *Principes de la nature and de la grace fondés en raison.* Edited by André Robinet. Paris: PUF, 1954.

———. *Sämtliche Schriften und Briefe.* Edited by the Akademie der Wissen-schaften. Darmstadt: Reichl, 1930.

———. *Textes inédits d'après de la bibliothéque provinciale de Hanovre.* Edited by G. Grua. 2 vols. Paris: Presses universitaires de France, 1948.

Lennon, Thomas. "The Cartesian Dialectic of Creation." In *The Cambridge His-tory of Seventeenth-Century Philosophy,* edited by D. Garber and M. R. Ayers, 1:331–62. Cambridge: Cambridge University Press, 1998.

Leslie, John. *Value and Existence.* Totowa, NJ: Rowman & Littlefield, 1979.

Lovejoy, Arthur. *The Great Chain of Being.* Cambridge, Mass.: Harvard University Press, 1936.

Lucretius. *On the Nature of the Universe.* Translated by R. E. Latham. Middlesex, England: Penguin, 1970.

Maimonides, Moses. *The Guide of the Perplexed.* Translated by Shlomo Pines. Chicago: University of Chicago Press, 1963.

Marion, Jean-Luc. *Questions cartésiennes II: Sur l'ego et sur Dieu.* Paris: Presses Universitaires de France, 1996.

Marmura, Michael E. *Probing in Islamic Philosophy.* Binghamton, NY: Global Academic Publishing, 2005.

Mates, Benson. *The Philosophy of Leibniz: Metaphysics and Language.* Oxford: Oxford University Press, 1986.

Mayer, Toby. "Ibn Sīnā's 'Burhān al-Siddīqīn.'" *Journal of Islamic Studies* 12 (2001): 18–39.

McGinnis, Jon. *Avicenna.* Oxford and New York: Oxford University Press, 2010.

———. "The Avicennan Sources for Aquinas on Being: Supplemental Remarks to Brian Davies' 'Kenny on Aquinas on Being.'" *Modern Schoolman* 82 (2005): 131–42.

———. "A Penetrating Question in the History of Ideas: Space, Dimensionality, and Interpenetration in the Thought of Avicenna." *Arabic Sciences and Philosophy* 16 (2006): 47–69.

McGinnis, Jon, and Reisman, David C. *Classical Arabic Philosophy: An Amnthology of Sources.* Indianapolis: Hackett, 2007.

Milbank, John. *Theology and Social Theory: Beyond Secular Reason.* Oxford: Blackwell, 1990.

Morewedge, Parvis. "A Third Version of the Ontological Argument in the Ibn Sinian Metaphysics." In *Islamic Philosophical Theology,* edited by P. Morewedge, 188–222. Albany: State University of New York Press, 1979.

Neuhouser, Frederick. *Fichte's Theory of Subjectivity.* Cambridge: Cambridge University Press, 1996.

Neville, Robert C. *Behind the Masks of God: An Essay Toward Comparative Theology.* Albany: State University of New York Press, 1991.

———. "Concerning *Creativity and God*: A Response." *Process Studies* 11, no. 1 (1981): 1–10.

———. *Creativity and God: A Challenge to Process Theology.* New ed. Albany: State University of New York Press, 1995.

———. *Eternity and Time's Flow.* Albany: State University of New York Press, 1993.

———. "From Nothing to Being: The Notion of Creation in Chinese and Western Thought." *Philosophy East & West* 30 (1980): 21–34.

———. *God the Creator: On the Transcendence and Presence of God.* Rev. ed. Albany: State University of New York Press, 1992.

———. *The Highroad around Modernism.* Albany: State University of New York Press, 1992.

———. *On the Scope and Truth of Theology: Theology as Symbolic Engagement.* New York and London: T & T Clark, 2006.

———. *Symbols of Jesus: A Christology of Symbolic Engagement.* Cambridge: Cambridge University Press, 2001.

Nishitani, Keiji. *Religion and Nothingness.* Translated by Jan van Bragt. Berkeley: University of California Press, 1982.

O'Rourke, Fran. *Pseudo-Dionysius and the Metaphysics of Aquinas.* Leiden: Brill, 1992.

Peghaire, Julien. "L'Axiome 'Bonum est diffusivum sui' dans le néo-platonisme et le thomisme." *Revue de l'Université d'Ottawa* 1 (1932): 5*–30*.

Pigler, Agnès. *Plotin, une métaphysique de l'amour: l'amour comme structure du monde intelligible.* Paris: Vrin, 2002.

Pinkard, Terry. *German Philosophy 1760–1860: The Legacy of Idealism.* Cambridge: Cambridge University Press, 2002.

Plato. *Platonis Opera.* Edited by E. A. Duke, W. F. Hicken, etc. New York: Oxford University Press, 1995–.

———. *Platonis Opera.* Edited by John Burnet. 5 vols. Scriptorum classicorum bibliotheca oxoniensis. Oxford: Clarendon, 1900–1907.

Plotinus. *Enneads.* Translated by A. H. Armstrong. 7 vols. Loeb Classical Library. Cambridge, Mass.: Harvard University Press, 1969–1988.

———. *Plotini Opera.* Edited by Paul Henry and Hans-Rudolf Schwyzer. 3 vols. Scriptorum classicorum bibliotheca Oxoniensis. Oxford: Clarendon, 1964–82.

Pseudo-Dionysius. *De divinis Nominibus.* Vol. 3, *Patrologiae cursus completes, Series Graeca.* Edited by J. P. Migne. Paris: Imprimerie Catholique, 1857.

———. *Pseudo-Dionysius: The Complete Works.* Translated by Colm Luibheid. New York–Mahnah: Paulist Press, 1987.

Regis, Pierre-Sylvain. *L'Usage de la raison et de la foy, ou l'accord de la foy et de la raison.* Edited by J.-R. Armogathe. Paris: Fayard, 1996.

Rescher, Nicholas. *Nature and Understanding.* Oxford: Clarendon, 2000.

———. *The Riddle Of Existence: An Essay In Idealistic Metaphysics.* Lanham, MD: University Press of America, 1984.

Ropohl, Heinrich. *Das Eine und die Welt: Versuch zur Interpretation der Leibnizischen Metaphysik.* Leipzig: Hirzel, 1936.

Rosen, Joe. "The Primacy of Asymmetry over Symmetry in Physics," c. 11 in *Physics and Whitehead: Quantum, Process, and Experience,* edited by Timothy E. Eastman and Hank Keeton. Albany: State University of New York Press, 2004.

Ross, James. "Aquinas's Exemplarism; Aquinas's Voluntarism." *American Catholic Philosophical Quarterly* 64 (1990): 171–98.

Rowe, William L. *The Cosmological Argument.* Princeton: Princeton University Press, 1975.

Rudolphi, Michael. *Produktion und Konstruktion: Zur Genese der Naturphilosophie in Schellings Frühphilosophie.* Stuttgart–Bad Cannstatt: Frommann-Holzboog, 2001.

Russell, Bertrand. *A Critical Exposition of the Philosophy of Leibniz.* 2d ed. London: George Allen & Unwin, 1937.

Scheler, Max. *Die Stellung des Menschen im Kosmos.* 15th ed. Edited by Manfred S. Frings. Bonn: Bouvier Verlag, 2002.

Schelling, F. W. J. *The Ages of the World (Fragment)*. Translated by Jason M. Wirth. Albany: State University of New York Press, 2000.

———. *Einleitung in die Philosophie*. Edited by Walter E. Ehrhardt. Stuttgart–Bad Cannstatt: Frommann-Holzboog, 1989.

———. *First Outline of a System of the Philosophy of Nature*. Translated by Keith R. Peterson. Albany: State University of New York Press, 2004.

———. *Ideas for a Philosophy of Nature as an Introduction to the Study of this Science*. Translated by Errol E. Harris and Peter Heath. Cambridge: Cambridge University Press, 1988.

———. *Ideas on a Philosophy of Nature as an Introduction to the Study of this Science*, translated by Priscilla Hayden-Roy, in *The Philosophy of German Idealism*, edited by Ernst Behler. New York: Continuum, 1987.

———. *On the History of Modern Philosophy*. Translated and edited by Andrew Bowie. Cambridge: Cambridge University Press, 1994.

———. *Philosophical Investigations into the Essence of Human Freedom*. Translated and introduced by Jeff Love and Johannes Schmidt. Albany: State University of New York Press, 2006.

———. *Sämmtliche Werke*. Edited by Karl Friedrich August Schelling. Stuttgart-Augsburg: Cotta, 1856–1864.

———. *System der Weltalter. Münchener Vorlesung 1828/27 in einer Nachschrift von Ernst von Lausaulx*. 2d ed. Edited by Siegbert Peetz. Frankfurt am Main: Vittorio Klostermann, 1998.

———. *System of Transcendental Idealism* (1800). Translated by Peter Heath. Charlottesville: University of Virginia Press, 2001.

———. *"Timaeus" (1794)*. Edited by Hartmut Buchner. Stuttgart–Bad Cannstatt: Frommann-Holzboog, 1994.

———. *Urfassung der Philosophie der Offenbarung*. Vols. 1–2. Edited by Walter E. Ehrhardt. Hamburg: Felix Meiner Verlag, 1992.

Schmaltz, Tad M. "Deflating Descartes's Causal Axiom." *Oxford Studies in Early Modern Philosophy* 3 (2006): 1–31.

———. *Radical Cartesianism: The French Reception of Descartes*. New York: Cambridge University Press, 2002.

Schröter, Manfred. *Kritische Studien: Über Schelling und zur Kulturphilosophie*. München: R. Oldenbourg, 1971.

Schulz, Walter. *Die Vollendung des Deutschen Idealismus in der Spätphilosophie Schellings*. 2d ed. Pfullingen: Neske, 1975.

Schurr, Adolf. *Philosophie als System bei Fichte, Schelling und Hegel*. Stuttgart–Bad Cannstatt: Frommann-Holzboog, 1974.

Shun Kwong-Loi. "Ideas of the Good in Chinese Philosophy." In *A Companion to World Philosophies*, edited by Eliot Deutsch and Ron Bontekoe, 139–47. Oxford: Blackwell Publishers, 1997.

Siger of Brabant. *Quaestiones in Metaphysicam*. Edited by Armand Maurer. Louvain-la-Neuve: Éditions de l'Institut Supérieur de Philosophie, 1983.

———. *Quaestiones in Metaphysicam*. Edited by William Dunphy. Louvain-la-Neuve: Éditions de l'Institut Supérieur de Philosophie, 1981.

Sim, May. "Categories and Commensurability in Confucius and Aristotle: A

Response to MacIntyre." In *Categories: Historical and Systematic Essays*, edited by Michael Gorman and Jonathan J. Sanford, 58–77. Washington, DC: The Catholic University of America Press, 2004.

———. "Harmony and the Mean in the *Nicomachean Ethics* and the *Zhongyong.*" *Dao: A Journal of Comparative Philosophy* 3 (2004): 253–80.

———. "The Moral Self in Confucius and Aristotle." *International Philosophical Quarterly* 43 (2003): 439–62.

———. *Remastering Morals with Aristotle and Confucius.* Cambridge: Cambridge University Press, 2007.

———. "Ritual and Realism in Early Chinese Science." *Journal of Chinese Philosophy* 29 (2002): 501–23.

Sleigh, Robert C. "Truth and Sufficient Reason in the Philosophy of Leibniz." In Chappell, Vol. 12, pt. II, 251–84.

———. "On the Two Great Principles of All Our Reasonings." In Chappell, vol. 12, pt. II, 285–308.

Smith, Gerard. "Avicenna and the Possibles." *The New Scholasticism* 17 (1943): 340–57.

Snow, Dale E. *Schelling and the End of Idealism.* Albany: State University of New York Press, 1996.

Solomon, Robert C., and Kathleen M. Higgins, eds. *The Age of German Idealism.* London: Routledge, 1993.

Spinoza, Benedictus de. *A Spinoza Reader: The "Ethics" and Other Works.* Translated by E. M. Curley. Princeton, NJ: Princeton University Press, 1994.

———. *Spinoza Opera.* Edited by Carl Gebhardt. 4 vols. Heidelberg: Carl Winter, 1925.

Stone, Abraham D. "Simplicius and Avicenna on the Essential Corporeity of Material Substance." In *Aspects of Avicenna*, edited by R. Wisnovsky, 73–130. Princeton, NJ: Markus Wiener Publishers, 2001.

Street, Tony. "Fakhraddin ar-Razi's Critique of Avicennan Logic." In *Logik und Theologie: Das Organon im arabischen und im lateinischen Mittelalter*, edited by U. Rudolph and D. Perler, 99–116. Leiden: E. J. Brill, 2005.

Sturma, Dieter. "Politics and the New Mythology." In *The Cambridge Companion to German Idealism*, edited by Karl Ameriks, 219–38. Cambridge: Cambridge University Press, 2000.

Suárez, Francisco. *Disputationes Metaphysicae.* 2 vols. Hildesheim: G. Olms, 1965.

Suchocki, Marjorie Hewitt. *The End of Evil: Process Eschatology in Historical Context.* Albany: State University of New York Press, 1988.

———. *God Christ Church: A Practical Guide to Process Theology.* Rev. ed. New York: Continuum, 1995.

Szlezák, Thomas A. *Reading Plato.* Translated by Graham Zanker. London: Routledge, 1999.

Thomas Aquinas. *De ente et essentia.* Vol. 43, *Sancti Thomae de Aquino Opera omnia.* Leonine edition. Rome: 1976.

———. *De veritate.* Vol. 22, *Sancti Thomae de Aquino Opera omnia.* Leonine edition. Rome: Editori di San Tommaso, 1975.

————. *In Librum B. Dionysii De Divinis Nominibus Expositio.* Vol. 2. Edited by Ceslaus Pera. Turin-Rome: Marietti, 1950.

————. *On Being and Essence.* 2d ed. Translated by Armand Maurer. Toronto: The Pontifical Institute of Mediaeval Studies, 1968.

————. *Prooemium* to *In duodecim Libros Metaphysicorum Aristotelis Expositio.* Rome-Turin: Marietti, 1950.

————. *Quaestiones disputatae De potentia.* Edited by Paul M. Pession. Turin-Rome: Marietti, 1965.

————. *Scriptum super Libros Sententiarum.* Vol. 2. Edited by P. Mandonnet. Paris: Lethielleux, 1929.

————. *Summa Contra Gentiles.* Translated by Anton C. Pegis. Notre Dame, IN: University of Notre Dame Press, 1975.

————. *Summa contra Gentiles. Sancti Thomae de Aquino Opera omnia.* Leonine edition, Vols. 13–15. Rome: Typis Riccardi Garroni, 1918–30.

————. *Summa theologiae. Sancti Thomae de Aquino Opera omnia.* Leonine edition. Vols. 4–12. Rome: S.C. de Propaganda Fide, 1888–1906. *Editio Leonina Manualis.* Rome: Leonine Commission, 1934.

————. *Super Boetium De Trinitate. Sancti Thomae de Aquino Opera omnia.* Leonine edition. Vol. 50. Rome: S.C. de Propaganda Fidei, 1992.

Tilliette, Xavier. *Schelling. Une philosophie en devenir.* 2 vols. 2d ed. Paris: Vrin, 1992.

————. *Schelling. Biographie.* Translated by Susanne Schaper. Stuttgart: Klett-Cotta, 2004.

Tu Weiming. "The Continuity of Being: Chinese Visions of Nature." In *On Nature,* edited by Leroy S. Rouner, 113–29. Notre Dame, IN: University of Notre Dame Press, 1984.

Vaught, Carl. "Being, Nonbeing, and Creation *Ex Nihilo.*" In *Interpreting Neville,* edited by J. Harley Chapman and Nancy K. Frankenberry, 147–64. Albany: State University of New York Press, 1999.

Viganó, Federica. "Schelling liest Platons 'Timaeus': Die Erneuerung zwischen Platon und Kant." In *Das antike Denken in der Philosophie Schellings,* edited by Rainer Adolphi and Jörg Jantzen, 227–35. Stuttgart–Bad Cannstatt: Frommann-Holzboog, 2004.

Voltaire. *Candide and Other Writings.* New York: Modern Library, 1956.

Ward, Keith. *Religion and Creation.* Oxford: Oxford University Press, 1996.

Waterlow, Sarah. *Passage and Possibility: A Study of Aristotle's Modal Concepts.* Oxford: Clarendon Press, 1982.

Weiss, Paul. *Modes of Being.* Carbondale: Southern Illinois University Press, 1958.

Wells, Norman. "Descartes' Uncreated Eternal Truths." *New Scholasticism* 56 (1982): 185–99.

Welte, Bernhard. *Religionsphilosophie.* 5th ed. Edited by Bernhard Casper and Klaus Kienzler. Frankfurt am Main: Verlag Josef Knecht, 1997.

Whitehead, Alfred N. *Process and Reality: An Essay in Philosophical Cosmology.* Rev. ed. Edited by David Ray Griffin and Donald Sherburne. New York: Free Press, 1978.

————. *Religion in the Making.* New York: Macmillan, 1926.
Wildman, Wesley J. "Ground of Being Theologies." In *The Oxford Handbook of Religion and Science,* edited by Philip Clayton. Oxford: Oxford University Press, 2006.
Wippel, John. *Metaphysical Themes in Thomas Aquinas II.* Washington, D.C.: The Catholic University of America Press, 2007.
————. *The Metaphysical Thought of Thomas Aquinas: From Finite Being to Uncreated Being.* Washington, D.C.: The Catholic University of America Press, 2000.
Wisnovsky, Robert. *Avicenna's Metaphysics in Context.* Ithaca, NY: Cornell University Press, 2003.
Yaḥyā ibn ʿAdī. "Establishing the Nature of the Possible." [In Arabic] Translated and edited by Carl Ehrig-Eggert as "Yaḥyā ibn ʿAdī: über den Nachweis der Natur des Möglichen." *Zeitschrift für Geschichte der arabisch-islamischen Wissenschaften* 5 (1989): 63–97 [Arabic], 283–97.
Yu Jiyuan. "The Language of Being: Between Aristotle and Chinese Philosophy." *International Philosophical Quarterly* 39 (1999): 439–54.
Zaborowski, Holger. "'Reason and Freedom remain our Schibboleth and the Invisible Church Our Point of Unity.' The German Idealist View of the Church and Its Political Implications." In *Church as Politeia: The Political Self-Understanding of Christianity. Proceedings of a Becket Institute Conference at the University of Oxford, 28 September–1 October 2000,* edited by Christoph Stumpf and Holger Zaborowski, 191–218. Berlin: Walter de Gruyter, 2004.
————. "Reason, Truth, and History. The Early Hegel's Philosophy of History." In *Hegel's Phenomenology of Spirit: New Critical Essays,* edited by Alfred Denker and Michael Vater, 21–58. New York: Humanity Books, 2003.
Zedler, Beatrice. "Another Look at Avicenna." *New Scholasticism* 50 (1976): 504–21.
————. "Why Are the Possibles Possible?" *New Scholasticism* 55 (1981): 113–30.
Zeltner, Hermann. *Schelling-Forschung seit 1954.* Darmstadt: Wissenschaftliche Buchgesellschaft, 1975.

Contributors

DANIEL O. DAHLSTROM, chair of the Department of Philosophy at Boston University, is the author of *Heidegger's Concept of Truth* (2001) and *Philosophical Legacies* (2008). A former president of the Metaphysical Society of America and currently presiding officer of the Heidegger Circle, he is the editor of *Interpreting Heidegger: New Essays* (forthcoming, 2011). His recent articles include "*Continentia*, Self-possession, and Resoluteness: What Is the Good of *Being and Time?*" *Research in Phenomenology* (2009); and "The Critique of Pure Reason and Continental Philosophy" in *Cambridge Companion to Kant's Critique of Pure Reason*, ed. Paul Guyer (2010).

LLOYD P. GERSON is professor of philosophy at the University of Toronto. He has written many books and articles on ancient philosophy, including *Ancient Epistemology* (2009); *Aristotle and Other Platonists* (2005); *Knowing Persons: A Study in Plato* (2004); *Plotinus* (1994); and *God and Greek Philosophy* (1990). He is the editor of *The Cambridge History of Philosophy in Late Antiquity* (2010) and *The Cambridge Companion to Plotinus* (1996); and editor and translator of, with John Dillon, *Neoplatonic Philosophy* (2004), with Brad Inwood, *Hellenistic Philosophy* (2nd edition 1997), and with H. G. Apostle, *Aristotle. Selected Works* (1992).

EDWARD C. HALPER is professor of philosophy at the University of Georgia. He is the author of *One and Many in Aristotle's Metaphysics: Books Alpha–Delta* (2009) and *One and Many in Aristotle's Metaphysics: The Central Books* (1989, reprint 2005). The final book in the series, *One and Many in Aristotle's Metaphysics: Books I–N*, is scheduled to appear in 2012. Halper is also the author of *Form and Reason: Essays in Metaphysics* (1993), along with some fifty papers in journals and books, including many on Hegel and Plato and others on Maimonides, Spinoza, and Nietzsche. Recent articles include "Aristotle's Paradigmatism: Book Iota and the Difference It Makes," *Proceedings of the Boston Area Colloquium in Ancient*

Philosophy (2007); "Hegel's Criticism of Newton" in *The Cambridge Companion to Hegel and Nineteenth Century Philosophy* (2008); and "Torah as Political Philosophy: Maimonides and Spinoza on Divine Law," in *Judaic Sources and Western Thought: Jerusalem's Enduring Presence* (forthcoming, 2011).

BRIAN MARTINE is professor of philosophy and director of the Humanities Center at the University of Alabama in Huntsville. He is the author of *Individuals and Individuality* (1984); *Indeterminacy and Intelligibility* (1992); and the first two parts of a trilogy in systematic philosophy (tentatively titled "Where Are the Philosophers Now?"), which are currently under review for publication. He has also published various shorter essays developing the themes of these central works. He serves as the chief administrative officer of the Metaphysical Society of America and on the Council of Administrative Officers of the American Council of Learned Societies.

JON MCGINNIS is associate professor of classical and medieval philosophy at the University of Missouri, St. Louis. His general research interest is in the history and philosophy of Aristotelian natural philosophy, with a particular focus on that tradition within the Arabic-speaking world. McGinnis has written numerous articles on various aspects of ancient and medieval science and philosophy. He is also the author of a general introduction to the philosophy of Avicenna in Oxford University Press's Great Medieval Series (2010); translator and editor of Avicenna's *Physics* (2009) from his encyclopedic work *The Healing*; and co-translator, with David C. Reisman, of *Classical Arabic Philosophy: An Anthology of Sources* (2007). McGinnis has been awarded a National Endowment for the Humanities Summer Stipend, two NEH Fellowships, and a Mellon grant, and has been a member of the Institute for Advanced Study, Princeton.

ROBERT CUMMINGS NEVILLE is professor of philosophy, religion, and theology and dean emeritus of the School of Theology at Boston University. He is the author of twenty-two books in those fields, ranging from *God the Creator* (1968) to *Realism in Religion* (2009).

NICHOLAS RESCHER is Distinguished University Professor of Philosophy at the University of Pittsburgh, where he has also served as chair of the Philosophy Department and as director (and currently chair) of the Center for Philosophy of Science. In a productive research career extending over six decades, he has established himself as a systematic philosopher of the old style with over one hundred books to his credit, ranging over all areas of philosophy, sixteen of them translated from English into eight other languages. Rescher has served as a president of the American Philosophical Association, the American Catholic Philosophical Association, the American G. W. Leibniz Society, the C. S. Peirce Society, and the Metaphysical Society of America, as well as secretary general of the International Union of History and Philosophy of Sciences. He was the founding editor of the *American Philosophical Quarterly*. An honorary member of Corpus Christi College, Oxford, he has been elected to membership in the American Academy of Arts and Sciences, the Royal Arabic Society of Great Britain, the European Academy of Arts and Sciences (Academia Europaea), the Royal Society of Canada, the Institut International de Philosophie, and several other learned academies. He was awarded the Alexander von Humboldt prize for Humanistic Scholarship in 1984, the Belgian Prix Mercier in 2005, and the Aquinas Medal of the American Catholic Philosophical Association in 2007.

TAD M. SCHMALTZ is professor of philosophy at the University of Michigan, Ann Arbor. He is the author of *Malebranche's Theory of the Soul* (1996); *Radical Cartesianism* (2002); and *Descartes on Causation* (2008). He is a co-editor of the *Historical Dictionary of Descartes and Cartesian Philosophy* (2003), republished in paperback as *The A to Z of Descartes and Cartesian Philosophy* (2010); and is the editor of *Receptions of Descartes* (2005). Among his recent published articles and book chapters are "Malebranche and Leibniz on the Best of All Possible Worlds," *Southern Journal of Philosophy* (2010); "Cartesianism in Crisis: The Case of the Eucharist," in *Theology and Early Modern Philosophy* (2010), "Cartesian Freedom in Historical Perspective," in *Descartes and the Modern* (2008); and "Occasionalism and Mechanism: Fontenelle's Objections to Malebranche," *British Journal for the History of Philosophy* (2008).

MAY SIM is associate professor of philosophy at the College of the Holy Cross. She is the author of *Remastering Morals with Aristotle and Confucius* (2007); and a contributor to *The Crossroads of Norm and Nature: Essays on Aristotle's Ethics and Metaphysics* (1995) and *From Puzzles to Prin-*

ciples? Essays on Aristotle's Dialectic (1999). Her articles comparing Eastern and Western philosophies in the areas of metaphysics, ethics, education, the environment, and human rights have been published in the *International Philosophical Quarterly*; *Dao: A Journal of Comparative Philosophy*; the *Journal of Chinese Philosophy*; and *Asian Philosophy*. She is currently working on a book-length project on a Confucian account of human rights.

JOHN F. WIPPEL is Theodore Basselin Professor of Philosophy at the Catholic University of America. He is the author of *The Metaphysical Thought of Godfrey of Fontaines* (1981); *Metaphysical Themes in Thomas Aquinas* (1984); *Boethius of Dacia: "On the Supreme Good," On the Eternity of the World, On Dreams* (1987); *Mediaeval Reactions to the Encounter between Faith and Reason* (1995); *The Metaphysical Thought of Thomas Aquinas* (2000); *Metaphysical Themes in Thomas Aquinas II* (2007); and co-author and co-editor, with Allan B. Wolter, of *Medieval Philosophy: From St. Augustine to Nicholas of Cusa* (Free Press, 1969); co-author, with B. C. Bazán, G. Fransen, and D. Jacquart, of *Les questions disputées et les questions quodlibétiques dans les facultés de théologie, de droit et de medicine* (1985); editor of *Studies in Medieval Philosophy* (1987); and the author of many articles and book chapters.

HOLGER ZABOROWSKI is assistant professor in the School of Philosophy at the Catholic University of America. His publications include *"Eine Frage von Irre und Schuld?" Martin Heidegger und der Nationalsozialismus* (2010); *Robert Spaemann's Philosophy of the Human Person: Nature, Freedom, and the Critique of Modernity* (2010); *Spielräume der Freiheit. Zur Hermeneutik des Menschseins* (2009); "Heidegger's Hermeneutics—Towards a New Practice of Understanding," in *Interpreting Heidegger: New Essays*, ed. Daniel O. Dahlstrom (forthcoming, 2011). He is co-editor of *Heidegger-Jahrbuch* (2004–) and of F. W. J. Schelling, *Philosophie und Religion. Text und Interpretationen* (= *Interpretationen und Quellen* 1) (2008); *System-Freiheit-Geschichte. Schellings Einleitung in die Philosophie (1830) im Kontext seines Werkes* (= *Schellingiana* 16) (2004).

Index of Topics

absolute, the, 142, 161, 162. *See also* nothing/
  nothingness; absolute
Absolute Idea (Hegel), 16, 178–79,
  182n27
abstractions, 182, 214, 215, 216
abyss, 46, 122, 167
action(s): in Chinese philosophy, 50, 54,
  55–56, 59; external, 3, 35, 38; God as agent
  of, 186n34, 186n35, 202. *See also* agency/
  agents; creation, act of
actual entities, 50n28, 78, 194–99
actuality, 15, 50, 173, 180
actualization, 53n47, 82, 226–27
agency/agents, 80, 96, 166–67, 223, 224, 225;
  God as source of, 15, 173–74, 186, 201–2.
  See also action(s)
alternatives, optimal. *See* Law of
  Optimality
ancestors, worship of, 55, 56
angels, 76n26, 77
annihilation, 90, 91
appearance, reality *vs.*, 22, 213
apperception, unity of, 185n32
appetite(s), 95, 96
appropriateness, virtue of, 56
argument(s): cosmological, 74n23, 109;
  from design, 25, 225; metaphysical, 5, 88;
  ontological, 74n23, 194, 210; physical, 75;
  from *posse*, 194; a posteriori, 10, 77, 131; a
  priori, 74n23, 77, 130, 172–73, 174, 180n25,
  185n32
artists, 193
association, determinate, 76
asymmetry, 4, 17, 46–48, 58, 193, 201
asymptotes, 130–31
atomic age, 126, 127, 141–43
atomism, 181

axiogenetic optimality principle, 23–24, 218,
  228
axiology, 24, 217–30

beauty, 33, 204
becoming, 2, 16, 22, 178, 201, 207, 213
beginning, Hegel's concept of, 181–82
being(s), 21, 32, 77, 95, 148, 163, 207, 210,
  215–16, 226; absence of, 140, 143, 144;
  Aquinas's concept of, 87–89, 178; causes
  of, 40, 59, 86, 111–16, 144, 178–79, 184; in
  Chinese philosophy, 3–4, 58; contingent,
  60, 133n21, 142, 143–45, 166–67; creation
  of, 144, 165; divine, 87–88, 204; God as
  source of, 13, 46, 90, 114, 134, 143, 164, 169,
  191, 223n7; ground of, 11, 44n8, 125–45,
  216; Hegel's concept of, 15–16, 178–79;
  Heidegger's concept of, 138; higher-level,
  173, 175, 182, 209; historicity of, 11, 142–43,
  144–45; indeterminate, 16, 71, 177–79,
  181–82, 185, 192, 200–201; individuality
  of, 142, 143; intelligent, 223; necessary,
  167; nothingness and, 16, 168, 178, 181–82;
  partaking of *ousia*, 30–31, 37–38; perfect,
  94, 122n20, 178; Plato's view of, 2, 210;
  positive, 20, 201; presence of, 140, 143,
  144–45; pure, 174, 200–201; self-relation
  of, 139, 182, 183; self-transforming, 178–79;
  sufficient reason principle and, 9, 138;
  transcendent, 141, 143, 178, 184; as will,
  138n32. *See also* angels; determinate
  beings; *esse;* fullness-of-being conceptions
  of God; God; God, existence of; Necessary
  Existent (Avicenna); non-being
being as being: Aquinas on, 6, 87–88;
  Aristotle on, 5–6, 84–85, 87–89; Avicenna
  on, 66, 86; Heidegger on, 139–40, 141

249

Index of Names

Acar, Rahim, 75n24, 79n33
Adam, C., 111n2
Adams, Robert Merrihew, 131n16, 131n17, 133, 133n20, 133n21
Adamson, Peter, 79n33
Adolphi, Rainer, 151n26, 157n57
al-Fārābī, Abu-Nasr, 69n13
Allen, Reginald E., 172n7
Ameriks, Karl, 146n1
Ames, Roger T., 56n59
Ariew, Roger, 174n11
Aristotle, 2, 4, 6, 8, 14, 15, 29, 29n1, 30, 31–32, 38, 39, 43, 50n29, 65, 68, 69–70, 69n9, 69n12, 75, 84, 85, 87–88, 113, 140, 140n35, 151n26, 170–72, 171n3, 172n6, 173, 175, 179, 207, 219, 221
Armogathe, J. R., 120n18
Arnauld, Antoine, 8, 113, 113n6, 113n7, 114, 115, 116, 117
Asmuth, Christoph, 150n20
Averroës, 87, 175, 175n13
Avicenna, 1, 4, 5, 65–83, 66n2, 68n7, 69n13, 71n17, 72n20, 73n21, 74n23, 76n26, 77n29, 78n31, 79n33, 81n39, 86, 86n6, 87, 88
Ayers, M. R., 119n15

Badawi, A., 65n1, 68n7
Baumgartner, Hans Michael, 150n21
Beaude, J., 120n16
Beck, Lewis White, 180n25
Behler, Diana I., 147n7
Behler, Ernst, 147n7, 152n29
Beiser, Frederick C., 146, 146n1
Bennett, Jonathan, 117, 117n12, 118, 119
Berthrong, John H., 44n8, 48n18, 50, 50n28, 52, 52n43, 54n52, 57n61
Blankenhorn, Bernhard, 104n50

Boethius, 87
Boler, John, 193n7
Bonsiepen, Wolfgang, 179n22
Bontekoe, Ron, 44n4, 60
Bowie, Andrew, 146n2
Bracken, Joseph A., 195, 195n15
Bragt, Jan van, 192n3
Breazeale, Daniel, 147n5
Buchheim, Thomas, 162n73
Buchner, Hartmut, 157n56
Burrill, Donald R, 225n9
Buschmann, Elisabeth, 81n39

Careil, Foucher de, 131n13
Carraud, Vincent, 111, 111n1, 112n5, 113n7, 114n8
Casper, Bernhard, 168n102
Cassirer, Ernst, 134, 134n23
Catan, John R., 172n6
Caterus, 111–12, 113
Chan, Wing-Tsit, 50n22, 50n23, 50n24, 50nn25;26, 52n38, 52n40, 52n41, 52n42, 54n51, 54n52
Chang Tung-sun, 60
Chapman, J. Harley, 44n3
Chappell, Vere, 129n7, 131n13, 131n16
Cheng Chungying, 44n4, 49n21, 51n37
Chou Tun-I, 44n8
Chu Hsi, 50, 54n52
Clarke, Samuel, 130
Clarke, W. Norris, 104n50, 130
Clayton, Philip, 191n1
Cobb, John B., Jr., 197n20
Confucius, 4, 44n8, 46, 48, 54, 55, 56–57, 57, 60
Copernicus, 148
Corrington, Robert S., 52n44, 53n47

257

Wippel, John F., 19n2, 84–106, 87n9, 88n13, 93n26, 94n27, 95n30, 105n52, 157n59
Wirth, Jason M., 162n72
Wisnovsky, Robert, 65n2, 81n39
Wolter, Allan, 192n5
Wood, Allen W., 167n99
Woodhouse, R. S., 134n23

Yaḥyá ibn ʿAdï, 69n13
Yu Jiyuan, 43, 43n1

Zaborowski, Holger, 11–14, 146–69, 148n10, 149n13, 152n32
Zayed, S., 68n7, 69n13
Zedler, Beatrice, 79n35
Zeltner, Hermann, 149n14
Zhangzai, 52n40, 52n42
Zhoudunyi, 4, 44, 46, 48, 58, 59, 60
Zhuxi, 4, 44n8, 46, 48, 50, 50n28, 52, 52n43, 54, 57, 58, 59, 60, 61

The Ultimate Why Question: Why Is There Anything at All Rather than Nothing Whatsoever? was designed and typeset in Minion by Kachergis Book Design of Pittsboro, North Carolina. It was printed on 60-pound House Natural Smooth, and bound by Sheridan Books of Ann Arbor, Michigan